Army Life in Virginia

The Civil War Letters of
George G. Benedict

Edited by Eric Ward

STACKPOLE
BOOKS

Copyright © 2002 by Stackpole Books

Published by
STACKPOLE BOOKS
5067 Ritter Road
Mechanicsburg, PA 17055
www.stackpolebooks.com

Printed in the United States of America

10 9 8 7 6 5 4 3 2 1

FIRST EDITION

Library of Congress Cataloging-in-Publication Data

Benedict, G. G. (George Grenville), 1826–1907
    Army Life in Virginia : the Civil War letters of George G. Benedict ; edited by Eric Ward.—1st ed.
       p. cm.
    Includes bibliographical references (p.) and index.
    ISBN: 0-8117-0139-5
    1. Benedict, G. G. (George Grenville), 1826–1907—Correspondence. 2. United States. Army. Vermont Infantry Regiment, 12th (1862–1863) 3. United States—History—Civil War, 1861–1865—Personal narratives. 4. Vermont—History—Civil War, 1861–1865—Personal narratives. 5. United States—History—Civil War, 1861–1865—Regimental histories. 6. Vermont—History—Civil War, 1861–865—Regimental histories. 7. United States. Army—Military life—History—19th century. 8. Soldiers—Vermont—Burlington—Biography. 10. United States—History—Civil War, 1861–1865—Journalists. I. Ward, Eric. II. Title.

E533.5 12th .B46 2002
973.7'443—dc21

                                    2001049743

To my grandmother Nancy Davis,
whose stories about her grandparents in the Civil War
started my interest in it.

And to Col. Gil Newby,
Norwich Class of 1942, as he and his generation
fought and won World War II,
and saved the world from a tyranny worse than slavery.

CONTENTS

ACKNOWLEDGMENTS

I wish to thank the many people who over the years helped me make this project a published reality. A few people were key in this endeavor, such as those at Stackpole Books, especially William C. Davis, Michelle Simmons, and Leigh Ann Berry, who took a chance on this unknown writer and published this work. I would like to thank Jeffrey Marshall and his staff, who were very helpful in my research at the special collections department at the Baily-Howe Library at the University of Vermont. They tolerated my many requests for materials over the years and made each research session productive. Thanks also to Paul Carnahan and Barney Bloom of the Vermont Historical Society, for their time, effort, and guidance.

Among the nonlibrarian help, I thank Bob Poirier, Norwich Class of 1966, who is the closest thing to a mentor I have ever had. His suggestions and friendship brightened many a day when it was needed, and he steered me toward untapped information that has been worth the effort in finding. Thanks to my brother Aaron, who did valuable footwork on loose ends on some of my research. And to my mom, Nancy, and my wife, Debby, for whom words are incapable of expressing the depth of my thankfulness for their help and prayers. Debby is the youngest "Civil War Widow" I know and has put up with dozens of trips to Civil War sites and research stops. She also edited my writing, among other tasks.

INTRODUCTION

The first histories written about the Civil War were soldiers' letters republished in their hometown newspapers. Through these articles, the community gained a sense of what these soldiers saw and experienced from a "you are there" perspective. Although these letters usually presented a clear and honest view of camp life, most were written by privates in the army, who, other than camp rumors, had little idea of what was going on or was going to happen next. Another problem was that the letter writers often sought to protect their readers, especially their families, from the realities of war. Despite these drawbacks, these letters are critical in firsthand accounts of Civil War history.

Of the thousands of soldiers who wrote to their hometown newspapers, George G. Benedict is one of the best of these writers, and one of the most interesting. Though he was a private for about half of his term of service, he was a decade older than the average private, more educated, and possessed political and social connections that the ordinary army private did not.

George Grenville Benedict was born on December 10, 1826, in Burlington, Vermont, the son of George Wyllys and Eliza Benedict. George Wyllys Benedict was a War of 1812 veteran who, after the war, attended and graduated from William College in Connecticut in 1818. In 1825, he and his family moved to Burlington, Vermont, where George Wyllys became the professor of mathematics and natural history at the University of Vermont. A year later, George Grenville Benedict was born, the second of four sons, and the one that most closely followed his father's footsteps in military service, teaching, and professional callings.

George Grenville earned his undergraduate degree from the University of Vermont in 1847. That same year, his father left the university to establish and operate several telegraph companies in the state. The younger

George worked with his father in the family business part-time until he earned his master's degree from the University of Vermont in 1850. He then moved to New York City and taught at the Washington Institute for a year, after which he returned to Vermont to work at the family business, the Vermont-Boston Telegraph company, founded by his father. Benedict worked with Vermont-Boston Telegraph for twelve years, rising through the ranks to company president in 1860. He remained in this position until 1862.

In 1853, two events shaped George G. Benedict's destiny. That year, his father acquired the *Burlington Free Press*. Benedict became its associate editor and started a career in journalism that lasted fifty-four years. He and his family turned the *Burlington Free Press* into Vermont's first daily newspaper via the Vermont-Boston Telegraph, which gave the *Burlington Free Press* quicker access to the news around the country and a competitive advantage over most other Vermont newspapers. In the coming years, the *Burlington Free Press* became one of the most influential newspapers in the state. The other event was Benedict's marriage to Mary Kellogg of Canaan, New York, on October 27, 1853. A daughter, Mary Frances, was born on June 3, 1857. Tragedy struck that same year when his wife died of consumption on November 9, 1857.[1] Benedict had little time to grieve, however, as caring for his infant daughter and work kept him busy.

In the summer of 1862, George Benedict was a man on the rise. He was a leader in his community, well traveled, well connected in the state, well educated, and wealthy by the standards of that day. On August 23, 1862, he enlisted in the Howard Guard, one of Burlington's militia companies for military service. Regimental records described him as five feet, nine inches tall, with a light complexion, blue eyes, and brown hair, and stated his occupation as an editor.[2] Why Benedict enlisted is not known. He did not have to serve and could have gotten an exemption as he was the postmaster of Burlington. In fact, he had to get permission to enlist from the postmaster general. While Benedict was in the army, his father took over as Burlington's acting postmaster. A possible reason could have been the nine-month term of service, which was short enough that he could serve without grievously disrupting his affairs. It is curious that Benedict and three other Vermont newspaper editors enlisted in these nine-month regiments at the same time. Perhaps a sense of duty or peer pressure influenced him. He was the only one of the four editors to remain a private after their muster into Federal service. Two of these four became executive officers in different regiments, and the third became Benedict's regiment's commissary sergeant. Benedict had the political pull and the social standing in the community to get a commission, but he remained a private until he was appointed second lieutenant in January 1863.

When Benedict became a soldier in the fall of 1862, he also became an army correspondent for his newspaper. In this position, he wrote thirty-one letters that were published in the *Burlington Free Press* during his term of service. He wrote from the camp at East Capitol Hill, Camp Vermont, the camp near Fairfax Courthouse, the camp at Wolf Run Shoals, and the field at Gettysburg, among other places. In these letters, Vermonters could read about the daily routine in camp; picket duty; the civilians near the camp; how soldiers celebrated Thanksgiving, Christmas, and New Year's Day; and the hazards of camp life and the battlefield. Benedict told the people at home what it was like in the army in a manner similar to Ernie Pyle in World War II some eighty years later.

The 12th Vermont saw little action against Confederate troops and never lost a man to enemy fire. The regiment's only time under fire was a brief firefight when Gen. J. E. B. Stuart's cavalry probed its position on the night of December 28. Since Stuart's cavalry found that the 12th's defensive position could not be taken without heavy losses, he wisely avoided attacking it. Nevertheless, Benedict and his comrades were not safe behind the lines, as his brigade commander and John S. Mosby demonstrated on the night of March 9, 1863. For the remainder of the spring of 1863, the 12th Vermont defended Wolf Run Shoals. A week before the end of their enlistment, the men were ordered to march with the rest of the brigade north to join the Army of the Potomac, which was marching to catch General Lee and his army. As aide-de-camp, however, Benedict remained with his brigade commander, Brig. Gen. George J. Stannard, at Gettysburg on a grassy knoll behind the Codori farm as Pickett's division advanced on them on the afternoon of July 3, 1863. Decades later, he was awarded the Medal of Honor for the part he played that afternoon in one of the Civil War's most famous charges.

Benedict was discharged ten days after Gettysburg, along with the other soldiers of the 12th Vermont, having completed their enlistments. After the war ended, he became active in veterans' affairs and Civil War history. He became Vermont's official Civil War historian and wrote three books, lectured, and published articles on the subject.

It is not known why Benedict never wrote a history of his regiment. Although he gave a brief overview of his regiment in two of his other books, the closest he came to a regimental history of the 12th Vermont was his last book, *Army Life in Virginia,* which was composed of edited versions of the letters he wrote during the war. While this book has the same title, it is not a reprint of that 1895 book. Instead, George Benedict's original letters are reprinted as they appeared in the *Burlington Free Press,* with the exception of their text format and the standardization of spelling and punctuation. These latters are augmented by information gathered from Benedict's personal papers, other Vermont newspaper Civil War articles and the letters printed in them, official documents from the 12th Vermont and her sister regiments, and three other unpublished letter collections. These all provide details that Benedict lacked as a witness to this part of American history and help place his letters in context. A larger picture of what Benedict and his regiment endured in their service to their country thus emerges, starting from Burlington and other towns in Vermont in the fall of 1862 to Washington, D.C., and its local area to Gettysburg in the summer of 1863 and back again to Vermont.

CHAPTER 1

A Call to Arms

In the spring of 1862, the Army of the Potomac was close enough to the Confederate capital at Richmond, Virginia, to hear city church bells toll the time. Its fall was all but assured, according to Union newspapers and to Gen. George B. McClellan. But McClellan overestimated his enemy's strength, and readers of the *Burlington Free Press* learned of battles such as Williamsburg, Savage Station, and White Oak Swamp in June and July 1862.

By the end of July, the Union needed more troops to stop this reversal of fortune. President Lincoln earlier that month had called for three hundred thousand troops for three years' service or until the Rebellion was crushed, whichever came first. But before most of those troops could take to the field, the Union had suffered another defeat at Bull Run, and General Lee and his army prepared to invade the North. This led Lincoln in August to call for another three hundred thousand troops for nine months' service. By this time, the pool of willing recruits had dried up, and this latest call for troops tested many states, as the Federal government gave itself the power to draft men needed to fight an increasingly protracted war.

Vermont had a difficult time with this call. It had already sent nine infantry regiments and provided replacements for those regiments as they suffered losses from disease and combat. According to the 1860 census, the state had a population of 315,000, with little growth, as many in the decades before the war had moved west to obtain better farmland and take advantage of other opportunities. In these two calls for troops, Vermont's quota was two infantry regiments of three-year men and almost five thousand nine-month men, or five infantry regiments. Vermont governor Frederick Holbrook and his adjutant general, Peter Washburn, both worked creatively to solve this problem using the few advantages they had. The nine-month enlistment option gave even the most reluctant recruit incentive to join during the late summer and early fall, as harvest season drew to a close. The state also paid its enlisted soldiers an extra $7 a month. Added to the Federal pay, this meant that a private from Vermont made as much as a first or orderly sergeant, five pay grades above the average private serving in the Union army.[1] This monetary dish was sweetened by the town selectmen's promise of a $50 bounty to each soldier who enlisted and served. If a man was drafted, he forfeited the extra $7 a month and the $50 bounty. In addition, he would serve three years instead of nine months. These considerations moved many a reluctant man to join the nine-month regiments rather than risk being drafted later.

The short enlistment also attracted men who might otherwise forgo service because of their position and community responsibilities. The August 16, 1862, *Burlington Free Press* reported:

> *Editors Going*—The Editors of Vermont, having done their best to send forward men to the army, are now beginning to go themselves. Dr. Cummings of Brattleboro *Phoenix,* has the honor of leading off—having enlisted two or three weeks since. Mr. Brown, Assistant Editor of Walton's *Journal,* is raising recruits for a company in Montpelier. John Cain of the Rutland *Courier,* has enlisted, and we perceive the names of G. H. Bigelow of the *Times,* and G. G. Benedict, of the *Free Press,* on the roll of volunteers in this place.

Andrew C. Brown and Charles Cummings became executive officers, or the seconds in command of the regiments of the 13th and the 16th Vermont Infantry Regiments. George H. Bigelow and George G. Benedict enlisted in the Howard Guard, their town's militia company. In a few weeks, George Bigelow became the commissary sergeant of the 12th Vermont. George Benedict remained a private for the remainder of 1862. All of these men wrote letters to their newspapers during their service, but George G. Benedict wrote more, and his accounts were from the soldier's point of view.

Benedict enlisted in the Howard Guard on August 23 at a war meeting at city hall on Church Street. In a war meeting, a city or town turned out to decide how to support the state's war effort. They also discussed and voted on plans to raise money to offer as enlistment bonuses and to support families of soldiers whose absence caused a hardship. At that meeting, seventy-

Pvt. George G. Benedict.
BENEDICT PAPERS, UNIVERSITY OF VERMONT.

nine men enlisted in the Howard Guard, filling part of Burlington's 155-man quota for troops.[2] Another nineteen men from Shelburne, a town about five miles south of Burlington, enlisted in the Howard Guard, as well as five men from South Hero, twenty miles north of Burlington. Thirty-seven of these men recorded their occupation as farmer, twenty as mechanic, thirteen as clerk, and nine as student. Other occupations included sailor and mason. The oldest man in the ranks was Pvt. Burnam Seaver, a forty-two-year-old mechanic from Burlington, followed by Lemuel Page, forty-one. The youngest members of the Howard Guard were ten eighteen-year-old recruits. Pvt. Guy Irish, standing at six feet, two inches, was the tallest man in the company. The shortest was Pvt. Morris Rice, a foot shorter than Irish. In this company, the men tended to be on the short side; only one other man was taller than six feet, and fourteen recruits were between five feet, three inches, and five feet, five inches, in height.

The Howard Guard selected its leadership in accordance with Vermont militia laws, electing the company officers on August 24, as reported in the *Burlington Free Press* the next day:

The organization of the Howard Guard which occurred on Saturday, took place with gratifying unanimity. Capt. Page received every vote but one. He is one of our most respected citizens, was long connected with company, was its First Lieutenant for a year or two, and is fully qualified by military knowledge, high character, and personal worth, for the position. He will make a *good* captain.

First Lieut. Wing, is a member of the firm of Wing & Smith, well known and highly respected manufacturers of this place. He has been active in getting the company together, brought with him into it, some twenty of its best members from the Pioneer shop, is a patriotic and whole-souled man, and will undoubtedly make an excellent officer. He received 75 of the 85 votes cast, for the 1st Lieutenancy.

Second Lieut. Loomis is a son of our townsman, Henry Loomis, Esq. He left College to join the 1st Regiment, served faithfully and with high credit throughout its four months' term of service; returned to his studies, and now, at the opening of his Senior year, returns to the army at his country's call. He is a fine, resolute and capable young man, and the company is to be congratulated on securing so promising an officer. He received a flattering vote, and his election was then made unanimous.

The elections were received with hearty cheers by the Company, each officer in turn receiving three [cheers] and a tiger [roar], and acknowledging the honor in a short and appropriate speech. Three cheers were then given for the presiding officer of the election, Hon. Geo. F. Edmunds. He responded in a few remarks, complimenting the Company on their spirited appearance, and on the unanimity and good feeling apparent among them. He said he knew they would stand by each other, never leaving a comrade, dead or alive, between them and the enemy. They had chosen good officers, and with a good Colonel and Brig. General, such as he trusted would be placed over them, they could not fail to do good service, and make a shining mark. The Company then after some less important business, adjourned to meet at the armory this evening at half past seven o'clock.

The material of the Company is *first rate.* It is composed mainly of the best class of the young merchants, mechanics and farmers of Burlington and Shelburne. Ten or twelve graduates and members of the Senior class of the University are among its members. If it ever has a chance to fight and does not fight well, we shall be disappointed. On August 26, 1862 The *Burlington Free Press* went on to report: At the meeting of the Guard, last evening, Capt. Page announced the appointment of non-commissioned officers, which were submitted to the Company for their approval and were unanimously approved. They will be found below.

Orderly Sergeant Rogers, is a young man of considerable military knowledge, and we are assured will fill capably that responsible position. The other Sergeants, and the 1st Corporal have all seen service in the 1st Regiment, and are tried and thorough soldiers.

The Company elected G. G. Benedict, *Treasurer,* in place of Wm. Loomis, resigned, and W. W. Walker, *Auditor.* The thanks of the Company were voted to E. C. Loomis, Esq., for a handsome donation of *one hundred dollars,* to the funds of the Company, which was announced at the previous meeting and received with three hearty cheers.

The Company is to meet regularly three times a day for drill.

The men elected Lemuel Page, a merchant, as their captain and commander; Herman Wing, a thirty-six-year-old manufacturer, as their first lieutenant and the second in command of the company; and William Loomis, a twenty-year-old University of Vermont senior, as their second lieutenant. Unlike most men now in the Howard Guard, Loomis was an original member of this company when it went south with the 1st Vermont Infantry Regiment in 1861. That service interrupted his studies at the University of Vermont. Now, in his senior year, he went off to war again.

Captain Page, in consultation with his officers, named the company's five sergeants and eight corporals the next day. The company, as far as the state of Vermont was concerned, was now organized and ready to serve.

The Howard Guard drilled three times a day, when the men were not squaring away their personal affairs, and waited for nine other companies to be recruited and organized to form the 12th Vermont Infantry Regiment. These other companies, formed by the start of September 1862, and in a few weeks were designated as: Company A, the West Windsor Guards; Company B, the Woodstock Light Infantry; Company D, the Tunbridge Light Infantry; Company E, the Ransom Guards, from the towns of Fairfield, Georgia, and St. Albans; Company F, the New England Guards, from

Capt. Lemuel W. Page.

1st Lt. Herman Wing.

2d. Lt. William Loomis.

NATIONAL ARCHIVES.

Northfield and Randolph; Company G, the Allen Grays from Brandon; Company H, the Saxton River Light Infantry; Company I; and Company K, the Rutland Light Infantry. Once these infantry companies had been recruited and organized, the company commanders elected the regimental commander, regimental executive officer, and battalion commander. After that, the regimental commander, in consultation with his officers, appointed the regiment staff, which consisted of the regimentals' adjutant, quartermaster, and chaplain; and the noncommissioned staff, which consisted of the regimental sergeant major, the quartermaster's sergeant, and the commissary sergeant.

The company commanders that formed this new regiment went to the Island House at Bellows Falls for its organizational meeting on September 20, 1862. Brig. Gen. Alonzo Jackman served as the governor's representative and ran the elections that selected the key regimental leadership. Jackman refereed these elections and ensured that Governor Holbrook's wishes were known and his candidate for regimental commander—Asa P. Blunt of St. Johnsbury—was elected. The company commanders elected Holbrook's choice for regimental commander, even though most of them never met him. Despite the political arm-twisting, Colonel Blunt was an excellent choice for this command. Before the war, he was a partner in the Fairbanks Scales Company, in St. Johnsbury. In June 1861, he had joined the 3rd Vermont Infantry and was appointed its adjutant. In the sixteen months since, Blunt rose rapidly in the ranks becoming the executive officer of the 6th Vermont Infantry, one of the 3rd Vermont's sister regiments. In this position, Lieutenant Colonel Blunt fought in the Peninsula campaign and was ready for a regimental command of his own when the 12th was being formed.

Blunt's second in command was Roswell Farnham of Bradford. Farnham was a thirty-six-year-old lawyer and captain of the Bradford Guards in the fall of 1862. He had served in the Bradford Guards as a first lieutenant during its service with the 1st Vermont Infantry Regiment in the summer of 1861. They saw little action, except for a skirmish at the battle of Big Bethel where the 1st Vermont suffered the state's first losses from combat and disease. Upon his return to Vermont in June 1861, Farnham became the state attorney for Orange County and the commander of the Bradford Guards when they were called to fill the state's quota in August.

Nathan T. Sprague, commander of the Allen Greys, was elected as major, the battalion commander's position, but he shortly resigned his commission for health reasons. Soon after, Levi Kingsley of Company K was elected in his place. Major Kingsley was another officer who had served in the 1st Vermont Infantry Regiment, in this case a second lieutenant in Company K. Now, like Farnham, he too was returning to Virginia. He was the regiment's third in command, and he commanded two or more companies if they were detached from the regiment, or the left or right wing in battle formation if the regimental commander or executive officer was knocked out of action.

Roswell Vaughan of Burlington was selected to be the regimental adjutant, who managed the regiment's administration and personnel paperwork, including promotions, demotions, punishments, discharges, and official communications between the 12th Vermont and higher headquarters. The adjutant also advised the regimental commander on personnel accountability. These numbers were used for the issuing of rations, ammunition, and pay, as well as a gauge of the regiment's capabilities. Adjutant Vaughan was a good selection for this position because of his prior work with the Federal army liaison officer, Maj. William Austine, on army personnel matters

12th Vermont Staff.
Left to Right: (Standing) Adj. Roswell Vaughan, Surgeon Granville P. Conn,
and Q.M. Harry Brownson; (Seated) Lt. Col. Roswell Farnham, Col. Asa P.
Blunt, and Maj. Levi Kingsley. Houghton Collection, University of Vermont.

involving Vermont troops in Federal service. Aiding him in these tasks were the regimental sergeant major, E. D. Reddington, and a clerk or two.

Harry Brownson of Rutland was appointed as the regimental quartermaster, who managed the regiment's supply system and worked through the army bureaucracy to provide the regiment's logistical needs, except for rations and ammunition after they left Vermont. Once the regiment was assigned to a brigade, the brigade's commissary department would procure its rations, and the brigade ordnance officer and his department procured its ammunition and related supplies. In the meantime, Brownson and his counterparts in the other nine-month regiments spent a great deal of time and paperwork to see that the regiment's housing, clothing, equipment, and fuel needs were met, as well as the storing and transportation of these supplies to the field as needed. Assisting Brownson in these tasks was the quartermaster sergeant, George Bigelow, and a clerk or two. Their first project was preparing the regiment's camp at Brattleboro, where the companies that composed the 12th Vermont would assemble to prepare for their muster into Federal service.

As the 12th Vermont's staff prepared for the rendezvous, the companies of the 12th had send-offs from their towns. These were usually town gatherings, where the company's commander and officers received gifts such as swords and pistols. The men of the company were given official recognition and sometimes a banquet after a speech from leading town citizens and their company commander. The Howard Guard's official send-off was on September 24 at Burlington's city hall, with Pvt. George G. Benedict as master of ceremonies. The city fathers gave Captain Page an infantry sword, officer's sash, belt, and pistol. Benedict's address to the gathering appeared in the *Burlington Free Press* the next day:

> Captain Page—Your fellow soldiers, officers, and privates of the Howard Guards have requested your presence here this evening, for the purpose of presenting to you some tokens of their regard, and they have placed on me the pleasant task of requesting your acceptance of the same, and of expressing the feeling of respect and esteem, on their part, which goes with the gift.—That feeling is something more than the common respect which is due from the soldier to his command. We are most of us, your fellow-townsmen, who have known and esteemed you for years. We have gone in to

this business with a tolerably distinct idea of what we are about. We have entered the army in no feeling of frolic or adventure. We go, because the good Government under which we have hitherto prospered is in danger, and has called for the help of its sons, because we believe that the cause of the Government is the cause of Human Liberty and equal rights, the cause of Christian order and just law; because we have no desire to see our nation divided into a Mexican chaos of petty republics; because we consider the Union to be something more than a rope of sand; because we love freedom for all men, and hate rebellion, and secession, and treason; because our friends have gone before us and are now standing on Southern battlefields, and we are anxious to place ourselves by their side and share their toil and danger; because we believe that to the 600,000 men, of whom we are a portion, will be given the honor of closing up this war, and to have had a share in that holy work will be glory enough for us, whether we live or die. We go, knowing that some thing is expected of the 300,000 nine months' men, and conscious that on each one of us rests, in a measure, the honor of our State. We know something of the risks to run, something of the foe we have to meet, something of the necessity of thorough discipline, and strict attention to duty in order to [attain] success.

We have selected you, with absolute unanimity, to be our Captain—because we believe you will be, as we have thus far found you to be, a careful instructor in our new business, a watchful guardian of our interests, as individuals and as a Company; because you will drill us as we wish to be drilled, and lead us as we wish to be led.

We present you these gifts, not by them to purchase an indulgence. We ask you not to abate a jot or tittle of a soldier's duty for any one of us. We give them to you because we appreciate you as a man and an officer. We have selected with some care this blade of trusty steel, this sash, revolver, and field-glass. We have endeavored to procure articles of some value of their own for actual service; but we trust that they will have an additional value for you because they are given by *your* men. Accept them as a pledge of faithful obedience, of good order, and hearty service on our part. We promise, in giving them, to stand by you as Vermonters should stand by a brother Vermonter, whether he has straps on his shoulder or not; to go where you send us and follow where you lead us. We hope under you to see active service, and to be able to show that, in our ranks we have no cowards or laggards.

We trust, whatever befalls the rest of us, that you will return from the war in safety. You *shall* so return if these stout arms and faithful hearts can protect you from injury and capture. We trust that you may return unharmed, in days to come, when peace is restored, when our country is again one, when a New England man can go from Maine to Texas, and express his honest, honorable opinions, without fear of tar and feathers. We trust you will be able to transmit these gifts to your children as mementos of the Great War for the Union, when the little State of Vermont sent 20,000 of her sons to the fight; and that, as you look on these gifts, you may never be ashamed of the time when you were Captain of the Howard Guard.

Captain Page then addressed his company as follows:

Brother Officers, and Fellow Soldiers—Accustomed, as I have been, to the pursuits of mercantile life, and not to making speeches, you must not look for one from me on this occasion. I do not know what I have done to merit these tokens of respect from you. In accepting these gifts, which are now the last resorts for the promotion of law and order, language cannot express to you what my feelings would have it. I make no promises as to what I shall do in the future, but I trust they may always be the instruments [to] inspire me with that zeal which knows no disgrace in the performance of my duty; I shall endeavor never to bring dishonor upon you as a company, or upon our beloved town and State. Should the fortune of war cause us to face the enemy, as probably it will, may God give us strength and firmness to uphold the honor of our Flag; and may that noble emblem of liberty, soon wave triumphantly over our land, and we become once more a united and free people; also may the God of Battles protect each one of us and return us safe to our family and friends. Again, fellow soldiers, I thank you.

The next morning, September 25 at 8:30 A.M., the Howard Guard left for the regimental rendezvous from the Rutland and Burlington railroad station located on the south end of the city on Lake Champlain. They joined the St. Albans company, the Ransom Guards, on the train as they headed south to Brandon, then east to Bellows Falls, collecting the other companies in their regiment along the way. George Benedict was among 1,022 men who had left home that day to become part of the 12th Vermont Infantry Regiment. These men made an interesting snapshot of Vermonters. Their average age was twenty-five. Pvt. Lawrence Banister of Company A and Pvt. Philip F. Jones of Company D were the youngest men in the regiment, both only sixteen years old, and Pvt. Elisha Smith of Company I was the oldest man in the regiment, at age fifty-nine. Four more men over fifty served in the ranks, along with seven who were over forty. The average height in the regiment was five feet, eight inches. The shortest man was Pvt. Silas Emery of Company F, who stood at four feet, five inches tall, and the tallest man was Cpl. Albert Sturgess of Fairfield, at six feet, five inches.[3]

Most of the men in the regiment had been born close to the homes they left that day, although 221 men were born outside of Vermont, mostly in New York and New Hampshire. Two men were born in what was now the Confederacy: Pvt. Edward C. Jackson of Company K, was born in Columbus, Georgia, and Pvt. David J. Lyon of Company G, in New Orleans, Louisiana. Seventy-eight were foreign born, mostly in Canada and Ireland, with a few from England, Scotland, France, and Germany. Pvt. Lewis Hemenway, a student serving in Company K, had the most unusual birthplace of any man in the regiment, being born in Bangkok, Thailand. Hemenway could have been the son of a sea captain or more likely a missionary, but a man who was born in Asia ending up in a Vermont infantry regiment in the Civil War made him a curiosity.

The regiment's records further document the men's occupations. The chief occupation was farmer (657 men). Next came mechanic (66), then blacksmith (15). Other occupations included doctor, lawyer, laborer, mason, and of course, newspaper editor.

Despite their different backgrounds, these men were now all part of the 12th Vermont Infantry Regiment, and soon the Union army, when they boarded the train that traveled south to Brattleboro on September 25, 1862. This began Pvt. George Benedict's life as a soldier and his letters home. It was also the moment when the men's lives changed too, for good or bad.

In Camp, Brattleboro
September 26, 1862

Dear Free Press:

My army correspondence must begin little back of the natural starting point, of our leaving Burlington. The uppermost thing in my mind, as I sit down to write, is the feeling of kindly interest in the Howard Guard, on the part of the citizens of Burlington, as shown by the tremendous concourse which crowded the Town Hall on Wednesday evening, to grace and give emphasis to our sword presentation to our worthy Captain—by the kind sentiments expressed and the hearty "God bless you," uttered there and then— and by what seemed to us the absolute turn out *en masse* of the town of Burlington to see us off the next morning. Those demonstrations touched every man in the Guard, I can tell you, and will not soon be forgotten by them. It was an unfortunate thing for us, that our departure was so hasty as to deprive most of us of the opportunity of giving the final hand-shake to our friends. It was our own fault, however. We should have been at the depot half an hour earlier.

Our ride to Brattleboro was a pleasant one. We were joined at Brandon by the Brandon Company, at Rutland by the Rutland Company, and at Bellows Falls, by the long train with the remainder of the Regiment. At every station, the people seemed to be out in multitudes, and from the doors and windows of every farmhouse on the way, the handkerchiefs were fluttering. The nine months' regiments are evidently objects of special interest among the citizens of Vermont—and I trust will fulfill the expectations of their friends. I am told that the arrival of a whole regiment, in camp, on the day set, is something unprecedented here.

We reached Brattleboro about half past four o'clock. The regiment formed in long column[s] and had a dusty march enough to camp, where, after considerable exertion on the part of Col. Blunt, it was finally formed into line, in front of the barracks. The companies are, most of them, like our own, deficient in drill, and have in fact, about everything to learn. They did, however, finally get into line parallel with the barracks (ten in number) without having

Camp Lincoln—Brattleboro, Vermont. BRADY COLLECTION, NATIONAL ARCHIVES.

the line of buildings moved to correspond with the line of men, which for a time, appeared to be the only way in which any kind of parallelism could be established between the two. The companies are composed for the most part, however, of men who will learn quick, and a few days of steady drill will tell another story. We broke ranks just at dark, received our blankets, woolen and India-rubber, selected our bunks and then marched off to supper, which was abundant and good enough for anybody, sauced as it was with a hearty appetite.

The barracks are plain houses of boards, without clapboards or battens, within which wooden bunks are ranged for the men, in double tiers. I cannot speak from experience as yet, as to their comfort, your humble servant having been among the fortunate individuals who constituted the first eight (alphabetically) of the company, and who were consequently, "detailed for guard duty." This phrase I found to mean in my case, a couple of hours of rest such as could be extracted from the soft side of a hemlock plank in the guard house, with sergeants and corporals and "reliefs" coming in and going out, and always in interested conversation, when not in active motion—then two hours (from 11 to 1) of pacing a sentry beat, musket on shoulder, over what by this time is a path, but then was an imaginary, and in the darkness, sometimes slightly uncertain, line on the dew-soaked grass of the meadow. Then about three hours more of that "rest" I have alluded to, (but this time I found the plank decidedly softer, and slept in spite of the trifling drawbacks mentioned). Then two hours more of sentry duty, and then—volunteers having been called for, for some special guard duty—two hours more of the same. By this time it was well into the morning.

On the whole it was quite a night, for the first one in camp. I rather liked it. To be sure, if the only proper business of the night be sleeping, it was not as successful a piece of business in that way as could be conceived of, but it was a very successful effort at guard duty. Not a rebel broke in, or a roving volunteer broke out, over my share of the line, and if there was no sleeping there was a good deal of other things. There was, for instance, a fine opportunity for the study of astronomy; ditto, for meditation. I read in the bright planets success for the good cause, and glory for the 12th Vermont, and mused—on what not. This was one of the finest opportunities to see the Connecticut Valley mist rise from the river and steal over the meadows, giving a shadowy veil to the trees, a halo apiece to the stars, and adding to the stature of my comrade sentinels till they loomed like Goliaths of Gath through the fog cloud. There was also the opportunity to see the morning break, not with the grand crash of bright sunrise, but cushioned and shaded by that same fog-bank till, the break was of the softest and most gradual. Who will say that these are not compensations, and who wouldn't be a soldier?

Today, up to noon, at which time, I write, the regiment is doing nothing but settle itself in its quarters. If it does anything worth telling, I shall try to tell it to you.

Yours, G.

Brattleboro is located in Vermont's southern corner on the Connecticut River. Across the river is New Hampshire, and ten miles down the river is Massachusetts. With the river and the railroad both running through Brattleboro, this city was a natural transportation hub for the thousands of troops and the supplies they needed. This was not the only reason why

Brattleboro was selected for the regimental assembly point, however. G. Frederick Holbrook, a native of the town, could easily watch the training and preparation of these new troops from his home when not attending to other business in Montpelier. It was also easy for the adjutant general's office, quartered ten miles up the river in Woodstock, to keep an eye on things. And the town was only about thirty miles, or an hour by train, from Norwich University, Vermont's only military college, and that helped with the training of these new soldiers.

Norwich University had a profound impact on the Union army in general, and Vermont troops in particular. It provided more officers for the Union than any school save West Point. Brig. Gen. Alonzo Jackman was Norwich's commandant of cadets and Vermont's adjutant general for the first year of the war. Later, Jackman advised Governor Holbrook in the selection of the regimental commanders of the nine-month regiments, and influenced the selection of key regimental leadership by chairing the regimental organizational meetings. The regiment had ten Norwich alumni— three officers, including Major Kingsley, and seven enlisted men—and their education helped their units. In addition, Norwich provided students as drill masters who were knowledgeable and experienced in using *Casey's Infantry Tactics,* the standard training manual for the Union army. As first lieutenants in the Vermont militia, they served as trainers and advisors to the company commanders in the instruction of their men in company drill. This was important, as most company commanders and the majority of their officers lacked the military experience to drill their men. These drillmasters gave the company commanders a knowledge base that they did not have.

The 12th Vermont moved into newly built barracks at their new camp, named Camp Lincoln. Close by was the 11th Vermont, a three-year regiment completing its preparation for service at Camp Washburn. The troops of the 11th Vermont left, but more infantry regiments soon replaced them.

Camp Lincoln, Brattleboro
September 29, 1862

Dear Free Press:

Special order No. 26, which was read on Dress Parade, Saturday night, assigned the Companies their letters and the Captains their rank. The arrangement is determined, I understand, by the dates of the commissions of the several Captains which in the state of chaos into which our militia matters in this State have fallen, were not as clearly defined as they might have been. We know that our Company would be among the first; all had hoped, and some had expected, that we should take the right of the Line; but it seems that cannot be. The Howard Guard is Co. C, and takes the honorable position of the Color Company. It is, as we well know, one of especial danger, but we take it cheerfully—and if we do not carry the colors where they ought to go, and protect them to the very last man, then we shall do less than we think we shall.

You have noticed, doubtless, some of the new appointments. That of Surgeon, is the most important one, in the estimation of the Regiment. With a good Colonel, Quartermaster and Surgeon, we are sure of being well led, well fed, and well doctored. I hope Dr. Ketchum, of Manchester, who has the position through the form of an election, but really by the selection of the Colonel, will prove to be just the man we want. The Assistant Surgeon, Dr. Conn, of Richmond, is very well spoken of, and will undoubtedly be a capable and efficient surgeon.

Major Sprague resigned, as I understand, by the medical advice of Brigade Surgeon Phelps.—His successor, Major Kingsley, is described as an able and excellent officer.

Our comrade Geo. I. Hagar is at present acting Sergeant Major of the Regiment, and performs the high duties with the promptness and efficiency which must be expected from his natural ability and experience. It must be owned that same article of *experience* is in demand in our Camp.—But experience is a fault some like that of youth, it is pretty sure to be remedied in time.

As yet we have been getting settled in camp. Tomorrow business begins, after the following order:

Reveille,	at	5 1/2	A.M.
Breakfast,	"	7	"
Surgeon's call,	"	8	"
Guard Mounting,	"	8 1/2	"
Company Drill,	"	9 to 11	"
Dinner,	"	1	P.M.
Company Drill,	"	2 to 4	"
Supper,	"	5	"

Dress Parade,	"	6	"
Tattoo,	"	9	"
Taps,	"	9, 10	"

The final inspection of the men of the Regiment by Dr. Phelps is going on from day to day. Our company is expecting to be inspected this afternoon, and to be mustered into U.S. service tomorrow. I suppose from all I hear, that the Regiment will leave here on Monday of next week.

Yours Truly, G.

The captain who had the earliest date of rank was the senior company commander, in command of Company A. The next most senior was in charge of Company B, and so on in the regiment. That was important, because in *Casey's Infantry Tactics,* each company was positioned in the regiment's formation according to the company commander's seniority. So at Camp Lincoln, the regiment formed up thus from left to right: Company B, Company F, Company G, Company C, Company H, Company D, Company E, and Company A, with Company K as the 1st Company of Skirmishers, and Company I as the 2nd Company of Skirmishers.

Benedict's reference to the color company being in more danger than other companies in the regiment was true. The color company maintained and guarded the regimental colors, which during the Civil War, were the regiment's rallying point. To obtain the regiment's colors was the goal of the enemy, and the color company marked the center of the regimental formation and usual location of the regiment's commander. But the officers and men of the 12th Vermont would not be in danger until they were mustered into Federal service.

Pvt. George I. Hagar, mentioned in Benedict's letter, was then acting as the 12th Vermont's sergeant major. Hagar was a twenty-six-year-old mechanic from Burlington, five feet, five inches tall, with blue eyes and light brown hair.[4] George Hagar was one of the few men who had served in the 1st Vermont Infantry Regiment but was the Howard Guard's first lieutenant in the spring of 1861. This time he either did not want to be an officer or could not get elected. Because of Hagar's administrative knowledge and experience of an infantry company and regiment, he was assigned to the regimental adjutant's office as a clerk. There he helped Adjutant Vaughan with the regiment's paperwork and kept the company orderly sergeant and his paperwork in order.

The schedule detailed in Benedict's letter became official in Special Order No. 2, dated September 30, 1862.[5] This schedule, with the exception of times, duties, and special circumstances, remained constant for the regiment throughout its service. After reveille and at dinner, each company held a roll call to account for its company soldiers.

Guard mounting was the changing of the camp guard at the regiment's guardhouse, where the new shift, or relief, was inspected and its leadership was informed if any orders or procedures had changed, or anything special had occurred during the previous shift. Then the old guard shifts were relieved and the new shifts went on duty.

At the company drills, soldiers trained under the company commander in the movements of what was known in *Casey's Infantry Tactics* as the "School of the Soldier." Here a soldier learned his individual movements within the company formation, such as dressing or aligning the ranks; marching; individual maneuvers; and weapon handling, including bayonet and loading drills. In short, he learned the skills he needed to fight in combat. Drill ensured that a soldier would follow his officers' orders while under fire, as it conditioned a soldier to respond automatically and instilled discipline and a sense of teamwork. Company drill also trained the soldiers in the "School of the Company," in which they practiced platoon and company movements and fighting as a unit. This required practice to perform effectively, and lives depended on it.

In the afternoon, the regiment, and sometimes the brigade, practiced what was known in *Casey's Infantry Tactics* as the "School of the Battalion." In battalion drill, the soldiers practiced what they had drilled in the morning, but over greater distances, in bigger battalion and regimental formations. Not only did this train the soldiers in the ranks further, but it also trained regimental and company-grade officers to handle their units. Colonel Blunt and his staff had the company officers receive additional training at night. Throughout their military service, Blunt taught the company commanders twice a week on military matters and *Casey's Infantry Tactics*. Lieutenant Colonel Farnham taught the regiment's first and second lieutenants the same thing, usually at the same time, in his tent. Then these officers trained their men.

Dress parade was a daily regimental formation in which the regimental commander and staff gauged the regiment's drill proficiency by its movements in the parade at the end of the day. Tattoo was the final roll call at the end of the day, an hour before lights-out. In a later letter, Benedict further described the soldier's routine, but from the field in Virginia.

Camp Lincoln, Brattleboro
Sept. 30, 1862

Dear Free Press:

Maj. Austine is expected here on Friday morning next, to muster in the 12th, which will be done on that day, provided the overcoats and other equipments shall have arrived and been distributed by that time. It is the intention of Gen. Washburn not to let the regiment pass out of his hands until it is *fully* equipped throughout. The quality of the articles thus far furnished us by Quartermaster General Davis, is a guaranty that our fit-out will be of the best. With our arms we are especially pleased. They are the Springfield rifle of 1862—the best arm in the world; light, strong, well-balanced, perfect throughout. The overcoats, belts, cartridge boxes and knapsacks remain to be furnished. I understand that they are on the way from New York, and will, probably, be received before this reaches you.

It has been found impossible to procure tents proper, and the regiment will be supplied on its arrival at Washington, with the little "shelter tents," so called—strips of duck, which, laid over some suitable sticks, make a shelter for a couple of men a-piece, lying on the ground, at night or in a storm, and are packed and carried on the shoulders of the men on the march. Of course, if we remain stationary for any length of time, we shall have huts, or at least sheds of brush to cover us.

The final inspection of our Company took place yesterday, conducted by Brigade Surgeon Phelps, assisted by Dr. C. T. Adams. The men as you probably know undergo the examination in *puris naturalibus,* in squads of about twenty at a time, and are required to march, kick, throw about their arms, &c., in a way which, under the sharp eye of Dr. Phelps, soon discloses any stiffness or disability. In conjunction with the very close individual inspection instituted at the time of enlistment it makes a pretty thorough piece of work.

There was found to be but one of our company with regard to whom there was any doubt as to his physical fitness for a soldier's duties—and he will probably pass. About a baker's dozen of the whole regiment have been inspected out—showing a remarkably high average of health and condition.—In fact Dr. Phelps remarked in my hearing that he had never inspected a regiment in which he found so few who must be thrown out.

I have no doubt that the regiment will leave for Washington, on Monday next.

Yours, G.

Benedict and his colleagues prepared for Federal service and drilled when the weather permitted it. In late September and early October, Vermont is cool, usually wet as fall arrives in its glory with the leaves turning color. These days can be known for their Indian-summer warmth, which can be hard to adjust to when the nights are cool.

The equipping of the men was difficult for Vermont, which was trying to field its regiments at the same time as other Northern states. Altogether, the states were attempting to equip more than half a million men at the same time. Since Vermont did not manufacture these items, State Quartermaster General Davis had a difficult time procuring uniforms, weapons, and other equipment. The 12th Vermont was affected by this problem, as were its sister regiments, except for its rifles. To be good soldiers, however, the men needed more than good arms, equipment, and uniforms; they needed good leadership, training, and—most of all—experience.

Camp Lincoln, Brattleboro
October 4, 1862

Dear Free Press:

An order was read at Dress Parade Thursday night, announcing the appointment of Col. E. H. Stoughton, to the position of Commandant of this Post, and his assumption of the duties of the station. He has established his headquarters just outside the grounds, and it is understood will proceed actively with the work of disciplining these 9 mos. regiments.

The overcoats, knapsacks, belts, cartridge boxes and haversacks were distributed yesterday morning, completing our equipment. The articles seem to be very good, with the exception, perhaps of the knapsacks and haversacks, which might be better, without injury to the service, or to the feelings of the troops. They are, however, I suppose, the best that could be procured. The whole form an amount of harness which strikes the unsophisticated recruit with a slight feeling of dismay. Is it possible, he says to himself, that all this pile of traps is only my share, and is all to be carried on my devoted shoulders? Why have they made them all so heavy? What earthly reason now, for cutting these straps out of such an almighty thick side of harness leather, and making them so broad, too? However, we took them all, and were, I trust, duly thankful for the same.

Yesterday afternoon was rendered memorable by our first knapsack drill. The orders were for a review of the regiment, fully equipped with knapsacks packed. The overcoats were, accordingly folded and placed within the knapsack; the change of underclothing, socks, &c., ditto; and the woolen blanket rolled tightly within the rubber blanket and then strapped on the top—the whole concern, with the straps, weighs, on an average about 35 pounds. There goes *science,* let me tell you, to the production of a skillfully packed knapsack.

This review was considered, I am told, quite a fine affair by the numerous array of spectators. Let me endeavor to give you an *inside* view of the affair, as it seemed to one in the ranks. *We* did not think it so fine. At 2 o'clock, then, each private hoisted on to his shoulders his knapsack packed as above, slung around his haversack and canteen, buckled on his cartridge box and shoulder-belt, and, musket in hand—took his place in the ranks. The sun has come out hot and it is a warm afternoon. About 15 minutes of waiting takes place before moving into line, in the course of which the luckless volunteer becomes distinctly conscious of a *weight on his back.* He straightens up manfully, however, and endeavors, when the orders come, to step out with his customary light step. But that he finds is not quite so easy. He is *logy*—He weighed 145 half an hour before, now he weighs 190. That knapsack gives an undue momentum to his about-face, and bumps uncomfortably against his neighbors as he faces from file to front. But we are in line now. The captain, astonished at the unwonted clumsiness of his men, labors hard, but with only moderate success, to "dress" them into a straight line, and there we stand, arms at shoulder. There is drumming and fifing and stepping into place of officers; but you notice little of what is going on. Your attention is mainly directed to a spot between your shoulder blades, which feels peculiarly. In short, it *aches.* This sensation gradually spreads through your back and shoulders, and is complicated with a sense of suffocation from the pressure of the straps across the chest. The perspiration bursts from every pore. You hear a groan from your comrade on the left, and are comforted a little to know that you have company in your misery; but it is poor consolation. That knapsack, strange to say, is evidently *growing* both in size and weight. It felt heavy before; now it weighs on you like a thousand [pounds] of brick. You cease to wonder at the breadth and thickness of the straps which support it—anything less strong would snap with the tension of such a weight. You haven't been in the habit thus far, of considering it a desirable thing to be detailed for guard duty; but, you now find yourself looking off at the sentries pacing to and fro with only their muskets to carry, and you wish you were on guard today. And now you are conscious of a sharp pain in the hollow of your right arm, from holding your musket at the shoulder for three quarters of an hour. Why *can't* they let us order arms for five minutes? But instead comes the order to wheel into platoons, and around the grounds we are marched for a weary hour.—We don't march good. We don't "right dress" and "left dress" good, we don't "wheel" good, and we don't *feel* good; but somehow or other, we get through with it—though a few of the more weakly or ailing ones drop out of the ranks—and we are still alive when marched to quarters and allowed to break ranks. It feels better now that it is done aching; but there are some I find, who express the deliberate opinion, that with all the need of drill and toughening for our work, two hours of knapsack drill, on a hot afternoon, was a pretty steep dose for raw recruits, the very first time. *I* don't say so, however, mind you. We shall all learn to like it in time, doubtless, but like olives, tobacco, and some other luxuries, one must get accustomed to it to really enjoy it.

At the close of Dress Parade yesterday afternoon, we were drawn up in hollow square, and a presentation of a handsome sword to Col. Blunt by the commissioned officers of the regiment, took place. The presentation speech was made by Chaplain Brastow and—was, I am told (we could not hear it) a very appropriate one. Col. Blunt responded in fitting terms, assuring the officers of his high appreciation of such a mark of their regard, saying that he was proud of his regiment, and that it should not be for want of his earnest endeavors, if it did not prove to be the best regiment ever sent from the State or that could be sent from it.

The sword is a beautiful one, of Ames' make, with two scabbards—one for field service, and the other richly gilt and chased.

After the Parade, the non-commissioned officers presented to the Colonel at his quarters, a pair of elegant shoulder straps. The Colonel again responded earnestly and well, thanking the givers for their confidence and regard, reminding them of the dangers and trials to be borne, declaring that to see his troops suffer would be the greatest pain for himself; but that he had rather endure all and end it with death on the battlefield, than to remain a laggard at home, in the hour of the country's trial.

After this, a presentation of a pair of shoulder straps to Major Kingsley, by the Rutland Light Guard, his former company, took place.

We are to be mustered into the U.S. service, reviewed by the Governor, and inspected in full marching equipment by Adjt. Gen. Washburn today. It will be a busy and hard day.

There is a camp rumor that the regiment is to go to New Orleans.

G.

Col. Edwin H. Stoughton, from Bellows Falls, Vermont, was an 1859 graduate of the United States Military Academy at West Point. Upon the outbreak of war, he resigned his commission and went home to Vermont, where he was selected to command the 4th Vermont Infantry in the summer of 1861. He served with distinction in the Peninsula campaign, and after the second battle of Bull Run, he took a leave of absence for health reasons and returned to Vermont. A month after his return from Virginia, Governor Holbrook selected him to command the regiments at Brattleboro during their preparations for Federal service. As Stoughton supervised these nine-month regiments, there was an understanding that he was to be promoted to brigadier general and command them once they entered field service. This promotion made the colonel, at age twenty-four, the youngest brigadier general in the Union army in the eastern theater. Only General Pleasanton's promotion of George A. Custer to brigadier general put a younger man in this position of authority in the East. In both cases, the wisdom of those decisions was tested in the field.

In the ranks of the 12th Vermont Regiment, Benedict learned that being a soldier was hard physical work in his knapsack drill on October 3. It did not help that he and his comrades were not used to moving around with their new equipment. A soldier of that era had an imaginary box of forty inches of space within the ranks in which to maneuver and fight. The extra weight and bulk of the equipment made this a tight fit for the men. Benedict and his comrades were lucky that this was a drill and not a twenty-mile forced march with full gear in the rain, with a battle to fight at the end of it.

Also on October 3, the officers of the regiment gave Colonel Blunt a sword made by Ames Armory of Chicopea, Massachusetts. Benedict could not hear Blunt's remarks, but one of his fellow soldiers recorded them:

> "Colonel—By the courtesy of these, my fellow-officers and comrades, I have been designated to present you with these insignia of your leadership. I do not refer merely, when I speak of your leadership, to your official relation to us, but chiefly to that native quality that determines you to be a leader of nature's make.
>
> "Men can make for themselves leaders after their own will. God makes them after His own pattern. There is a difference between the office and the character, and they are too often separated. We are proud to find in you those sympathies that draw us to and around you, and still a certain native energy that commands and controls. These native credentials give sanction to those official credentials by which we are to recognize you as *our* leader.
>
> "Where you lead, therefore, we shall dare to follow—not only obediently, but confidently and cheerfully. It is very satisfactory for us to feel, too, that your quality has been thoroughly tested.

"Look at the scabbard and you will find our recognition of the value of such a test of patriotism, nerve and daring. Lee's Mills, Williamsburg, Golding's Farm and the rest—these for you and for this regiment have a great meaning and value, as the scenes thro' which you passed to prove yourself worthy to lead such a body of men as are now under your charge. Be assured of the full confidence of these officers that you have earned this regiment, and it is yours. And now be pleased to accept these their gifts, as tokens of confidence, respect and affection, and God go with you to strengthen and guide."

The colonel was so much affected that his voice quivered with emotion as he responded substantially as follows:

"Gentlemen—Accept my sincere thanks for this testimonial of your regard, and believe me when I say that it is wholly unexpected, and at the same time all the more gratifying.

"Acts are the best evidences of a man's character, and I have as yet done nothing which in the least entitles me to be the recipient of such beautiful presents, yet this is gratifying, being as I am sure it is so thoroughly unalloyed, and dissevered from any of the lower motives which sometimes influence men.

"I know it is spontaneous, and I believe it is heartfelt.

"I am pleased at the confidence which you thus by this testimonial repose in me.

"This confidence, though premature, I trust may not have been misplaced, and I hope that you may never have reason to regret the occurrences of this day.

"I have great reason on my part to feel proud of both officers and men, and I anticipate that the good character we have thus far sustained will be confirmed by time and service; that the Green Mountain State may also feel proud that she has sent into the field this regiment to aid in sustaining the best government on earth, and perpetuating those glorious institutions which have been handed down to us stained in the blood of our fathers.

"I shall not distract you, but shall endeavor to make this what it should be—the best regiment that has left the State.

"Let us co-operate with each other and success will be ours."

The sword presented to the colonel is one of Ames make, and is a magnificent thing.—I have seldom seen one so massive and rich. It is appropriately inscribed—

Presented to Colonel Asa P. Blunt,
By the Officers of the 12th Regiment VT. Volunteer Militia.

On the reverse was beautifully engraved a national shield having enclosed the names of the battles he was personally engaged in, and in all of which he proved himself a brave and thorough soldier:

Lee's Mills, Williamsburg, Golding's Farm, Savage Station,
and White Oak Swamp.

Afterwards the non-commissioned officers of the regiment presented an elegant pair of shoulder-straps to the colonel. The sword is of exquisite workmanship, and is provided with two scabbards, one for service and the other for exhibition.[6]

The camp rumor that the regiment was going to New Orleans was false. It probably began because of the War Department's new policy of sending newly formed regiments to General Banks's command, which was preparing for an expedition operating in the Gulf of Mexico.[7] Benedict did not know that arrangements had been made for his regiment to stay in the eastern theater. Camp rumors were as much a part of camp life as hardtack and salt pork. Given the large number of men living together in close proximity, with little knowledge of where they would be sent, rumors naturally spread. In time, some of them turned out to be true, but most were not.

On October 6, Benedict wrote about one of the more important events for the regiment—its muster into Federal service on October 4:

Camp Lincoln, Brattleboro
October 6, 1862

Dear Free Press:

Our review by Gov. Holbrook and Inspection by Generals Davis and Washburn, and Col. Stoughton, commanding the post, Saturday was not so tedious as we expected. One man of our company fainted and two or three fell out before it was over; but most of the men agreed that it was on the whole an easier job than that of the day before. For one, my knapsack was sensibly less mountainous in size and weight, and my gun feels less like a six pounder howitzer. I presume both will continue to decrease in respect of ponderosity, as my muscles become habituated to the new pull on them.

The Regiment was mustered by companies into the U.S. service, in the afternoon, by Major Austine, who declared after he had administered to us the oath of allegiance, that he felt proud of the Burlington Company. The Guard responded to the compliment with three cheers for the Major. One man of the Bradford Company declined to take the oath, but thought better of it shortly, and with tears begged the privilege of taking it, which was granted. Another of the Rutland Co. also declined to take the oath and stood to his refusal. What makes his case more singular, is that the man, was one who served in the 1st Regiment, throughout its term of service, and was a good soldier.

Yours, G.

The mustering officer for Vermont, Maj. William Austine, was an 1838 West Point graduate with service in the Seminole and Mexican Wars. When war broke out in 1861, he was a major assigned to the 3rd Artillery regiment in San Francisco. On February 20, 1862, he retired from active service due to disability resulting from exposure in the line of duty. He was then assigned to Burlington as the disbursing, recruiting, and draft officer of Vermont. In this position, he was the Federal army's official representative and took care of personnel issues such as mustering new units, discharges, enlistments, and deserters, and served as liaison to state government. Only a Federal officer could muster state troops into Federal service, and Austine was that officer for most Vermont units sent into Federal service.

For the 12th Vermont and the other four nine-month regiments, muster went like this: Austine, with the regimental commander and regimental adjutant, inspected the regiment's personnel paperwork, including each soldier's descriptive rolls and clothing account records; the regimental order book, in which were recorded all orders to the regiment from higher headquarters; and most important, the muster rolls, in which were recorded details of the soldiers' service, including their pay and rations.

If these documents were in order, then Austine inspected one company at a time to determine its readiness.[8] He counted the men to ensure that the company had at least the seventy-one needed for muster, and he inspected their uniforms, equipment, and arms to see if they were fit for service. As for the arms, the 12th Vermont had Springfield muskets, which were the standard Union infantry rifle of that time. The 14th, 15th, and 16th Vermont received French and Belgian castoffs, which many of the soldiers thought were as dangerous to themselves as they were to the enemy. Better rifles were hard for the state to come by, however, and these poor-quality muskets could be exchanged before the regiments entered field service. Once the company was fit for Federal service, Austine read the ninety-six Articles of War to the company, and then has the men take the oath of allegiance, thus officially mustering these men into Federal service. The oath of allegiance for the soldier was thus:

"I (the name of the soldier), do solemnly swear that I will bear true allegiance to the United States of America, and that I will serve them honestly and faithfully against all their enemies and opposers whatsoever, and observe and obey the orders of the President of the United States, and the orders of the officers appointed over me according to the rules and articles for the government of the armies of the United States."[9]

A man could back out at the last moment, as did one soldier in Company K, who did not take the oath. Once a man had taken the oath of allegiance to the Federal government, if he then changed his mind and deserted, he faced punishment, which could be as severe as execution by firing squad. Two of Benedict's fellow soldiers, Pvt. Henry Martin and Pvt. Julian Parote, both of South Hero, deserted that night after being paid their enlistment bonus and state pay. But a telegram to their county sheriff beat them home, and they were captured and returned to the 12th Vermont to serve out their enlistment. There also were other privates in other regiments who did not show up for regimental training camp or deserted after their muster. Many made good their escape, probably into Canada, which shares a common border with Vermont.

What George Benedict and the men of the 12th and the other regiments did not realize was that their muster into Federal service marked the beginning of their nine-month enlistment. Benedict and his comrades had enlisted on August 23 and received the state pay of $7 a month for enlisted men, but that did not count toward their nine months. The restarting of the clock did not affect Benedict and his company as much as other companies that had enlisted at the same time as the 12th Vermont but were mustered in other regiments a month or two later. This caused some grumbling in the ranks, especially in the 15th and 16th Vermont Infantry Regiments, which had not yet arrived at Brattleboro when the 12th Vermont left it for Washington.

Within two weeks, from September 28 to October 4, Benedict and his fellow soldiers were transformed from civilians into a regiment of Union infantry. They were equipped and organized, yet were unfamiliar with the basics of their new profession. Colonels Blunt and Stoughton knew this, as they were experienced and had seen combat with the 1st Vermont Brigade. Luckily for the men of the 12th Vermont, they were shipped to Washington during the lull after the Antietam campaign and remained there, instead of immediately joining the Army of the Potomac. They did not share the same fate as the 14th Connecticut Infantry, which was a month and a half older than the 12th Vermont. The 14th Connecticut was assigned to the Army of the Potomac two weeks after its muster and found itself at Antietam, where it suffered heavy losses. The 12th Vermont and its sister regiments did not share that fate, but their service still had its costs.

CHAPTER 2

Camp at East Capitol Hill

On September 17, 1862, eight days before the 12th Vermont arrived in Camp Lincoln, the Army of the Potomac fought the Army of Northern Virginia outside the small Maryland town of Sharpsburg. That one-day battle along the Antietam Creek was the costliest in American military history, with a total of 26,134 casualties.[1] Lee and his army were stopped, and Confederate hopes for foreign recognition were dashed. However, McClellan allowed Lee's army to slip away, when he could have destroyed it in Maryland. Nevertheless, McClellan believed that he had saved the Union in the face of overwhelming odds. But his failure to engage and crush the Confederate army allowed the war to continue for two and a half more years, costing thousands more lives on both sides. In the weeks after the battle of Antietam, the Army of the Potomac recovered by receiving new regiments and other replacements to replace its losses.

At Camp Lincoln, the newly mustered 12th Vermont was now officially a part of the Union army. No one in the ranks knew when and where they would be sent. Many wondered whether they would be joining the Army of the Potomac or General Bank's Gulf of Mexico expedition.

As the 12th Vermont waited for transportation, the area around Camp Lincoln became crowded. The local inns and hotels overflowed with the men's relatives, and more troops and their friends and families were on their way to Brattleboro. The 980 men of the 13th Vermont arrived in camp on October 1 to begin their muster and training, and on October 6, the 14th Vermont, another nine-month regiment of 980 men, arrived. The 12th Vermont finally had its transportation arranged and was to leave that day, perhaps on the same train in which the 14th arrived. But Benedict and his comrades soon discovered that nine-tenths of army life is waiting for the other tenth to happen.

Washington, DC
October 10, 1862

Dear Free Press:

The camp of the 12th, at Brattleboro, presented a busy appearance last Tuesday morning. The thousand operations preparatory to breaking up of camp were in active progress. The quarters were full of friends of the soldiers, many of them ladies, who were seated here and there and plying busy fingers in taking the last stitches for their brothers and friends, before bidding them the final goodbye. The men were generally in good spirits, and anxious to be off. By eleven o'clock, every knapsack was packed and the regiment in line, and at half past eleven—the time set, to a minute—it marched from Camp Lincoln.

The day was a *very* hot one, and the sun blazed down, with midsummer power. The 13th, Col. Randall, escorted the regiment to the depot. Col. Stoughton, the acting Brigadier General of the post, took command of the column, and in order probably to show the regiment to some of his Brattleboro friends, took them by a circuitous route through the streets to the depot. The march of nearly two miles in the hot sun was a pretty hard one for the boys; but as they passed the depot, where I was stationed on special duty, I was glad to see that Company C marched as stoutly as the stoutest, and that in the little party of stragglers, (perhaps twenty or thirty in all) who had fallen out on the way, and who brought up the rear, there was not a man of the Howard Guard. Through some unaccountable neglect of the railroad companies, though the day and hour of our departure had been set for nearly a week, *no cars* were in readiness to take on the regiment, and we had to wait until they were brought from below. The regiment was accordingly marched half a mile down the river to a shaded meadow, and allowed to "lie off" for the remainder of the day. A barrel of good things sent from Burlington by Mr. Beach, supplied our company with all they could eat, and some to spare to the rest, and the afternoon passed comfortably away. At six o'clock a train of empty cars arrived, and the work of embarkation commenced at seven. The cars were too few in number however. Some freight cars had to be rigged with seats manufactured on the spot (I believe our officers considered themselves fortunate in not having to wait until cars and all were manufactured for the occasion) and it was ten o'clock before we were fairly under way. Before this, our kind friends had taken their leave, by the trains in each direction, and the actual departure was as quiet as that of any train of thirty loaded cars.

Let me mention here the kind offices of your townsman, Wm. Brinsmaid, who took up his quarters with us on Monday, worked like a beaver in helping the boys pack up their things, took charge of a big pile of valises and bundles to be taken home, and remained till the last man in camp to pick up things and see that all was off in proper shape. It was a valuable bit of service.

The delay in getting away was a disgraceful one for the railroad managers; but was a fortunate thing for the regiment. Had it been packed away into the cars, as it came heated from the march, and been compelled to ride all the remainder of that hot day, the men would have suffered. As it was, they lay around in the shade during the afternoon, took the rail in the cool moonlight, and had the pleasure of a daylight boat-ride through the Sound. The night was a splendid one, and the ride down the beautiful valley of the Connecticut, which seemed doubly beautiful in the liquid moon-light, was a notable one for every man who had a particle of sentiment in his soul.

At Springfield (which we reached about 1 o'clock) we were received with a rousing salute of 50 guns. Preparations had also been made on the supposition that we should arrive about supper-time, to supply refreshment to the troops; but the delay upset the kind arrangement. We made little stop there or anywhere, but swept on down the river. We reached New Haven at 5 o'clock, spent exactly an hour in changing the men and the baggage from the cars to the "large and splendid steamer" *Continental,* and were off for New York. The boat barely touched at Peck Slip, and then went on to Jersey City, where we debarked about noon. Col. Howe had provided there a dinner of soup and bread, which was served promptly, and we were off again by rail for Washington.

I can give little time and space to the thousand times told story of the passage of a regiment from New York to Washington. We had the customary wavings of handkerchiefs and flags, demonstration of God-speed all along the way, the usual—and it is all the more noticeable and praise-worthy because it *is* usual—substantial welcome, in the shape of hot coffee, good bread and butter, and meat, &c., served by the kind hands of the ladies and gentlemen of the Union Relief Association, in Philadelphia; and the customary delays in getting from Baltimore to Washington. Up to Baltimore we made steady and reasonably rapid progress, reaching there at six o'clock Thursday morning. Then came a march of a mile and a half across the city, six hours of tedious standing with stacked arms, near the Washington depot, varied by breakfast at the Relief Rooms, when we were stowed away in freight cars and started out of the city. The train took 600 other troops besides our regiment, and numbered 34 heavily loaded cars, the men covering the tops as well as filling the insides of the cars. We made slow progress, waiting three or four hours at Annapolis Junction, and reached Washington at 9 o'clock Thursday night. Supper was given us in the not very sweet or savory halls of the "Soldiers Rest," and in the huge white-washed barns attached thereto, the boys finally laid themselves down to sleep as best they might, on the hard floors, many preferring to take their blankets and sleep on the ground outside. Today we are to go into camp, somewhere about Washington, exactly where I cannot say at this present writing.

The behavior of the regiment throughout the whole journey, elicited expressions of surprise and admiration from the railroad and steamboat men and the citizens of every place at which we stopped. One of the managers of the Relief Association at Philadelphia said to me: "We have a good many regiments through here—*thirteen* this week, and on an average two regiments a day, now-a-days—and I think I have never seen a regiment of a thousand such *universally* well-behaved, orderly and gentlemanly men."

I should like to write something of our Colonel and other officers, but I must close this hurried letter. Our company is all here to a man, and all are well. I shall write you next from camp.

Yours, G.

For most of the men in the 12th Vermont this was the first time they had been to their nation's capital, or even away from their hometowns. Now these men had arrived at a city they had only heard about in the newspaper, and one that was bigger than any city in Vermont. Washington was a city of contrasts, with magnificent buildings such as the Capitol and White House along with pigs and other farm animals loose in the unpaved streets. The city, now in its second year of war, was an armed camp. The Confederate capital at Richmond was only ninety miles away, with the Army of the Potomac and the Army of Northern Virginia in between. Fortifications alone could not stop a Confederate attack. Troops to man those fortifications were needed, too. The men of the 12th Vermont were to learn more about that duty.

The regiment's two-day trip to Washington did not start or end smoothly. When the train did not arrive as arranged, Colonel Blunt, Lieutenant Colonel Farnham, Quartermaster Brownson, and the railroad manager must have had a long and frustrating afternoon, which did not end when the train that did arrive lacked the cars needed to transport the troops. While most of the soldiers were not happy about the situation, it likely was even worse for Benedict, who owned stock in and was a member of the board of directors for the Vermont Central Railroad, which transported the regiment down the Connecticut River valley to the port of New Haven, Connecticut. Nevertheless, Blunt decided to use the train that did arrive so as not to waste more time in moving his regiment south. That was the start of an interesting journey to Washington for the regiment, as it traveled down the Connecticut River valley, marking the first leg of a trip that thousands of Vermont troops had made. The planning, organization, and coordination in this process could and sometimes did break down on these established routes.

Benedict mentions the meal provided by Col. Frank A. Howe, state agent for Vermont in the New York City area, but does not explain why it was memorable for the 12th Vermont and her sister regiments as they headed south. Though Howe had more than likely worked hard to supply these incoming regiments with food and water, he failed with the main course. That dish was an inedible porridge the troops called "Jersey stew." Decades later, every soldier still remembered what "Jersey stew" was.

As the 12th Vermont headed south, the locals greeted them respectfully as men going to do their part for the Union cause. Benedict fails to mention, however, that as soon as the regiment crossed the Mason-Dixon line, all of this changed. Once the regiment arrived in Maryland, residents ignored them as occupiers or disliked them as invaders. The eastern part of Maryland was pro-Confederate, and violence often developed. The Union garrisoned troops in this region of Maryland and guarded every railroad bridge between Philadelphia and Baltimore. When the regiment reached Baltimore, the men thought of the Baltimore riot of April 19, 1861, when the 6th Massachusetts Infantry Regiment marched through the city to take the train to Washington. In the ensuing violence, three soldiers and twelve rioters were killed, after which Federal troops occupied the city.

The 12th Vermont's delay at Annapolis Junction was caused by railroad priorities and other problems. Blunt took the opportunity to send Adjutant Vaughan and Quartermaster Brownson on another train to arrange rations and quarters for the 12th regiment in Washington.[2] But by the time these two officers reached Washington, a few hours ahead of the regiment, they could do little, as the duty day was over and most offices were closed.

The same morning that Benedict wrote this letter, Blunt and Vaughan reported to Gen. Silas Casey's headquarters at 568 14th Street at 8:00.[3] Casey's division headquarters served as the starting point for any regiment or battery that joined the Union army in Washington. Casey was responsible for getting these units to army standards and finishing their equipping before sending them out to the major commands. This meant that a constant parade of regiments and batteries flowed in and out of camp. That morning, Blunt received orders to march the 12th Vermont to the camp on East Capitol Hill. He was assisted by a divisional guide. Then the final phase of equipping and training began, as Benedict's next letter describes.

Camp on E. Capitol Hill, Washington
October 12, 1862

Dear Free Press:

The 12th had taken up its temporary quarters when I wrote last, at the Soldiers Rest, near the Capitol, in this city. On Friday at 11 o'clock came the order to move, and we filed out upon the Eastern Road, to our present camp, some thing over a mile East of the Capitol. It is upon the wide, high, level plain called Capitol Hill.

Around us are the camps of numerous regiments. To the South of us, but hidden from our sight, runs the Eastern Branch of the Potomac, and across it are the Virginia heights with four or five forts in plain sight crowning the more prominent elevations. The ground on which we are encamped, has but two or three trees in a

square mile, and having been the site of numerous camps, is not
overstocked with grass. Some of the men looked a little blank as they
saw the bare cheerless surface of Virginia clay, on which they were
to pitch their tents, and some blanker yet when they took in the
length and breadth of the little strips of canvas, which were to be
our only shelter from sun and storm. These "shelter *tents*" are made
of a couple of strips of light cotton duck, about five feet long and
four feet wide, which button together at the top or ridgepole of
the concern. They are pitched by straining over the muzzles of a
couple of muskets set upright, and so form a little tent, with both
ends open, until closed at one, by hanging over it a blanket under
which two men may huddle and sleep at night. A *short* man can be
covered by them when extended at full length; a man of ordinary
height must "draw up" his feet or let them stick outside. We got
our ground laid out and tents pitched by dark, and officers and
men were by that time hungry enough to enjoy their supper of
three crackers a piece (there was no fuel to cook anything with,
and our cooked rations had spoiled on the journey) and tired
enough to drop off quickly to sleep, with but a blanket between
them and the ground. Most of us however, were waked at midnight by rain driving into our little tabernacles. My comrade
turned out, and hung our rubber blankets so as to keep out the
most of it for us, and we dropped to sleep again, to sleep soundly
till morning.

These are mere trifles of a soldier's everyday life; but they are
what many of your readers, who wish to know just how their boys
are living while away, wish to know about, and so I put them on
paper.

Next day our Colonel and Quartermaster got the strings of red
tape, which hang around the various departments of supply, thoroughly pulled, and by two o'clock, a train of a dozen army wagons
came filing into camp with fuel, rations of good bread, beef, pork
and potatoes, forage, and, last but not least, *tents,* procured for us,
by much exertion, by Col. Blunt. These were quickly made to take
the place of the others, and were viewed with intense satisfaction
by the men. They are not the biggest things in the world—are in
fact the simplest form of tent proper, wedge shaped and holding six
men apiece lying closely side by side; but they are *tents*—can be

closed against the weather, and will answer well our turn while here. When we take the field, we must take the others again.

We shall now begin the work of active drill, and will soon, I trust and believe, be in fighting order.

We have already been visited by many of our friends of other regiments—by Quartermaster Dewey, Capt. Erhardt, Sergeant Morse, E. Walker and others, of the Cavalry whose camp is across the river; but several from the 11th Vt, which is in camp about four miles out on this side; by Lieut. Carey of the 13th Mass, whose fine regiment of 1,100 men has now 700 in hospital, sick and wounded, and is reduced by losses (in battle mainly) to 191 men; by Lieut. Willie Root, of the 22nd Conn. which was in camp close by us yesterday, but today has struck tents and moved away to Chain Bridge; and others, whose brown and hearty faces it was pleasant to see.

We begin to realize that we are a part of the big army of the Republic—and that a single regiment is but a *little* part of it. Camps surround us on every side.—Six thousand men, they say came into Washington the day we did, and some come every day. They come, encamp, and disappear, the rest know not whither. Our thousand is but one of a hundred thousand, and its best blood—which will be given as freely as water, if need be—will be but a drop in the red tide which the demon of Rebellion causes to flow.

What can be done for any regiment, our Colonel will do for this. Cool, spirited, industrious, considerably experienced, feeling deeply his responsibility, one who fears God, and regards man when worthy his regard, who appreciates the character of the men who are under him, who is stern when necessary, and yet kind by nature and practice, he has the qualities, unless I am greatly mistaken, which will make him a model Colonel. The men already feel attached to him—and the sentiment will strengthen greatly, I think, as they know more of him. He will be well seconded by his staff—and if the 12th does no service it will not be the fault of its officers, as I believe. We are to be temporarily brigaded in our present camp, with the 22d and 27th New Jersey. One or two of our Company have had slight ailments; but there has been no serious illness among them as yet.

Yours, G.

Benedict's letter shows that conditions in camp at Washington, D.C., with the Union army were much different from those at Camp Lincoln. Those who had thought that they were roughing it at Camp Lincoln, where they lived in barracks and were well fed, must have been dismayed by their new camp at East Capitol Hill. This camp was a dusty pit when dry and a mudhole when it rained. Benedict's regiment was lucky that Blunt actively worked on the regiment's supply and housing situation as soon as possible. Blunt, more than anyone else, got the army supply system to issue his regiment tents, rations, fuel, and forage in the space of a day. This took some skill, which Quartermaster Brownson lacked. But Brownson and his staff were learning from Blunt and getting experience that helped them in the months ahead.

Benedict and his regiment came from a small state, and for them, ten thousand troops was probably more people than they had ever seen in one place at one time. This number would have been equal to the population of several Vermont counties. Every soldier who saw these camps and troops spread out on Capitol Hill would always remember that he was a part of a large undertaking. This included the people Benedict mentioned from other regiments. Q.M. Archibald S. Dewey, Capt. Joel B. Erhardt, and Sgt. Cornelius W. Morse were from Burlington and had enlisted a year before Benedict.[4] They served in the 1st Vermont Cavalry Regiment, the first cavalry regiment raised in New England, and the only one Vermont fielded during the war. The fact that other Vermont regiments were close by helped the 12th Vermont's morale. The men could often visit friends and family members in those regiments when they were off duty. More Vermont nine-month regiments soon arrived, and they spent their time on East Capitol Hill training and preparing to take the field.

Camp Casey, East Capitol Hill, Washington
October 14, 1862

Dear Free Press:

The health of the 12th is on the whole good. Two or three of the Burlington Company and some twenty-five out of the entire Regiment are suffering from minor ailments, brought on in most cases by exposure on guard duty or sleeping in damp clothes; but with a spell of fair weather (thus far it has been rather cool, damp and variable) these will soon be on duty again. There has been thus far but one case of a dangerous character, which terminated fatally last night. I am told that the deceased—John B. Taggart, of Company F—was a man of bad habits, which aggravated his disease. He died in one of the permanent hospitals of Washington, to which he was removed.

We are giving strict attention nowadays to company and battalion drill, and shall soon be able to make a presentable appearance.

The 13th arrived yesterday afternoon, after a comfortable passage from Brattleboro, and has gone into camp today about half a mile West of us, between us and the Capitol. It is to be brigaded with us, and the 25th and 27th New Jersey under command of Col. Derrom of the 25th New Jersey, who is assigned to the temporary command of the Brigade. We are for the present attached to Gen. Casey's Division of the "Reserved Army Corps for the Defence of Washington," and it is the general impression among the men that we may remain here for some weeks, and possibly months. There is, however, nothing in our situation to prevent our being ordered to march any day.

Of Col. Derrom, our acting Brigadier, I know nothing except that I am told he is a German, and an old soldier. I have formed a favorable opinion of him from his first Order of duties for the Regiment, on which "Evening prayer at 8 P.M." has a place, weekdays, and which dispenses with the inspections of Sunday which in many Brigades make Sunday the most laborious day of the week. Our Sunday order, at present, is as follows: "Church Call, morning, at 10½ A.M., Divine service (voluntary) 11 A.M." "Church Call, afternoon, 3½ P.M. Divine service (positive) 4 P.M. All drills and parades except church and dress parade, are omitted on Sunday."

Our chaplain returned to us today after an absence of four days, having been under rebel rule at Chambersburg in the meanwhile. He left us at Baltimore to accompany a Vermont lady, on her way to her brother an officer in the 3rd Vt. who was lying at the point of death, at Hagerstown; and was returning by way of Chambersburg, on Saturday, when the rebels occupied the town. He thinks there were about 1,500 of them. They were well mounted, and well clothed as far as the stolen U.S. clothing went—the men under strict discipline and perfect control of the officers, who conducted themselves for the most part in a very gentlemanly and orderly way. Private persons and property were strictly respected. They left in a great hurry, amounting almost to a panic.

The chaplain being with us, the order for evening prayer was observed this evening. The Regiment was massed with closed ranks, in the dim twilight, and Mr. Brastow offered an earnest and appropriate prayer.

I find soldiering no lazy business, thus far, and have literally no time to write a longer letter today.

Yours, G.

P.S. An order read at Dress parade tonight, directs the Captains to hold their companies in readiness to march at a moment's notice. Forty rounds of ammunition apiece have been distributed today.

While the other Vermont nine-month regiments arrived and trained, the 12th Vermont lost its first man to disease: Pvt. John B. Taggart, a thirty-nine-year-old farmer from Northfield. The news of his death quickly reached the regiment. Taggart had been moved to a hospital located in the Odd Fellows Hall in Washington, D.C., where he died of an enlarged heart, according to the doctors.[5] While every soldier knew that death and injury on the battlefield was a possibility, death by disease was unexpected, though it was more of a threat in the Civil War as two men died of disease for every man killed in combat.

Benedict's regiment was still in limbo when the first of its sister regiments, the 13th Vermont, arrived in Washington on October 13. Its commander, Col. Francis V. Randall, was a lawyer by trade and veteran of the Army of the Potomac. As a captain, Randall raised Company F of the 2nd Vermont Infantry Regiment and fought at the first battle of Bull Run. Captain Randall then honed his trade at Camp Griffin during the winter of 1861–1862 and saw action with his company on the Peninsula the following spring. In August 1862, his division commander, Gen. William T. Brooks, authorized Randall to be a recruiting officer to help the 2nd Vermont make up losses that the regiment had suffered since it had left Vermont the spring before. While back in Vermont that fall, Gov. Frederick Holbrook tapped Randall to command the 13th Vermont. Now he and his command joined the 12th Vermont, along with the 25th and 27th New Jersey Infantry Regiments, in a provisional brigade.

In the Civil War, an infantry brigade was the smallest unit that could operate and feed itself. It was the largest tactical formation in the army and the principal fighting formation. It consisted of more than three infantry regiments but usually five regiments in the fall of 1862, with one or two artillery batteries attached to it. Later in the war, when attrition eroded a regiment's troop strength, other regiments were assigned to reinforce the brigade up to seven regiments. For example, in the fall of 1862, the 26th New Jersey reinforced the 1st Vermont Brigade, doubling its effective strength on paper. But the 26th New Jersey was unproven in combat and thus not trusted by veteran troops in battle. The Vermonters' opinion was not improved when this regiment soon gained the reputation of being light-fingered with anything that was not nailed down. However, the state of Vermont soon sent replacement troops to reinforce the regiments that composed the 1st Vermont Brigade.

The next higher unit in the army was the division, usually composed of three infantry brigades and supporting units. At East Capitol Hill, the 12th Vermont was assigned to a provisional division under the command of Maj. Gen. Silas Casey, a sixty-two-year-old Regular army veteran who had fought in the Mexican War. Casey commanded the 3rd Division, IV Corps, during the Peninsula campaign, yet he excelled in training raw recruits for the army. He wrote *Casey's Infantry Tactics,* which became the Federal army's official training manual in August 1862. In the fall of 1861, Casey was selected by McClellan as the drillmaster of the Army of the Potomac. In this position, Casey managed the army's training that fall and winter and got the Army of the Potomac into fighting trim. After the Peninsula campaign, he was reassigned to Washington, where he supervised the training and preparation of the new regiments in the East before their assignment to the Army of the Potomac or other commands. In addition to these administrative duties, he commanded one of the infantry divisions assigned to the defense south of the Potomac, which manned the city's fortifications.

Chaplain Lewis I. Brastow's observations in Chambersburg noted by Benedict were related to J. E. B. Stuart's ride against McClellan in October 1862, conducted to embarrass McClellan and to raise a little hell in the area. The Confederate cavalry under Stuart went to Chambersburg, Pennsylvania, to pay its first visit to this Northern town during the war. Here, Stuart merely burned an ordnance train that had been captured from the Confederates when Union cavalry escaped from Harpers Ferry that September. The Confederate cavalry was nearly brigade strength, well armed and mounted from captured Union guns and horses. In the fall of 1862, Union horsemen were not equal to the Confederates in leadership, organization, and training. As for Benedict's remark that these troops left almost in a panic, though the Confederate cavalry may have left in a hurry, it could outrun and outmaneuver Union infantry and had little fear of Union cavalry in the fall of 1862.

Camp Casey
East Capitol Hill, Washington
Oct. 18, 1862

Dear Free Press:

Reviews have been the order of the day with us for three or four days past. On Wednesday, the four regiments temporarily composing this Brigade, viz, the Vermont 12th and 13th, and the 25th and 27th New Jersey, were reviewed by Colonel Derrom, colonel commanding. The men were ordered out in "full marching order," which means with knapsacks packed, haversacks and canteens slung, 40 rounds of ammunition in the cartridge box, and arms and equipments all complete. We were in harness about two hours and a half, but the day was cool and shaded, and it did not come hard on us. The good appearance and behavior of the troops brought out the following General Order from the Acting Brigadier:

Headquarters, [2nd] Brigade,
Casey's Division,
Camp Casey, Capitol Hill, Washington
Oct 16, 1862

GENERAL ORDER No. 5

The Colonel commanding this Brigade, takes pleasure in giving credit to the several Regiments of this Brigade, for their smart appearance and general good order on Review yesterday. The States, they represent, as well as our common Country, may be proud of them. The material is excellent, indeed cannot be surpassed, and it rests now with the Officers of the Brigade, whether this material shall be properly moulded or not. To do this, requires much devotion to duty, and a strict attention to the rules and regulations of the United States Army, which will be their pride; and it is hoped the officers will be examples of neatness, good order, and military efficiency to the men.

A true soldier is the most courteous of men—obedient, firm, systematic, temperate and orderly, trusting in God at all times, and in all places.—Soldiers! aim each to be this perfect soldier.

By order of A DERROM—Colonel Commanding.

Next day the Brigade was reviewed by General Casey. This time I was not in the ranks, but detailed on special duty, and so had an opportunity to see the display. To the four regiments above named was added the 14th Massachusetts battery of Flying Artillery, six pieces. As I looked down the long line (half a mile or more in length) of bayonets, it looked to me like an array of 10,000 men, and I began to have some conception how grand a display a parade of fifty or sixty thousand must be. Of course I watched closely the marching and military appearance of the different regiments, and was proud to find the 12th Vermont, though the newest regiment on the ground, the 13th Vermont excepted, incontestably superior to any other on the ground.—This I am sure was not partiality on my part. I *tried* certainly to be perfectly fair in my judgment, and if I found that we were inferior in drill to the New Jersey regiments, as we might naturally be expected to be, having been in camp days to their weeks, to own it. But it was not so. Our officers were the most soldierly and spirited in appearance, our men the brightest in their looks, the quickest into line, the most uniform in marching, the most elastic in their step, the promptest in the simple evolutions ordered. And this was also the opinion of far better judges that I can be, General Casey having freely expressed his surprise at such proficiency in so new a regiment, and having transmitted to Col. Blunt an expression of his especial gratification with our appearance, which was read to us, with the added thanks of our good Colonel, at dress parade next evening. While we were out on Review, the Inspector of Camps, of Gen. Casey's Division took the opportunity to inspect the camps of the Brigade, and put a new feather in our cap, by declaring that he was glad at last to find in that of the 12th, a camp to which he might point other regiments, as an example of order and neatness.

Yesterday was given to Battalion drill, and today we have had another grand review, by Gens. Banks and Casey, of the troops of the two provisional Brigades of General Casey's Division. These, when the order for review was issued, comprised eight regiments of New York, New Jersey, Connecticut and Vermont troops, with two batteries, but a sudden order called two of them to the field last night, and but six regiments with the two batteries were on the ground. I wish I had the time to describe this review as I would like to—but I must cut it short.

The day was bright and the display a very fine one. Again the 12th took high honors. It is true the 15th Conn. surpassed them a little, and only a little in marching; but then the Connecticut regiment has been *three months* in camp, is a particularly good regiment, and its company lines were not over two-thirds the length of ours—an important consideration, superiority of numbers always adding correspondingly to the difficulty of maintaining a perfect line, in marching and wheeling.

It would have done you good to see the 12th alongside other good regiments. And we are as proud of our Field officers as they are of the men. Col. Blunt is an officer who always attracts attention by his keen eye, finely cut features, lithe and well formed figure, and perfect horsemanship. He rides a fine dark bay horse, of English blood and training, presented to him by Thaddeus Fairbanks of St. Johnsbury. Our Lieut. Col. Farnham, with nothing of show in his composition—for he is a very quiet as well as attentive and efficient officer—is a very showy officer, the effect being due to his handsome face and figure, and to the beautiful and fiery bay horse which he rides. Our Adjutant too, as you know, is a right handsome man, and rides a fine jet black Morgan stallion. Of course I wouldn't say these things where they could hear them, for they are modest men; but it is the simple truth, whoever says it, that there were no more soldierly and spirited looking officers on the ground, from Major Gen. Banks down, than the Vermont officers, or better horses than the Vermont horses. I may include in this remark, Col. Randall of the 13th, who rides a splendid chestnut charger.

The Brigades, after review, were marched down to the city, in column, through Pennsylvania Avenue to Gen. Casey's Headquarters near Long bridge, and then back to camp, making in all a march of six miles or more. The boys stood it well. They are getting toughened, I think, pretty rapidly, as a whole, although many suffer from diarrhea and colds. The list of sick men in hospital, however, does not average over twenty, none of them being very sick.

I find on looking over such of my letters as have returned to me in the *Free Press,* that I have omitted many things of interest to us here, and consequently to our friends at home. The advent of our mule teams is one. I ought to remember that, I am sure, for I traveled many a footsore mile, accompanying the officer who was sent to obtain them, over the pavements of Washington, from one army officer to another, before we secured them. We have five teams of four mules each. The driver rides one of the wheel mules, and drives by one single rein attached to the head of one of the leaders. They were but half broken when we took them, and do not understand English at all. There is no such word as *"whoa"* in the negro dialect, the monosyllable *"yay"* taking its place, and they do not always mind that. Their yay is not yay—nor their neigh a neigh proper, by any means.—The scene was a rich one, by all accounts, when our Vermont boys took them up Pennsylvania Avenue, the first day, on their way to camp. They cleared their side of the street as effectively as a charge of cavalry, and came within one of riding over one of the street railroad cars, horses, passengers and all. But I cannot tell every thing. If I jot down hastily now and then a circumstance or scene of interest, it is the most I can do.

Yours, G.

At Camp Lincoln, the men considered a dress parade with two regiments a big spectacle. Now, a few weeks later, a grand review with two brigades in their division and full marching order was of only passing interest. The reason for a grand review was the same as that for a dress parade— so that the divisional and higher-level commanders could gauge the men's training and combat readiness. It also instilled pride in the soldiers in the ranks, showing them that they were part of something big. And it showed how well brigade and regimental commanders moved their troops and put them through their paces. It was believed that if a commander and his regiment performed well on the drill field, they could fight well in battle.

The grand review of October 17 with the two brigades of Casey's division was held for Maj. Gen. Nathaniel Banks, then commander of the Washington military district. Banks was a forty-six-year-old politician, a self-made man from Massachusetts who had started in the mills of Waltham and eventually became speaker of the House of Representatives. At the outbreak of the war, his political connections got him his general's stars and then into trouble. Banks was more a politician than a soldier and lacked the administrative skill and military talent needed to be a good combat commander. His most famous battle was Cedar Mountain, in which Maj. Gen. Thomas Jackson defeated him. That was the end of Banks's career in the East, and perhaps would have been for the rest of the war had it not been for his connections. Soon after his defeat at Cedar Mountain, he was transferred to his present command before being tapped to command the Department of the Gulf. His luck did not improve over the next few years in the Department of the Gulf, however.

Benedict mentions Colonel Blunt's, Lieutenant Colonel Farnham's, and Adjutant Vaughan's horses in the review. Civil War infantry officers used horses only in reviews and for transportation while not in a combat zone, because officers on horseback drew enemy fire. Most horses in volunteer infantry regiments were gifts, not government mounts. Blunt's horse was a gift from his former employer, Thaddeus Fairbanks, who managed Fairbanks Scale and Measures Company of St. Johnsbury. Farnham had received one of his horses from the town fathers of Bradford.[6]

Mules pulled the wagons that carried the regiment's supplies and tents, and by the end of the war, army mules were a legend. In his classic account on the life of a Union soldier, *Hard Tack and Coffee,* John Billings wrote a full chapter on this animal. He recounted that mules survived the rigors of military service better than horses. A mule was more sure-footed and ate anything to survive in the field, whereas a horse might starve without forage or grass. Despite those advantages, mules had their drawbacks in army operations. Mules would not go into battle because they panicked at the sound of close gunfire and the sight of explosions. And they could not pull as great of a load as a horse. So mules took over the hauling of supplies in the rear areas during the war, freeing up horses to serve in artillery and cavalry units. The mule's overall performance, combined with its stubborn and sometimes violent behavior, added to the legend of this animal. A minor example was the 12th Vermont's mule charge up Pennsylvania Avenue while being brought back to camp by a work detail from Company C. As funny as that event may have sounded to the readers back home, however, it caused a fatal injury to a member of Benedict's company.

Camp Casey
East Capitol Hill, Washington
Oct. 23, 1862

Dear Free Press:

The *health* of a regiment is apt to be a matter of considerable interest to its members, and to their friends. The health of the 12th may, I suppose, be called pretty good. The longest sick list, as yet, has been 32 privates and 6 officers. Only two or three of these can be called very sick—some are merely home-sick; while on the other hand, there are to be added, in making a complete account, a number suffering from ailments not severe enough to figure in the regimental reports. The men, as a general thing, have a considerable repugnance to going into hospital. The hospital is a large tent, kept warm by stoves, in which the sick men lie, on straw, placed on the ground, as the Government does not furnish cots. It *looks* a little hard; but it is a good field hospital, and they are better off than many in and around this city. The sick and wounded men in the permanent hospitals in Washington, Georgetown, and Alexandria, number *thirty-four thousand*—an army in themselves. Many of these are in tents, for want of houses, and many I fear, from what I hear, suffer for want of suitable care. The Government is now building on the plain here, not far from our camp, some immense one-story wooden buildings, for a general hospital, which, when completed, will give the covering of a roof to thousands who now shiver in the hospital tents.

To return to our own regiment and company—our hospital steward, Mr. Hard, is a kind, skillful and faithful man; the hospital orderly, Wm. B. Lund of Co. C, is also a trusty and excellent man; the chaplain also interests himself heartily in the sick men. So far as they can secure it, all our sick will have kind and suitable care. I do not speak of the surgeons. As for Dr. Ketchum, I prefer to wait awhile before saying much about him. Dr. Conn, the Assistant Surgeon, has been sick himself, with a fever, ever since our arrival, and has been able to do nothing. He is improving, I am told. None of our Burlington boys have been seriously ill, thus far, with the exception of W. W. Walker, who has a combined attack of fever and ague and dysentery—and but one of our company (Collamer) can be called dangerously sick. He was suffering terribly with dysentery and vomiting yesterday. Today he has been removed by Cpt. Page, who will let no man of his company suffer if he can help it, to a comfortable private boarding house in the city, and one of our best men left in charge of him.

On many, probably on the majority of the men, the out-door life and abundance of exercise have a very favorable effect. They eat heartily, sleep soundly, enjoy themselves pretty well, and grow fat and hearty daily. Most, however, have worn out, thus soon, the romance of soldiering, and are ready to own that the life of a private soldier is a rather rough one. There are some discomforts about tent-life on East Capitol Hill, it must be owned. What do you think of a bath of 36 hours' duration in Washington *dirt?* That is what we have been enjoying yesterday and today. It has been quite dusty for a day or two, and you must remember that we are on the bare surface of this Maryland clay denuded of grass for the most part, and easily ground into the finest, most adhesive, and most disagreeable dust in the world—the dust of Washington. It had sifted pretty thoroughly over and into everything in our tents, when yesterday morning the wind began to blow. It commenced before light with a furious gust, which woke our thousand sleepers, and many other thousands around us, to find the dust pouring in, in almost solid masses, upon us, through every opening and crevice. We sprang up and with blankets and overcoats closed the openings; but the dust was still there, kept in constant motion by the slatting of our canvas walls, and the only way was to lie down again and take it as it came. What a dirty crew crawled out of tents that morning! And it was of little use to brush or wash—which latter habit, by the way, has to be indulged with moderation in our camp, for we are *short of water.* There is water in the Potomac, and in some wells around us, but these latter are drawn on constantly by other regiments as well as our own. The one nearest us, on which we relied almost entirely has given out; and having to be brought a considerable distance, water is now a luxury if not a rarity, in the camp of the 12th.—The wind kept up and the dust with it, and it is not fairly down yet. It is a peculiar life, when you must eat, breathe, and drink earth, instead of food, air and water. You open your mouth, it is as if some one put in a spoonful of pulverized clay. You put your hand to your hair, it feels like a dust brush. You touch your cheek, there is a clod. You place your finger in your ear, it is like running it into a hole in the ground. You draw from one of the dust holes in your clothes, the mud stained rag which a few hours since was your clean handkerchief, and wipe a small pile of "sacred soil" from the corner of either eye. You look on the faces of your comrades, they are of the earth, earthy. The dust penetrates every fibre of every article of clothing; you feel dirty "*clear through.*" But it is no use to attempt to describe it; it is unutterable—this plague of dust. It has not prevented, however, the company and battalion drills, and a *Brigade* drill by General Casey of this brigade and the 11th Mass. Battery attached to it, came off today. It was emphatically, a dusty affair.

There are frequent movements of regiments about us. On the whole more come than go. The 25th and 27th Maine, and the 14th New Hampshire, have arrived within a day or two, and are encamped close to us. The latter is under marching orders, however, and will be off tomorrow. Two or three of these neighboring regiments have fine brass bands, and so we have good music around us, on some of the clear mornings. There is talk of organizing a Band for the 12th, from the musical talent in the ranks. I think it will be done, if there is any prospect of our remaining stationary for any length of time. Our Drum Major, Perley Downer, has been made Brigade Drum Major of this provisional brigade. Company C received him, after dress parade last evening, when the order for his promotion was received, with presented arms and three cheers to which Major Downer responded in an appropriate and characteristic little speech.

FRIDAY MORNING.

The dust storm is over. The frost lies this morning thick and white on the ground—the first one of the season here. The sick are all doing well, except Captain Savage of Co. A, who has been delirious and ran out of camp in his shirt and drawers last evening. He was found a while later in the barracks of a neighboring regiment. I must close in haste.

Yours, G.

Besides army camps and fortifications, hospitals sprang up in and around Washington once the war started. Benedict gives a good picture of the medical services available to him and his comrades during their service. Care for a sick or injured soldier started at the regiment's surgeon's call, where the man saw his regimental medical staff. If they could not provide treatment, the soldier was moved to the brigade hospital, then the divisional or general hospital, as the need for care grew. It was common practice to keep a soldier as close to his regiment as his condition allowed, both to boost his morale and to ensure that the soldier returned to his regiment instead of becoming lost in the hospital system or being discharged home.

Benedict writes about the growing number of sick men in the hospitals as disease started to take its toll. The account of Capt. Charles Savage, who commanded Company A, is odd as, until then, Benedict wrote about the regiment's officers in near glowing terms. Benedict's account is at least embarrassing to Savage, and one wonders if he was still fit to command. Benedict never mentions Savage in his letters again, and no other newspaper, except for the *Brattleboro Phoenix,* which reprinted the account from the *Burlington Free Press,* mentions Savage's delirium. What is known is that Savage was a thirty-four-year-old farmer from West Windsor, Vermont. He remained Company A's commander for its term of service, showing that he had the health and temperament to command it. If he had not, Savage would have been replaced, as one of his colleagues later was.

In the meantime, the 12th Vermont was still living in the dust of Camp Casey. A few days later, the 14th and 15th Vermont Regiments arrived in Washington, but they probably did not feel lucky with respect to the timing of their arrival.

Camp Casey
East Capitol Hill, Washington
Oct. 26, 1862

Dear Free Press:

We have had a regular *soaker* today, hard rain all day: tents soaked through, camp ground swimming, mud 5 to 15 inches deep; nothing done but to keep the water out and eat our meals. It is raining harder than ever, since dark. I have just been out and made a raise of a couple of shelter tents, which we have thrown over our tent, and hope thus to keep the water from dripping on us. I think it will work first rate. The ground is soaked, however, so that the tent pins have but a slight hold, and a gust of wind, as high as one we have had here, would bring down half the tents in the regiment.

Some of our boys, who have been down to the camp of the 13th, say that we are much better off than they—their ground is softer, and they have not made themselves half so comfortable as we.

We are all pitying the poor fellows of the 15th, which arrived here at six o'clock this morning, and was to leave in about three hours after for Camp Chase, involving a march of 3 or 4 miles in the rain and mud. The 14th was sent up to Chain Bridge, night before last—all of which shows that the Vermont regiments are not to make a brigade together at present.

I have just learned that the 15th did not march today; but remained in the barracks near the Railroad Depot. I am glad to hear it. It would have been hard on them to march 4 miles and then pitch camp in this storm. I think, from what I hear tonight, that we are likely to remain here a while longer; but all is uncertainty as to army movements, from the very nature of things.

G.

Benedict and his comrades had heard that the five nine-month regiments from Vermont would be combined to form a brigade like the 1st Vermont Brigade, but the posting of the 14th and 15th Vermont to another camp made them wonder if that could still be the case. This was important to these men, as the 1st Vermont Brigade was one of the best in the Army of the Potomac and a source of pride to the state of Vermont. Being in the 2nd Vermont Brigade would give these men the possibility of being just as good. But they would have a lot of work to do first. The 1st Vermont Brigade was created on November 18, 1861, when Col. William F. Smith went to his friend and West Point classmate, Maj. Gen. George B. McClellan, then in command of the Army of the Potomac, and had the 2nd, 3rd, 4th, 5th, and 6th Vermont Infantry Regiments organized into the 1st Vermont Brigade.[7] Not surprisingly, William F. Smith became the 1st Vermont Brigade's commander.

The 1st Vermont Brigade was an exception to the rule, however, because the Federal government discouraged state brigades. The War Department held that mixing regiments from different states into brigades prevented any one community from suffering heavy losses by spreading that possible risk around. It was also thought that competition among these regiments made such a brigade more combat effective than a single-state brigade. Though the Federal government did gain relief from the political cost of regimental losses, these brigades were not as combat effective as the Confederate infantry brigades, the majority of which were composed of regiments from the same state and were more combat effective throughout the war. Vermont did have some political muscle, however, and the five regiments were brigaded together.

Camp Casey
East Capitol Hill, Washington
Oct. 28, 1862

Dear Free Press:

All of the Vermont Regiments are now here, the 16th having arrived yesterday. As the 14th and 15th were sent across the Potomac on their arrival, we had about given up the expectation that the new Vermont Regiments would be brigaded together. But last night an order came, brigading them, under command of Colonel Blunt, and establishing their post, for the present, on East Capitol Hill. The New Jersey regiments with which we have been brigaded, are on the march today, and the Vermont Regiments which were sent across the river, will come back, and be posted near us. The 16th went into camp right over against us last night. They slept under the little shelter tents—if sleep they could, for it was a very cold night, the ground damp, and covered with white frost this morning. They would have had a rather a poor look too, if left to themselves, for something to eat, as they got into camp too late to get up their cooking arrangements; but they were not allowed to go hungry. The 13th Regiment had them to supper last night, and the 12th invited them to breakfast this morning. Each company entertained the company of the corresponding letter, and Company C, of the 16th, who were the guests of the Howard Guard, thought they got a first rate breakfast, and acknowledged our hospitality before they filed away, with three hearty cheers for the 12th, and three for Company C, of Burlington. The men of the 16th are a fine, hearty looking set of men, and behaved like gentlemen, as they doubtless are.

The brigading of the Vermont Regiments is particularly satisfactory to our regiment, as the men feel sure of being in good company along side of Vermonters, and many of both officers and men have personal friends in the regiments. We were all, also gratified that the honor of commanding the Brigade should fall to our Colonel, and the receipt of the order was made the occasion for a little demonstration of the esteem and affection which the men of the 12th feel, and are always glad to express, for Col. Blunt. Company C, first got the news, just after dark last evening, and turning out, they filed down to the Colonel's tent, led by Capt. Page, and gave three cheers for "the Vt. 9 months Brigade, and Colonel Blunt commanding." This called out the Colonel, who made one of the little speeches, which he makes so happily, because he attempts nothing high sounding, but expresses unaffectedly the emotions of his heart, and stops when he gets through. He congratulated the men on the brigading of these five fine Vermont Regiments, who, he felt sure would live side by side, and fight side by side like true comrades. He explained the order, so far as it affected himself—that the position of Col. commanding fell to him by virtue of his rank as senior Colonel; that it was merely temporary, could last only till a Brigadier General should be placed over us, as he trusted a good one soon would be; that it would not take him from his men of the 12th, and that he *would not be taken from*

them except by an imperative call of duty, such as he trusted would
not come—that the kindness and good feeling he had met with
from both officers and men of this regiment, was all he could ask
and more than he deserved, or could think of without emotion—
that to remain the Colonel of the 12th was the highest honor he
desired, and to make the regiment what it could be and should be
was his utmost aspiration. "We have hitherto, my boys," said he,
"seen but the pleasantest part of a soldier's life. Thus far we have
known little of trial and suffering, and nothing of danger. The
rough times are yet to come. When they come we must meet them
like men, each doing the very best he knows how to do, for the
cause of the country, for the honor of our State, and for the credit
of the 12th, and looking to God to grant us success. I know I can
trust *you,* and I am proud and happy if you can trust *me.* I shall try
not to disappoint the trust."

With such hearty words he dismissed our company, which
retired only to make room for other companies, who came up in
succession, each to cheer the Colonel and call him out for a
speech, the Drum Major and Field music winding up the series
with a salute and Yankee Doodle. On the whole it was quite a little time, for an impromptu one.

I wrote of *dust* when I wrote last; we have had a touch of a different kind of experience since.—Day before yesterday, our first
steady rain set in. It came down steadily all day; but not hard
enough to cause us any *especial* discomfort. All the orders for the
day with the exception of the guard mounting and calls to meals,
had the go-by, and the men kept closely within their tents. At
night however, the air grew colder, the wind higher, and the rain
heavier. Our tents, which are not new, had hitherto kept out the
rain pretty well; but did not prove impervious to the big drops driven by the storm. They were stopped in a measure, by the canvas,
but a portion came right through, spattering in our faces, covering
our blankets with a heavy dew, and running down the *inside* of the
tent, in streams.

Things began to have a decidedly damp look for the privates.
There is considerable virtue however, in good woolen and India
rubber blankets; and most of us succeeded in cuddling on and
under them, in some shape, so as to get some sleep without dream-
ing of the Flood.

About four o'clock in the morning it stopped raining and began to pour down in sheets. Our company streets became rivers, the whole camp ground was deluged. The water in some parts of the camp overran the trenches around the tents, and poured in upon the inmates. The ground soaked to mud, ceased to hold the tent pins, and many a luckless soldier had to turn out in the storm and drive his stakes anew. It was a juicy time all around.

But daylight came, with much apparent difficulty, at last, and the question of *breakfast* began to stare us in the face. We were cold, wet, and as we now perceived, *hungry*. The storm had filled the kitchen trenches with water, instead of fire. Evidently there was no chance for anything *hot*, but should we have anything at all but rain soaked bread? Some companies did not. The good cooks of Co. C, however, had been equal to the emergency—had kept their fires burning, while there was any possibility of doing so, and provided in the night against the contingencies of the morning. We had a good breakfast of bread, beef and pork, and thus fortified within, possessed our souls in patience, till the storm broke away, as it did about 9 o'clock. It was hard rain, I think, even for this locality, and left a pond of many acres, which still remains in front of our camp where our parade ground has been heretofore. The day came off clear and cold, and before night the blankets were sufficiently dried to sleep comfortably in. Another wet night would probably have added considerably to the length of our sick list; as it was but few over the average were reported.

I spoke of our cooks above, and now wish to add that our company feels especially favored in respect of cooks. Three more careful and industrious, and excellent men for such a purpose, than Warren, Griffin, and Crane, of Co. C, it would be hard to find *anywhere*. Their good care of us has an important bearing on the health and comfort of the company, and I trust we were duly thankful therefore.

Yours, G.

The official creation of the 2nd Vermont Infantry Brigade was Casey's Division General Order No. 27. This order organized just one of several scores of infantry brigades in the Union army at the time, but it was almost a year before the impact of that decision became apparent. This general order made this brigade the main part of General Casey's division for the majority of its enlistment, instead of sending it to the Army of the Potomac, where the majority of the men wanted to serve.

Company C hosted its counterpart in the 16th Vermont for breakfast on October 28. The 12th Vermont and her sister regiments took turns feeding the 16th Vermont until it was on its logistical feet within a day or two after its arrival. Company C of the 16th Vermont, commanded by Capt. Asa Foster, was recruited from Plymouth and nearby towns on August 21, 1862. Located in the southeastern part of Vermont, Plymouth was the birthplace and boyhood home of Calvin Coolidge, the thirtieth president of the United States. The fact that these Vermont companies and regiments took care of each other when they did not have to, showed they had a high level of unit cohesion. Unit cohesion meant that a unit stuck together and more than likely fought better than those lacking it. Though sharing rations may seem a small matter, it meant that these officers and men would not let their counterparts down in other, more difficult situations.

The cooks of the 12th Vermont's Company C were Thomas Warren, a thirty-five-year-old farmer from Burlington; Henry F. Griffin, a twenty-nine-year-old butcher from Essex Junction; and William O. Crane, a twenty-year-old clerk from Burlington. Cooks were excused from most drills, as handling the rations and preparing food for nearly a hundred men a day kept them busy. They got the company's rations of hard or soft bread, vegetables, and meats from the regiment's commissary sergeant. Then they prepared the rations for the troops, which included butchering and cutting up steers for fresh beef rations, making coffee, and baking beans three times a day, unless they were on the march.

In the Civil War, enlisted men received either camp or marching rations. A camp ration consisted of up to a pound of fresh bread and a pound of fresh or salted pork or beef a day, as well as vegetables, usually potatoes or peas, often served in soups or stews, depending on what the commissary stocked and the vagaries of the transportation system at the time. A soldier also received coffee to wash it all down, along with some sugar. With the camp rations, the next challenge was to cook them. Outside their cook shack, the Company C cooks dug a cooking pit four by six feet wide and two feet deep, in which they burned wood for hot coals. They cooked the rations and made coffee in large pots with handles through which they inserted a wooden pole to lift them out at mealtime. The soldiers each had a mess kit consisting of a tin plate, cup, fork, knife, and spoon, which they cleaned themselves.

Marching rations were issued so that a soldier could prepare them himself on the move. They consisted of hardtack and three-quarters of a pound of salt pork or beef each day. Hardtack was a hardened biscuit about two and a half inches square and three-eights to one-half inch thick. Hardtack was edible depending on how old it was and the conditions in which the hardtack storage boxes were kept before issue. If the storage depot did not keep it dry and out of the weather, it became the hardtack of legend that was hard enough to break teeth or deflect bullets. At that stage, a soldier soaked the crackers in water or coffee until they softened up. The daily ration per man ranged from six to ten crackers a day. A soldier also got a pound of ground coffee with sugar per week. The soldier stored marching rations in his haversack, but it held only about five days' rations. So if a soldier was issued more than that, he ate the extra or had it transported by the regimental wagon, although the wagons and the troops usually got separated on the march.

Officers' rations differed from enlisted rations. Officers received an allowance for food and bought their rations directly from the commissary department or another vendor, such as a local farmer or a sutler. The company-grade officers, captains and lieutenants, usually ate the same rations as their men since it was easier and their allowance was not that large. Field-grade officers and their staff had different arrangements. Colonel Blunt and Lieutenant Colonel Farnham and their mess had Pvt. John A. Peach of Bradford from Company G, as their personal cook. Therefore, these officers and their mess had a much more varied diet than the average soldier. Though soldiers complained about their rations during their service, most wrote home telling their friends and family they were getting fat off them. Rations were also supplemented by foraging in the local countryside and food boxes from home.

Camp, 2nd Brigade, Casey's Division, Virginia
Oct. 30, 1862

Dear Free Press:

"Change sweepeth over all," said or sang the plaintive Mother-well, and we find the line to have as much truth as poetry in the army. Yesterday, at this time, every man in the 2nd Vermont Brigade thought we were good for a stay for some days, if not weeks, on East Capitol Hill. The Vermont Regiments had been brigaded together. The 14th and 15th, ordered across the Potomac on their arrival, had been ordered back and were busily establishing themselves in camp near us. It was reasonable to suppose that some time for drill in Battalion and Brigade Evolutions would be granted, *before* sending us forward. All the other regiments about us had been ordered away, leaving our Brigade alone, on East Capitol Hill. *Some* troops would, of course, be left there, and we must be the ones. So reasoned officers and men, and the conclusion was easily reached that we should stay where we were for the present. In this conviction, many of the 12th began making themselves more comfortable in camp without delay. Lumber was procured at $25 a thousand and upwards. Our little A tents, in which we enacted the daily and nightly miracle of stowing 6 men, with 6 muskets, &.—about as much harness as is allotted to so many horses in a well arranged stable, together with the bedding, baggage, and crockery and tinware, household furniture and goods and chattels, all and sundry, belonging to said family of 6, in a tent seven feet square on the ground and tapering in a wedge to the height of 6 or $6^{1}/_{2}$ feet—these little tents were elevated on the sides of boards, by which contrivance their original capacity is almost doubled and the comfort of the occupants at least trebled. Shelves were rigged, pegs put in to hang guns and trappings on, floors laid, and a hundred little contrivances to enhance order and cleanliness and comfort discussed and tried. With what satisfaction we looked at our new structures made, all but the roof, by our own hands! How we enjoyed a residence in which we could stretch our arms at length above our heads, and sit around the sides without doubling together like so many jackknives! With what complacency did we think of our own thrift, and look forward to days and weeks of such comparative luxury! Alas for the folly of human expectations! With nightfall came the order to move into Virginia, and here we are tonight, five miles the other side of the River, our new acquisitions left far behind us, and not a saw mill or lumber yard this side of Washington or Richmond, so far as we know. They may talk of the sorrows of leaving the ancestral roof-tree, the hearths around which boyhood's days were spent, and youth's and manhood's memories clustered; that can be described; but, the

pangs with which we left our wooden walls, and floors, are indescribable. But such is life in the army. We have, however, some
consolation tonight. A guard was left in our late camp and our kind
Colonel and Quartermaster have promised that if the wagons can
be procured to transport it, our lumber shall follow us hither.

The five Vermont Regiments broke up camp at daybreak this
morning. The order was to form in line at 7½ and march at 8.
Col. Blunt, commanding, is a prompt man, and expects and secures
promptness in those of his command. At half past seven the line
was formed, and at eight the long column marched. It swept down
Pennsylvania Avenue, a goodly array of stout, intelligent, spirited
men, as eye ever looked on. The march was a very comfortable
one for the men, as a whole, and our present camp, which is about
a mile beyond Camp Seward, back of Arlington Heights, bids fair
to be a great improvement on our late one, as far as the camping
ground and nearness to wood and water is concerned. I shall have
to reserve a description of it for a future letter.

You have heard before this, by telegraph, of the death of young
Collamer, of Shelburne. It is the first gap made by death, in the
ranks of Company C, and we feel it keenly. He was a very amiable
and excellent young man, with the making in him, to all appearance, of a stout and hearty soldier. His disease was uncontrollable
from the first, by medical skill, and he had as good care and attendance as Washington could afford. It had, on the first seizure and
throughout, I am told, symptoms which excited in his physicians
and friends, some suspicions of poisoning. The attack followed the
eating of a pie, bought of some peddler or sutler, I believe, but how
well founded the suspicions may have been, no one could say. No
personal malice towards one so inoffensive and gentlemanly in his
bearing towards all, could have had any share in it, if the painful
suspicion should be true. Capt. Page saw him every day, and he had
the kind and constant care of Pierson and Curtis, two of our best
men and well-skilled nurses. For a day or two the doctors thought
he might rally, but he did not agree with them. "I shall die in three
days," he said, one night, and in three days he died, peacefully, even
happily, for he had made his peace with God.

There are no very sick men of our company; and I believe we shall find our present Camp, on new ground, not tainted by the stay upon it of so many successive thousands, a healthier one than the old one. How long we shall stay here no one can say. We *suppose* it will be some little time.

Yours, G.

Other than having to leave their lumber behind, Benedict and his comrades were happy to get the order to move out. For the most part, they were sick of the dust, wind, rain, and mud of their camp on East Capitol Hill. As the men packed and readied themselves, there was a high level of excitement over their first move as a brigade. The march down Pennsylvania Avenue, despite its length and physical demands, was a morale boost as a crowd gathered to watch the men, marching in defense of their nation. They headed into Virginia, closer to the war they had enlisted to fight.

The tragedy involving Pvt. George Collamer was Benedict's first mention of a death in his company. It had come as an unexpected shock to the men. Collamer was an eighteen-year-old farmer from Shelburne, the nephew of Jacob Collamer, then one of Vermont's U.S. senators. It was not likely that Collamer died of food poisoning, as no one else got sick at the same time, and the chances that a peddler or sutler would poison only one soldier were remote. Pvt. Richard Irwin, another member of Company C, wrote to his family that George Collamer died from a kick from one of the mules that he, Collamer, and Benedict had brought into camp a few days before.[8]

Serious accidents in camp were common, and they took a toll on the regiment. For example, Lieutenant Colonel Farnham sprained his foot when his horse fell on it on October 19. He was lucky, as no bones were broken, but it laid him up for a week or two. By the time he had recovered enough to ride a horse, the 12th Vermont received orders to move on October 29. The next morning, Farnham rode his horse at the head of the 12th Vermont as Benedict and the others marched to a new camp closer to the war in Virginia.

CHAPTER 3

Camp Vermont

As October 1862 drew to a close, President Lincoln could see that he had a problem with his principal field commander, Maj. Gen. George B. McClellan. McClellan had not moved the Army of the Potomac for six valuable weeks after the battle of Antietam. The president, Secretary of War Edwin M. Stanton, and Maj. Gen. Henry Halleck tried everything to persuade McClellan to march his army south, but to no avail. Finally Lincoln visited McClellan and the Army of the Potomac at the Antietam battlefield on October 1. After four days spent visiting field hospitals, reviewing troops, and meeting with McClellan, Lincoln left for Washington with the belief that McClellan and his army were about to move. When this still did not happen, what little trust Lincoln had for McClellan evaporated. Telegrams and orders continued to pester McClellan to move. But even Stuart's raid of October 10–12 had little effect on the Army of the Potomac's activity.

On October 26, McClellan finally started the Army of the Potomac marching south toward Culpeper Courthouse. From there, the army could either attack Fredericksburg, about thirty miles to the southeast, or go through the Wilderness and attack Richmond before winter closed in and stopped active operations. McClellan was not in a hurry to reach Culpeper Courthouse, however, as the Army of the Potomac took eleven days to march thirty-five miles. By the time the lead elements of the Army of the Potomac arrived in Warrenton, Virginia, near the Rappahannock River, tensions between Washington and McClellan were at the breaking point. As the Army of the Potomac moved south, thus extending its lines of communication, units located around Washington were redeployed to protect them. One of these units was the newly formed 2nd Vermont Infantry

Brigade, which included the 12th Vermont. They were finally moving south, and sooner than they had expected.

Picket Station Number 35, Union Lines,
Mount Pleasant, Fairfax Co., Va., November 1, 1862
Five Miles from Mt. Vernon

Dear Free Press:

You see the 12th is making some progress. We are on "the Richmond Road," if not on the road to Richmond.

I promised in my last, I believe, some description of the first camping ground of the Vt. 2nd Brigade on the soil of the "Mother of Presidents," but our stay in it was not long enough to make it worth while to spend much time and paper on a description. We pitched our tents on the edge of a clean, inviting stretch of oak timber not far from the famous "Munson's Hill." A few rods in the rear ran a stream of the clear sweet water which we find the Virginia streams composed of. The contrast between the spot, and the bare Sahara like surface of East Capitol Hill, was delightful to us. Here was a mat of furzy grass between us and the ever lasting clay; here was shade in the heat of day—the midday sun is hot here, yet—here was *wood*—wood to burn if we wished a fire any-where—forked sticks for toasting forks, and clothes horses and gun racks, to be had for the cutting; wood to *whittle,* when one had time to indulge in that Yankee pastime.—Here was overflowing water in abundance. How different from that stretch of desert where not a sliver for a toothpick could be had at less than $25 a thousand, and water only came through much tribulation, and by the pailful for a company. It was a right pleasant spot, and we voted at once that we wanted no better for winter quarters, if there was no fighting for us to do this fall.

We lost no time now in waiting to see if we should stay here some days, but began at once to be comfortable. The lumber on which to raise the tents, for some of the boys, had followed them, and was put at once to its proper use; others split out flat shooks and made them answer well in place of boards. Others stockaded their tents with small logs, and filled the cracks with fringes of cedar. The camps (the five regiments were stretched along side by side) hummed with activity. The woods were filled with men, apparently on a big picnic. It lasted just one day! Orders were out for a grand Review on the parade ground of Fort Albany, near by us, on Saturday morning. The regiments marched out to it at ten o'clock only to be turned back by orders for two regiments to strike tents and march at once—and at twelve o'clock, the 12th and 13th were in line of march. Our A tents we left behind us and we carried on our knapsacks, each man his half, the little shelter tents. At half past 12 we started for Alexandria, Col. Randall, in the temporary absence of Col. Blunt, taking chief command, and the 13th leading. Col. Randall had ridden ahead, and our gait for the first two miles was set by an inexperienced officer of the 13th, who probably forgot that men could not march with heavy knapsacks on their backs, at the pace of his fast walking roadster, without feeling it. It was a very hot day. The men sprung to it, at a smart walk for the long legged ones, and on the keen jump for the short men.

We passed some squads of old reg'ts. "Where is the fight, boys?" was the first question. "There must be one," they added "men are not marched like that unless they are wanted in a *mighty* hurry." We got a rest in two miles, in time to save a third of the two regiments from falling out; but the men had got "blown" at the outset, and it made the whole march a pretty hard one. We passed through Alexandria about four o'clock; as we entered the city we passed through the camps of the paroled men and convalescents, which line the road. They came out by hundreds to see us go by, and laughed at our well stuffed knapsacks. "You're green," they said, "You'll heave them away before you march many more marches. Then you'll see where you missed it." "We see where *you* missed it," replied Dick E—— the funny man of our Company, whose supply of "chaff" is inexhaustible—"it was when you hove away that *soap and towels* so soon." This hit at the unwashed appearance of the first spokesman and his crowd, brought a roar of laughter from three hundred hearers, and "the uncalled for remarks" dried up suddenly. After a halt on the outskirts of the city, we passed across Hunting Creek, to a camping ground in a field on the southern side.—The march was one of about ten miles, and we were glad at its close to pitch our little tents in a hurry, eat our rations, brought with us in our haversacks, and drop off to sleep. We discovered first, however, that we had marched by a route about three miles longer than the true one for us, and that we were to picket a space of six miles, in the Union lines around Washington, left unguarded by the marching of Sickles' Brigade, which left with many thousand other troops, the day before, to reinforce Sigel. Two companies of the 13th were at once sent off (it was now dark) on that duty; our turn came the next day.

After dinner on Sunday we marched South on the Mount Vernon road about a mile and a half to our present Camp; and within fifteen minutes after our arrival, four companies were detailed for picket duty. Co. C was of the number, and so your correspondent, who was among the first to get a taste of guard duty, was also among the first to try picket duty. I found it (as it has often been described) the pleasantest part of soldiering. We were marched off rapidly two or three miles farther into the country to the brow of the high ground which looks off the valley of the Potomac, stretching many a mile in a varied scene of meadow and timber now glowing with the bright colors of the American Autumn, to the South, and far away to the west to the lands on the Accotink. From this point the line of picket stations extended three miles in each direction. The extreme on the left reaching to the Potomac. Two companies were taken to the right and companies C & D waited till the officer, an aide of Gen. Casey, who was to place us, returned from placing the others. As we waited we heard the first sound of actual conflict. From the Northwest came, distinct and unmistakable, the sound of cannon from the distant battlefield, of which you have the news, though as yet we have but uncertain rumors of it. For the hour and a half we waited there, the booming was incessant. It mostly died away however, before we started along the line. We were hurried along just at nightfall, leaving now one, now two, now three, now a reserve of ten or fifteen men, at the posts. A dilapidated log hut, a booth of boughs, or the shade of a big oak, gave shelter, and fires of brush or rails, were burning at each. For twenty-four hours we were to stand guard here, making ourselves as comfortable as we choose.—My own position, is on the Estate of Mt. Pleasant, in front of the residence of Mrs. W., its owner. From the brow of the high level plateau on which the home is located, I have before me a view of almost unsurpassed interest and beauty. Away below winds the Potomac through a magnificent valley, woodland and meadow varying the prospect, and evergreens relieving with green, the bright coloring of the oak forest. Directly in front lies Mt. Vernon, the house hidden by an interposing ridge; but the Estate plainly in view. To the left is Fort Washington, built in 1812 and now occupied by Union forces. The mansions of the wealthy "first families," are visible between the trees, here and there. It is a *magnificent* view. I had four hours of watch, from 11 to 3, at night. It was a mild night, sometimes a little clouded, anon the full moon, bringing out the prospect almost as by daylight. Four or five picket fires gleamed brightly along the line; but the night was still as death. There was no sound of armies or man or beast. I could bear personal witness to the fact that it was "quiet on the Potomac."

There is nothing very exciting in the duty. We know well that there are no rebel forces near us—but it is true after all, that we are at the front, doing actual duty, for the first time, with loaded arms, and that no armed body is between us and the lines of the enemy. I would like right well now to describe this old house, 150 years old, and the peculiar features of this scene and duty; but the Relief is now in sight to take our places, and I must prepare to march back to camp.

The health of the regiment is very good. Lieut. Wm Loomis, of Company C, is now acting as Adjutant of the 12th, adjutant Vaughan being A.A.A.G.—acting assistant Adjutant General. Two men, one in Co. I, another in Company K, shot themselves accidentally with their revolvers yesterday—one through the hand, one through the ankle.

Yours, G.

On October 30, the 2nd Vermont Brigade was ordered to Camp Seward near Arlington Heights to finish readying itself for field service. However, divisional headquarters ordered Colonel Blunt to provide two regiments the next day for picket duty south of Hunting Creek, which was just south of Alexandria. The two regiments were to replace Gen. Dan Sickles's brigade as it marched south as part of the Army of the Potomac. Blunt selected the 12th and 13th Vermont because they were the most combat ready in the brigade. (The other regiments were still using old,

unserviceable French and Belgian muskets.) Blunt stayed with the majority
of his brigade at Camp Seward in case they had any snags with army
bureaucracy. This put Colonel Randall, as senior officer, in command of the
two regiments as they marched south.

The new uniforms and fully packed knapsacks of the men of the 12th
and 13th Vermont signaled to all veteran troops along the way that these
men were new and had yet earned the respect of the veterans. But Company C had someone in the ranks who would not take guff even from the
veterans: Pvt. Dick Irwin, whom Benedict refers to as Dick E——. Irwin
was a twenty-six-year-old streetcar conductor from Burlington who gained
the reputation of being Company C's wise guy and cynic. This view of him
is reinforced in the letters he sent home, which were preserved and give an
interesting counterpoint to those of Benedict and his other comrades. Irwin
joined the Howard Guard to get his enlistment bonus, but more impor-
tantly, to avoid being drafted into a war he did not believe in. He was an
ardent Democrat and did not believe the war was just, although he did not
move to Canada to avoid service. When the call for troops came, Irwin felt
that spending nine months in the army was far better than spending three
years, and he joined the Howard Guard along with Benedict. Irwin was
relieved that the 12th Vermont was only doing picket duty and not marching into combat at this time.

As Benedict and his comrades discovered, picket duty was similar to
sentry duty, but rather than guarding a camp or building, they guarded a
likely avenue of approach by the enemy. The picket force was posted ahead
of a regiment's main body and acted as a human trip wire to control or
warn of the enemy's movement, as well as any escaped slaves, deserters, or
civilians crossing into their lines. A picket line's length and breadth were
determined by the terrain and the expectation of enemy contact. A picket
post was usually set so that it and other picket posts could see and support
each other by fire when the need arose. The picket line Benedict describes
was not long, being composed of just two companies and with only a third
of the men on the picket posts at any given time in four-hour shifts.

A picket reserve was located fifty yards or more behind the picket posts
in a defensible place, usually a prominent terrain feature such as a house,
barn, big tree, or field fortification. The picket reserve usually served as the
place where new shifts went to relieve the picket posts and off-duty men
could relax, as well as a rallying point if the picket posts were pushed back or
a staging area for the posts' relief during an attack. Then the picket reserve

Pvt. Richard J. Irwin.
IRWIN PAPERS, UNIVERSITY OF VERMONT.

commander, usually a sergeant, would decide whether to stand and fight according to his special orders, calling for reinforcements or falling back to the company or regimental reserve.

The last part of the picket line was the company or regimental reserve position, located fifty to a hundred yards behind the picket reserve. At Company C's picket reserve, the men were allowed to relax and eat, yet had to move at a moment's notice if called upon to support the picket reserve. The men rotated on set four-hour shifts that seemed to them to drag on, whereas their eight hours off passed quickly.

Camp Vermont near Alexandria, Va.
Nov. 7, 1862

Dear Free Press:

The camp of the Vermont 2d Brigade, in this place—two miles south of Alexandria, on the Mt. Vernon road has been christened

"Vermont," since I wrote you last. And today it looks more like Vermont, than Virginia is wont to at this time of year. We are enjoying a veritable *snowstorm*. It began at 7 o'clock this morning, has fallen steadily, and now at 7 P.M., at least *five inches* of snow lies upon the ground. Several gentlemen, who spent last winter in Camp Griffin, Va., assure me that there was no such fall of snow in this region in all last winter.

It is not thawing at all; the air is chill, and it will freeze sharply tonight. It is a sufficiently notable thing to be announced by telegraph, and I doubt not that a large amount of sympathy and concern will be expended by our Vermont friends tonight or tomorrow, as they read of half a foot of snow in Washington, and think of their soldier sons and brothers shivering under canvas, or standing on picket in the storm. But I think there is little suffering in this regiment. Not that a small A tent (our tents followed us hither from Camp Seward) soaked with moisture from damp snow, is the most warm and cheerful habitation imaginable; but it can be closed tight enough to keep the snow from actual contact with its inmates, and by piling on what woolen clothing he has, in all shapes, a healthy man can keep up the warmth of his body and snugging closely to his comrades, sleep with some approach to comfort.

But our Vermont boys, are not restricted in all cases, to the means and appliance for comfort furnished them by Uncle Sam, and are, I find apt to be equal to most emergencies. They are to this, at any rate. A couple of our old soldiers, formerly of the 1st, set us the pattern of a tent stove, two or three days since. A piece of sheet iron, a foot or two square, bent at the edges, so as to form a shallow pan, was inverted over a hole in the ground of corresponding size; a tube of bent sheet iron, leading from the outer air to the bottom of the hole provides air, and a joint or two of rusty stove pipe, eked out with one or two topless and bottomless tin cans, makes a chimney which draws like a blister plaster. It don't *look* much like a stove; I can't say exactly what it *does* look like—as near as anything, I should think like to the very young offspring of a cross between the Monitor and a Dutch oven; but it answers the purpose famously. Its chimney, smoking furiously this morning amid the flying snow flakes, gave the hint to our boys, and half the Co. C were off at once

Picket Post at the Old Barn at Wolf Run Shoals, Virginia. HOUGHTON COLLECTION, UNIVERSITY OF VERMONT.

for material wherewith to build similar non-descripts. They rummaged a deserted camp near us, and came back loaded with pieces of old stove pipe and scraps of cast and sheet iron, which were quickly put together; and as I looked up our company street an hour ago, I saw the rusty pipes sticking out of the ground by the side of more than half the tents, the curling smoke from each telling of warmth and comparative comfort within.

There were some, however—the tent hold of which your humble correspondent is a member among them—who were not enterprising enough to search for, or lucky enough to find, the needful supply of old stove pipe and sheet iron.—We stood our dinner of boiled pork, bread and coffee, in our damp tent, ate it in rather sour and meditative silence, and held a council of war at its close. Something had got to be done; our toes and fingers and noses were *cold,* our straw and blankets were damp. We must have a *fire;* how to get it in available shape was something of a question. Our sole supply of metal was in our dinner furniture before us. The problem was—given a table knife and fork, a tin cup and tin plate, to extemporize therewith a stove, pipe and chimney. But we set to work and Mr. Ericsson himself could not have done more with the same material. With the knife and cup we excavated a hole in the firm and adhesive clay which forms the floor of our tent; its top was a little less in circumference than our tin plate, its bottom, a foot or more below the surface, was somewhat larger. A hole was then dug outside the tent, sloping inward till it nearly met our excavation inside, and the bottoms of the two were connected by a passage two inches in diameter, worked through with the knife. From the top of our circular cavity within, a trench was made extending outside the tent, and covered by a brickbat, which turned up most opportunely when most needed.—The tin plate was placed over the hole, and the thing was done. You perceive the nature of the invention. This planet on which we dwell forms the body of our stove. The tin plate is both door and top of the same. The small hole at the bottom is the draught, the trench at the top is the flue! We fill it with hardwood chips, light a fire, and it works quite as well as we expected.

The heating surface was pretty small, it is true; but we kept the old plate red hot by assiduous feeding. In an hour or two the ground around began to be sensibly dried and warmed. A dry spot developed itself, as soon as the snow stopped falling, in the canvas of our tent, over the stove, and extended slowly along the side— the temperature rose sensibly within—and when by a fortunate stroke of policy we were enabled to substitute a sheet iron mess pan for our dinner plate, thus quadrupling our heating surface, we had all the heat we needed. We can no longer see our breath, within our linen house; we laid our bread on the top of our stove and had hot toast with our tea for supper; and the prospect is that we shall sleep tonight pretty warm and dry.

NOVEMBER 8, 1862

So we did, though the night was a very sharp one. Our snow stands the sunshine well today, and will not be wholly gone, I think, before tomorrow.

Nearly half the regiment is off on "fatigue duty" today. This, it seems, is the military term for the process which is said to be McClellan's *forte*. In common English it is called *digging*. The defensive strength of Fort Lyon, half a mile to the North of our camp, is being increased by some formidable outworks, and fifteen hundred men from our Brigade are to enjoy daily for a while, the privilege of digging the trenches and throwing up the breastworks.

Orders are out, moreover, for us to build log huts for winter quarters. This looks like wintering us here, though it is quite within the range of possibility, that we shall build and leave for others to occupy. There are other indications, however, which point toward a somewhat protracted stay here. If so, Camp Vermont is worth a line or two of description. The 12th is encamped on a sloping hill side, by a stream of good water, and in close proximity to the family mansion of the manor of "Spring Bank." Of this, Mr. George Mason is the proprietor—an old gentleman, who in this great contest between the Government and rebellion, announces himself as *neutral,* and had in token of his position a white flag hung out, when our regiment, without saying "by your leave" marched into his grounds. A written notice attached to a tree, informed all whom it might concern, that Mr. George Mason could accommodate no person, outside of his own family, in his house, and had stuck this up to save applicants the pain of a peremptory refusal. Nevertheless, I perceive that Col. Blunt has his headquarters in a small wing of the mansion, and the barns are filled with the horses of the regiment. One of the old darkies of the establishment hit it about right, as one of his brother contrabands expressed some astonishment at the summary exclusion of his master's cows from their wanted stalls for the accommodation of yankee horses: "Ole Massa might a' been nuff of a Union man to hang out the stars and stripes, den he got sarved better."

Around us, within a circuit of a quarter of a mile, are the other regiments of our brigade. There are woods close by to furnish us timber and fuel, and though it is not as sheltered and pleasant a place as our last encampment, we can make ourselves comfortable here, beyond a doubt.

The 14th, 15th, and 16th are to have their old French and Belgian muskets exchanged for Enfield rifles in a day or two, and will then do their share of picket duty. Some of your anxious readers may have supposed, possibly, from the fact that we are doing picket duty, that we are in the face of the enemy, or somewhere near it. Such is by no means the case. It is true that, with the exception of some cavalry videttes, there are no armed bodies between us and the rebels on the direct line south; but the rebel lines are twenty or thirty miles to the south and west of us, and are likely to be farther off rather than nearer. Our only danger at their hands is from a raid, and to that we should be liable, it seems, as far north as Chamberstown, Pa., and how much further, Gen. Stuart, C.S.A. only knows. We do not intend, however, to let that active gentleman through, about here. Our pickets are tolerably vigilant, and have thus far brought into camp three prisoners. One was a horridly dirty and animated, externally, specimen of humanity who turned out to be an enstray from the convalescent camp at Alexandria, who had wandered beyond our lines, perhaps with the intention of deserting. The others profess to be deserters from the rebels, and have been taken for safekeeping to Fairfax Seminary.

Col. Blunt continues to be the capable and popular commanding officer of this Brigade. Col. E. H. Stoughton, is, I hear, assigned to the command of a Brigade in Gen. Brook's division of the Army of the Potomac—a high honor for a young man of twenty-two.

Yours, G.

The snowstorm came as a surprise to everyone in the area, especially to the Vermonters, who had supposed that the Virginia climate was better than that of their own state, where the winters were usually long and cold. Yet this snowstorm was early even by Vermont standards. With this winter weather, rumors began to circulate as to whether the brigade would stay at Camp Vermont for winter quarters. While this talk made its rounds in camp, the more pressing need of heat for the tents concerned the men. Their only source of heat were whatever crudely built stoves the men could improvise.

McClellan had taken a personal interest in designing the defenses of Washington the previous winter. Several forts had been constructed, as well as miles of earthworks and roads to move the large numbers of men needed to defend the capital from the Confederates, who were then encamped at winter quarters near Centreville, twenty miles from Washington, D.C. With the Union's disastrous summer of 1862, this effort continued as the men improved existing forts and constructed new ones. The Federal government did not provide enough money to hire laborers to finish the job quickly, so

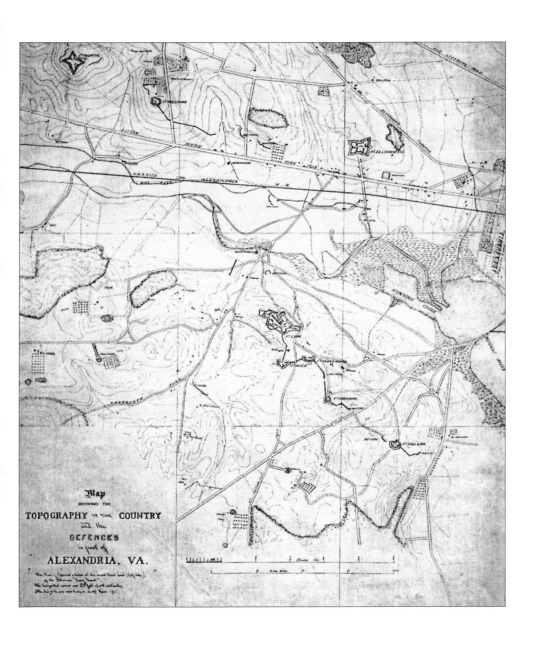

Washington's defenses south of Alexandria. NATIONAL ARCHIVES.

troops that were assigned to or stationed in the defense of Washington, and were close enough to the work sites, got the job of constructing these fortifications with picks and shovels. Benedict and his comrades were kept busy digging until another mission and movement a month later.

As the weather grew worse, the Vermonters began working to improve their camps. With one snowstorm and cold weather upon them, Benedict's company and the regiment constructed stockades, or wooden walls, for their tents. The men's quarters took on the look of log cabins, with their tents forming the roofs. They accomplished this in whatever spare time they had left after fort construction and picket duty.

George Mason, the owner of the land on which the 2nd Vermont Brigade camped, was unhappy about the brigade's stay. Mason was an old and disheartened man in the fall of 1862. Named for his grandfather, the George Mason who signed the Declaration of Independence, Mason was considered a member of a first family of Virginia, or FFV. Most Vermonters considered the FFVs the people most responsible for the war and thought them traitors. Mason was a slaveholder, yet many of his slaves had managed to escape. Now the rest of his estate suffered, as nearly five thousand soldiers settled on his land. Mason felt that the guards posted to protect his outbuildings, rail fences, and other property were there to imprison him and his family. He complained to officers and government officials to move the brigade elsewhere. Civilian officials did not listen to Mason, as military necessity overruled his rights. In addition, the commander of the reserve corps defending Washington, Maj. Gen. Samuel P. Heintzelman, questioned Mason's loyalty, having spent the prior winter at Spring Bank where he endured the same pleas as Colonel Blunt. Mason publically characterized himself as neutral, but his loyalty was questioned by most of the 2nd Vermont Brigade's officers and soldiers, since he flew a white flag at his house and refused to take the oath of allegiance to the Federal government. Furthermore, Mason's brother, John, was the Confederate representative to Great Britain and a household name in North America because of the Trent Affair the fall before.[1] For the first few weeks at Camp Vermont, Colonel Blunt had his headquarters in the west wing of Mason's mansion, further increasing tension between Mason and the Vermont troops. Ultimately, Colonel Blunt moved it because he could not stand Mason's whining.[2]

Benedict's information on Col. Edwin H. Stoughton was incorrect by two years on his soon-to-be brigade commander's age, and on his next army assignment. That was something Benedict and his comrades learned three weeks later, and it was not with General Brooks's division or the 1st Vermont Infantry Brigade.

Camp Vermont—Near Alexandria, Va.
Nov. 14, 1862

Dear Free Press:

You have discovered that I make little or no mention of army movements; nor do I indulge in criticism or speculation on the course of the war in any of its parts. Such matters I leave to the correspondents from Headquarters. My object is to give your readers, so many of whom have friends in the ranks, some idea of our life and business as seen not from the officers marquee, or the reporter's saddle, but from the tent of the private. I have nothing to write, consequently, about the change in the chief command of the army, or its probable results. You can judge of them better than we; I may say, however, that there has been no meeting in the 2nd Vermont Brigade, in consequence of Gen. McClellan's removal, and that any change that promises more active and efficient service for the army, will have our hearty approval, as a portion of the same.

In the absence of anything especially exciting, let me try and describe, briefly, an ordinary day in camp. You are, perhaps, familiar enough with the regular arrangement of tents in a regimental camp. The tents of the Colonel and his Staff are commonly disposed in a line at the rear of the camp. In a parallel line with them are the tents of the line officers, each captain's tent fronting the street of his company. The company streets run at right angles to the line of the officers' tents, and are of variable widths, in different camps, according to the extent of the ground. In our present camp they are about 25 feet wide. On each side are the company tents, nine on a side, a foot or two apart, facing the street on each side. At the inner end of the street, on one side, is the "Cook Tent," occupied by the company cooks and stores, and in front of it is the "Kitchen Range." Whose patent this is, I cannot say. It differs from most others I have seen. It is composed of a trench, 4 feet long and 2 deep, dug in the ground. In the bottom of this the fire is kindled. Forked sticks at the corners, support a couple of stout poles, parallel with the sides, across which are laid the shorter sticks on which hang the kettles. With this apparatus, and an oblong frying pan, of formidable dimensions—say three feet long by two wide, is done all the cooking of the company.

The first signs of life, inside of the lines of the main Guard, are to be seen at these points. The cooks must be up an hour or two before light, to get their fires started and breakfast cooking. The fires are, on the cold mornings (and most of the mornings are cold) objects of attraction to those of the soldiers who, for any reason have lain cold—too cold to sleep. These come shivering to the fires, and watch the cooks and warm their shins, till Reveille. There are stoves now, however, of some sort, in most of the tents, and almost all can be as warm as they wish at any time.

At daybreak, the Drum Major marshalls his drum and fife corps at the centre of the line, and the Reveille arouses, with scream of fife and roll of drum, the sleeping hundreds, lying wrapped in their blankets under the canvas roofs. The reveille is a succession of five tunes, of varying time, common and quick, closing with three rolls, by the end of which each company is expected to be in line in the company street. The men tumble out, for the most part, just as they have slept, some with blankets wrapped about them, some in slippers and smoking caps, some in overcoats.—In line, the orderly sergeant calls the roll, and reads the lists of details for guard police, fatigue duty, &c. After roll call, many dive back into their tents and take a morning nap, before breakfast, others start in squads for the brook, which runs close by our camp, to wash. The fortunate owners of wash-basins—there are two in our company—bring them out, use them, and pass them over to the numerous borrowers; other wash in water from their canteens, one pouring on the hands of another. "Police duty" comes at $6\frac{1}{4}$, and is performed by a squad under direction of a corporal. This varies slightly from the popular notion of such duty—which is commonly supposed to consist in wearing a star, standing round on city street corners, and the occasional diversion of clubbing some non-resistant citizen. "Police duty" in camp, corresponds to what, when I was a boy, was called clearing up the dooryard. The sweeping of the company streets, removal of noisome or unsightly objects, grading of the grounds, and work of similar character, come under this head. At half past six comes the "Surgeon's call." This is not a call of the Surgeon, who is not expected to appear in company quarters, unless for some special emergency; but of the orderly sergeant, who calls for any who have been taken sick in the night, and feel bad enough to own it and be marched off to the Surgeon's tent, when after examination, they are ordered into hospital or on duty, as the case may require. Breakfast takes place at 7, by which time in well ordered tents, the blankets have been shaken, folded, and laid away with the knapsacks in a neat row at the back of the tent, and the soldiers start out, cup in hand, for the cook tent, where each takes his plate with his allowance of bread and beef or pork, and fills his cup with coffee. Some sit and eat their breakfast on the woodpile near the fire; but most take all their meals to their tents. The straw covered floor is all the table, a rubber blanket the table cloth, and sitting round on the ground like so many tailors, we eat with an appetite which gives to the meal a zest almost unknown before we "went a sogering." Our meals do not differ greatly, the principal difference being that we have cold water instead of tea or coffee, for dinner. The rations are beef, salt and fresh, three-fifths of the former to two of the latter, both of fair quality; salt pork, which has uniformly been excellent; bread, soft and hard, the for mer equal to first rate home made bread, the latter in size, taste and quality resembling basswood chips—very wholesome, however, and not unpalatable; rice, beans, both good, and potatoes occasionally; coffee, rather poor, and tea ditto. Butter, which when good, is one of the greatest luxuries in camp, cheese, apples, which with most Vermonters, are almost an essential and other knickknacks, are not furnished by government; but may always be bought of the sutlers, at high prices. Our company are great hands for *toast;* and at every meal the cookfires are surrounded with a circle of the boys holding their bread to the fire on forked sticks, or wire toast racks of their own manufacture, and of wonderful size and description. So we live, and it shows to what the human frame may be enured by practice and hardship, that we can eat a meal of good baked or boiled pork and beans, potatoes, boiled rice and sugar, coffee and toast, and take it not merely to sustain life, but actually with a rel-ish—curious, isn't it?

Dinner is at 12, Dress Parade at $4^1/_2$ and Supper at $5^1/_2$. The heavy work of the men fills the intervals. This varies; at Capitol Hill it was company and Battalion Drills. Here it is digging in the trenches of Fort Lyon, and cutting lumber in the woods nearby, for our Winter quarters. Evenings are spent very much as they would be by most young men at home, in visiting their comrades, playing cards and checkers, writing letters, and reading. A private occupation of a leisure hour, with the smokers, is the carving of pipes from the roots of the laurel, found in profusion in the woods here. It is a slow business, in most cases beginning with a chunk about half as large as one's head, which is reduced by slow degrees and patient whittling to the small size of a pipe bowl. Another common, but not so delightful pastime, is the washing of one's dirty clothes. Many of our men have learned to be expert washers, and that without washboard or pounding barrel. Those who have pocket money, however, can have their washing done by the "contraband" washwomen, who have been on hand at every camp we have occupied.

At half-past eight the tattoo is sounded by the full drum and fife corps, playing several tunes as at Reveille, when the company is again drawn up in its street and the roll called. At nine comes "Taps," when every light must be out in the tents, and the men "turn in" for their night's rest. The ground within the tents is covered with straw or cedar branches, on which are spread the rubber blankets; this is the bed, the knapsack is the pillow. There is no trouble with undressing; our "blouses," or flannel fatigue coats, pantaloons and stockings, sometimes with overcoat added, are the apparel of the night, as of the day. We slip off our boots, drop in our places side by side, draw over us our blankets; and sleep, sound and sweet, soon comes with every eyelid. The man who can sleep at all, in camp, commonly sleeps soundly and well.

I spoke in the beginning of this letter of the absence of anything exciting in camp. We have since had something particularly exciting for Company C—the arrival of the boxes of good things from our kind friends in Burlington. We had had warning of their coming and were anxiously awaiting them. They reached camp after dark last evening; but the sound of wheels and the noise of unloading before the Captain's tent told every one that they had come, and an eager crowd hurried to the spot. A couple of pickaxes were quickly put in use. The covers flew off as if blown upwards by the explosive force of the good will and kind feeling imprisoned within, and the parcels were quickly handed out to the favored ones, who thereupon quickly disappeared within the tents, from which shouts of joy and laughter would come pealing as the things within were unpacked. What unrolling of papers and uncovering of boxes, and uncorking of jars and bottles and munching of good things in every tent! A bevy of children were never more pleased with their presents in holiday time, than we with our home luxuries, made doubly delicious by our confinement to army fare, and trebly valuable because they were from the friends *at home.* The whole thing was pronounced worthy of our Burlington friends and emphatically *"bully."* I beg you will divest this word of anything of coarseness or slang it may have heretofore had. It is the adjective which in the army expresses the highest form of admiration, and is in constant use from the Colonel and chaplain to the lowest private. When the soldier has pronounced a thing *"bully,"* he can say no more. I wish you could have heard—and if you had and listened sharply I think you might, the cheers and tiger [roar] which after roll call at tattoo last night were given by Co. C, "for our friends in Burlington."

The health of the regiment is improving. We have but thirteen men on the sick list, and none dangerously ill.

The picket line our Brigade is guarding, has been moved out several miles, and now runs about two miles this side of Mount Vernon. The weather is fine and the spirits of the men good. But they do not take very kindly to the "fatigue duty" on the trenches. They think they had rather be engaged in chasing or fighting rebels than in "strategy," however important the latter may be in all wars.

Yours, G.

Lincoln relieved McClellan of command on November 9, 1862. McClellan had done wonders training and organizing the Army of the Potomac, but he never used that army to destroy the Confederate army, making his work irrelevant. Lincoln held on to this general even after he became a thorn in the side of the Union war effort, as General McClellan remained popular with his troops, and the president did not want to adversely affect the midterm elections on November 4. Nevertheless, these elections were a disappointment for Lincoln, because his party barely retained control of Congress. Some in Washington privately feared that if McClellan was relieved, he would march his army on Washington instead of Richmond, and take over. This did not happen, however, and on November 9, Maj. Gen. Ambrose Burnside took command of the Army of the Potomac.

In this letter, Benedict provides a superb view of camp life. One can almost smell the beans baking and the beef roasting, and sense the steady routine that marked life in camp. Soldiers on both sides had regulated schedules that kept them busy and out of trouble until it was time to march or fight. The routine Benedict writes about was fairly common on both sides, except that the Union forces were better supplied than the Confederate ones.

In Benedict's Civil War letters published in the *Burlington Free Press,* he mentions sutlers only a few times. This seems curious as sutlers were fixtures of camp life. A sutler was a merchant who ran a store out of a tent in camp with the sanction of the regimental commander and the approval of a higher authority. In the 2nd Vermont Brigade's case, that authority was Gov. Frederick Holbrook. According to army regulations, each regiment was authorized one sutler, who provided a wide variety of items, from fresh fruit to pencils, to the men of the regiment for a price. Since the sutler had a monopoly within the regiment, he usually priced his goods accordingly. That did not endear him to his customers. But if they wanted what he was selling, they had to pay what he asked. If a sutler was too overbearing with his prices and treatment of his customers, a mob of soldiers might clean him out while the officers were out on duty. However, the soldiers did not realize the costs and risks involved in providing such goods to the soldiers. The sutler was, after all, a businessman who was there to make a profit. If the regiment suddenly moved, the sutler was on his own and could become a target for Confederate troops or guerrillas.

The 12th Vermont's first sutler was Edwin Vaughan, brother of Adjutant Vaughan. Sutler Vaughan contracted typhoid fever and died on December 6, 1862, in Washington, D.C.[3] The 12th's next sutler was Mr. Stearns, and he and his wife became acquainted with Lieutenant Colonel and Mrs. Roswell Farnham in the months to come. However, for Benedict and his comrades in the 12th Vermont, camp life and its duties were more of a concern.

Benedict writes from the view of the private and does not touch on the routine for noncommissioned and commissioned officers, who had more responsibilities. They had to do more than their men, as they had to lead them by example. The officers trained the noncommissioned officers when the men were released from duty. The officers trained on Tuesday and Thursday nights from Colonel Blunt and Lieutenant Colonel Farnham to prepare them to train their men and to expand their military knowledge.[4] Then there were other duties, such as inspecting the guard twice a day.

Staff personnel had better working conditions than the others, because they did most of their work indoors, yet they had to deal with the ever present and sometimes mind-numbing paperwork of the army bureaucracy. The typical day of Pvt. George Hagar, the adjutant's clerk, started with roll call, as he went to the first sergeants to get their morning reports and then checked them for accuracy. Next, he spent several hours getting the regimental strength report ready for the brigade's assistant adjutant general's office. Then he worked on the regimental order books, copying any new orders and circulars that had been handed down. Private Hagar made copies of each new directive or order for each company in the regiment to insert into their company orderly book. Hagar also substituted for Sergeant Major Redington when he was ill, which he was for the first month of their service, thus adding to Hagar's work load.[5]

Benedict vividly describes the morale boost that the letters, newspapers, and food boxes from home provided the soldiers. Hundreds of thousands of letters made their way back and forth to the soldiers on both sides of the war. These letters and hometown newspapers kept the men informed on what was happening back home and helped alleviate homesickness, as the majority of soldiers had never traveled more than fifty miles from where they lived before their enlistment.

It is amazing how quickly the mail moved to and from Washington. Most of Benedict's letters took, on average, about five days to get from Virginia to Vermont. A soldier would write and post his letter with the regimental postmaster, usually the chaplain or someone else designated by the regimental commander to take care of the regiment's mail. The postmaster took the mail to a post office in a nearby town or train station, and the postal system did the rest. If a soldier or his family wanted a faster mode of transport, such as for food boxes, they sent them by the express delivery service of the nineteenth century, Adams Express, which delivered freight via the railroad in just a couple days.

Camp Vermont—Near Alexandria, Va.
Nov. 24, 1862

Dear Free Press:

Death has again invaded the circle of our Company, and has taken one of our comeliest and best. We miss William Spaulding much, and mourn for him sincerely. We did not expect to bring back all we took away from Burlington, but if asked which would probably be of the first to yield to the exposures and risks of this hard life, who would have pointed out that fine handsome boy? It seems hard that such should be sacrificed of the demon of rebellion. He had in him, unless I am mistaken, the making of a first rate soldier, and a worthy and useful man. The regularity and hearty devotion with which he performed all his military duties, from the day of his enlistment till disabled by sickness, was matter of remark; and his tall figure and pleasant face, in the first file of the company, was always a pleasant sight to everyone. All who knew him here were his friends, and he had not an enemy, I presume, in the world. He began to lose flesh and strength while we were on Capitol Hill, without any apparently sufficient reason, and finally went into the regimental hospital; grew better, was pronounced fit for duty by the Surgeon, was placed on guard at a private house near here, where he had the shelter of a roof and more comforts than he could have in camp, caught a severe cold, and died in a day or two, from congestion of the lungs. Captain Page, Lieut. Wing, the Chaplain and Surgeon, did all they could for his relief and comfort after he was thus attacked, and with two of his comrades, were with him when he died. He received the intelligence that he must die calmly, said he was ready, sent a few words of parting remembrance and admonition to his friends, and passed away quietly from earth. His death has cast a shade over the Company, and we ask ourselves, "who will be the next?"

One of the Line officers, Lieut. Howard of the Northfield Company, died in the hospital on Friday, from inflammation of the brain. The two deaths were made the occasion of some impressive remarks by Chaplain Brastow, at Divine Service yesterday, preaching from the text, "So teach us to number our days, that we may apply our hearts unto wisdom."

Many as are the contrasts between our life in the army and that we led at home, there is none greater than that between our Sabbaths there and here. As we stood at regimental Service yesterday, our chapel a vacant spot before the Colonel's tent, our heads canopied only by the grey clouds drifting swiftly to the southwest, and the chill November wind blowing through our ranks, I could not but cast back a thought to the quiet and comfortable New England sanctuaries most of us have been wont to worship in, and notice some of the differences. But we were thus much better off than most of the regiments in the army, in that few of them, probably, had, or have commonly, any Sabbath service at all.

We had four days of almost incessant rain, last week—Tuesday, Wednesday, Thursday, and Friday. I have been thinking of going into some description of the special delights of such a time, for men living in small tents and sleeping on the ground; but I forbear. Our friends at home expend on us all the sympathy we need, without any detailed account of our "blue" times. I have the facts, however, for an essay on Virginia *mud,* whenever I get time to write it, and I assure you it is a *deep* subject.

Orders were out for a grand review on Thursday at Fort Albany, six miles from here, of all the forces on this side of the river, including of course our Brigade. It was the third and hardest day of the storm. A countermand was confidently expected; but none came, and at nine o'clock, the 12th, with three other regiments, took up its line of march through the mud and rain. The mud varied from a thin porridge of one part red clay to three parts water, to a thick adhesive salve of three parts clay to one of water—there or thereabouts—I may not give the proportions exactly. It was a hard march. The foot planted in the red salve alluded to, is lifted with some difficulty, and then comes up a number of sizes larger, and three or four pounds heavier. A mile or two of such marching tries the sturdiest muscles. But the march of our boys was that of a host of conquering heroes. They took the whole country—along with them, on their soles. In the lack of any affection on the part of the inhabitants, it was delightful to find such a strong attachment

on the part of the "sacred soil." These were the main compensations. We couldn't see, somehow, the mysterious connection
between this tramp through the mud, and the business of crushing
out the rebellion, on which we came down here; and when a mile
beyond Alexandria, a courier met the column with orders to
return at once to camp, the suspicion that when you got down to
the root of the matter you would find that all might just as well
have stayed in camp, became general. The substance of the proceeding was that four thousand men had a march of eight miles in
a storm which made the bare idea of a review an absurdity—that
was all. Perhaps "somebody blundered."

The winter quarters for this regiment are to be long log huts,
one for a company, made of logs set endwise in the ground, on
which a roof of boards will be placed. They make slow progress.
The truth is this Brigade has a *good deal to do.*—Our regiments have
a picket line of six miles to guard, the nearest point of which is five
or six miles from Camp. They furnish a thousand men daily, in
good weather, to dig in the trenches of Fort Lyon. They have to
cut the timber for their winter quarters, and construct the same,
and they have to fill up the interstices of time with the much
needed *drill.* If Uncle Sam's $20 a month is not pretty generally
earned, so far, in this Brigade, some of us are much mistaken.

The picket service is becoming arduous. The pickets are out 48
hours. At many of the stations no fire is allowed, and special vigilance is enjoined, so that little sleep can be obtained; and with all
precautions there is a chance of meeting a shot from some of the
rebel spies and straggling guerrillas which occasionally hover
around the outer circles of our lines. Saturday night a couple of the
Shelburne boys in our company were thus fired on. Add to these
inconveniences the special discomforts of rain and deep mud, and
picket service becomes anything but romantic.

A sad event occurred on Wednesday on the picket line. A Corporal of the 14th Regiment while instructing a soldier how to halt
and cover with his piece any suspected enemy approaching the station fired off his gun, shooting the man through the breast. The
wound was a terrible one, and I am told the man must die.

I noticed in a letter from the 13th regiment in the Daily *Times,*
a week or more ago, a sweeping statement that but few of the arti-

cles sent from home for the comfort of sick soldiers ever reach them, owing to the fact that the officers appropriate them to their own use. There may be individual cases of that sort, perhaps many of them, take the army through; but that such theft from sick men, of the things they prize most, is *customary,* in our Vermont Regiments, I do not believe. I *know* that in the hospital of the 12th the things sent in for the soldiers, are put to their proper use, with scrupulous care. I am a frequent visitor at the hospital and have been glad to note the improvements added daily, for the comfort of its inmates. Its area has been enlarged, while the number of patients has decreased. It is floored and boarded up on the sides. Neat iron bedsteads have been supplied, and the sick men sleep on beds, between sheets furnished by the Ladies' Relief Association of Washington. It is to the credit of Surgeon Ketchum that his hospital is comfortable, far beyond the average. Mr. S. Prentice, of the Committee of the Vermonters' Relief Association, Washington, is a frequent visitor, and brings supplies of needed articles.

The visit of the Committee of the Ladies of Burlington, Mrs. Dr. Thayer and Mrs. Platt, to our Camp yesterday, accompanied by Mrs. Chittenden and Dr. Hatch, was a most agreeable surprise for our Company. It was a double pleasure to see faces from home, and *Ladies'* faces, which are decided novelties in Camp.

Your printers make curious work with some of my sentences. I undertook to say, in a recent letter, that there had been no *mutiny* in this Brigade, in consequence of McClellan's removal; your types made it "no *meeting,*" which is another thing entirely, though it may be equally true.

The weather has come off fine, clear and frosty after the storm.

Yours, G.

Pvt. William Spaulding was a twenty-year-old clerk from Burlington, who died of disease on November 19. A second lieutenant, Knowlton P. Howard, of Company F, a thirty-three-year-old farmer from Northfield, died of disease two days after he resigned his commission to return home to Vermont for care. The 12th Vermont lost ten men to disease and accident from the time it left its home state until it left Camp Vermont, and the winter weather surely would add to that number. Four more men were discharged

for disability or resigned for health reasons.[6] An officer could resign his commission for cause at any time, but an enlisted soldier was discharged for
health reasons only if an army surgeon found him no longer fit for service.

As November drew to a close, the 12th Vermont saw and heard about
elements of the Army of the Potomac moving south to an unknown destination. These movements affected Benedict and his companions, as three
regiments from the 2nd Vermont Brigade were ordered to picket duty near
Union Mills, Virginia, and near the Bull Run battlefield area to replace
other troops that had been moved forward on November 26. This resolved
the problem with working on Fort Lyon, since everyone in the 2nd Vermont Brigade was on picket duty, with no troops to spare. The 13th, 14th,
and 15th Vermont Regiments marched and then took a train to Union Mill
to the picket lines.

Camp Vermont—Near Alexandria, Va.
Dec. 6, 1862

Dear Free Press:

One or two noticeable occasions have broken the quiet mo-
notony of our camp life since I wrote you last. The first was the
departure of three Regiments of the Brigade, which took place ten
days ago. The order came at 8 o'clock in the evening, and the
"bully 13th," as its boys delight to call themselves, was on the
march through our camp at nine, the 14th and 15th following with
little delay. The 12th had received orders to pack knapsacks and be
in readiness to move at a moment's notice, and our own camp was
meantime all astir with the bustle of preparation. The night was
dark and rainy, and as the other regiments passed on the double
quick through our camp, their dark columns visible only by the
light of the camp fires, our boys cheering them and they cheering
lustily in response, the scene was not devoid of excitement. Every
man in the ranks believed that such a sudden night march to the
front meant immediate action, and the cheerful haste and hearty
shouting showed that the prospect was a welcome one. The 12th
would have gone with equal cheerfulness; but the expected order
for us to fall in did not come. We have remained, doing picket
duty, sharing the labor with the 16th. The service takes about all

the effective men of each regiment, one going on for 48 hours, and then being relieved for the same length of time by the other. The marching to and from consumes the best part of another day, making in effect, 3 days hard duty, out of every 4. As the weather has been cold, and most of the boys get a little sleepy at night while out, they have found the duty pretty severe; but they take it, for the most part, without murmuring. The return of the other regiments, all three of which have come back to us, will, however, greatly lighten the service hereafter.

Thanksgiving was the second "big thing" of the past fortnight. Twasn't quite what it would have been, had the six or seven tons of good things sent to different companies from Vermont, arrived in season; but yet it was emphatically a gay and festive time. An order read at dress parade the evening of the 3rd, announced that in accordance with the request of Gov. Holbrook, his Thanksgiving proclamation would be read before the regiment on the morrow, and the soldiers would be relieved of all unnecessary labor. The 4th was as fine a day as is often seen anywhere; perfectly clear, air cool and bracing, but not cold, sunshine bright and invigorating. The boys of Company C made some fun over their Thanksgiving breakfast of hardtack and cold beans, but possessed their souls in patience in view of the forthcoming feast of fat things, on the way; for we had heard that our boxes from home were at Alexandria, and the wagons had gone for them before light. At ten o'clock, the regiment assembled for service. The proclamation was read by Chaplain Brastow, and was followed by an excellent Thanksgiving discourse, with the usual religious exercises. At its close, Col. Blunt addressed the regiment, expressing his feelings of sincere thankfulness that he could see around him so many of his men, in health and comparative comfort; urging a hearty and orderly observance of the day, and inviting the men to meet their officers after dinner, on the parade ground in front of the Camp, for an hour or two of social sport and enjoyment. Shortly after, the teams arrived, with but three or four of the forty big boxes expected, and the unwelcome news that the rest would not reach Alexandria till the next day. The things sent from Vermont on Friday, for the most part reached us in season; those sent on Saturday failed by a day. All the companies save one were in the same predicament. Co. I had a big box, and made a big dinner setting table in the open air, to which they invited the Field and Staff officers. Two or three men of Co. C, received boxes, with as many roast turkeys, which they shared liberally with their comrades, so that a number of us had regular Thanksgiving fare, and feasted with good cheer and a thousand kind thoughts of the homes and friends we left behind us. We knew that they were thinking of us at the same time. If each thought of affection and good will had had visible wings, what a cloud of messengers would have darkened the air between Vermont and Virginia that day!

At two o'clock, the regiment turned out on the parade ground in front of our camp, at the Colonel's invitation. He had, with his customary thoughtfulness, procured a *football*. Sides were arranged by our excellent Lieut. Col. and two or three royal games of football—that most manly of the sports, and closest in its mimicry of actual warfare—were played. The Lieut. Colonel, Chaplain, and one or two captains, mingled in the crowd, on a level with the men; Captains took rough-and-tumble overthrows from privates; shins were barked and ankles sprained; but all was given and taken in good part and with the utmost good feeling. Many joined in games of baseball, others formed rings and watched the friendly contests of the champion wrestlers of the different companies; others laughed at the meandering of some of their comrades, blindfolded by the Colonel, and set to walk at a mark. It was a "tall time" all round. Nor did it end with daylight. In the evening a floor of boards, hastily laid upon the ground, furnished a ballroom, of which the blue arch above was the canopy and the bright moon the chandelier. Co. C turned out a violin, guitar and two flutes for an orchestra; some other company furnished another violin, and a grand Thanksgiving ball came off in style. I did not notice any satin slippers—the "light fantastic toe" was for the most part clad in army shoes, or "*gunboats*" as the men call them, on the occasion, and the nearest approach to crinoline was a light blue overcoat; but the list was danced through, from country dances to the Lancers, nevertheless, and the gay assembly did not break up till half past nine P.M.

So ended the Thanksgiving day proper; but the enjoyment of the bigger portion of the creature comforts sent us from Vermont is yet to come, for our company. The great bulk of our Thanksgiving boxes came yesterday after the regiment had gone out on picket, our turn for which came yesterday morning. The few left behind in camp have opened some of the perishable articles, which they doubtless are enjoying, though the surroundings of booths of brush and picket fires almost extinguished by the snow, are hardly what one would choose. The cold snap will help preserve the cooked meats, however, and there is enough for a bountiful feast, when they come in tomorrow.

The Thanksgiving dinner for the Officers mess of Co. C, came off today, and was, I assure you, a highly select and recherche affair. It was a sufficiently notable occasion to justify this public allusion, and I trust I may be pardoned for mentioning that the board was spread in the capacious log shanty of Maj. Kingsley and was graced by the presence of the amiable lady of Col. Blunt, who has been domiciled in camp for a week or two past, also of the Field and Staff officers of the 12th, with the Chaplain and Surgeon of the 15th. I enclose a copy of the bill of fare, in the composition of which I suspect our humorous Drum Major, and my editorial brother of the Quarter Master's department, had a hand. It was on brown wrapping paper, like the Southern newspapers. Every thing on the bill was also on the board, mind you, sumptuous as it may seem. The good things said and done I do not feel at liberty to report:

Bill of Fare.

Shantic De Kingsley.

THANKSGIVING DINNER.

Camp Vermont, December 6, 1862.

TABLE D'HÔTE.

SOUP.

Nary.

ROAST.

Turkey, Mount Vernon Sauce.

ENTREES.

Pate de pullets, Cochon Sauce,

Fillet de Boeuf—a la smoke,

RELISHES.

Butter, Chittenden Co. Kohl Slaw,

Cheese, Stationary, Chow Chow,

Salt, *ordinaire,* Sultana Sauce,
Pepper, *a la contraband,* Tomato Catsup,
Pickles, *a la confusion,* Sauce de Savoy.
VEGETABLES.
Potatoes, Hibernian & Carolinian,
Onions, *aux fragantes.*
PASTRY.
Mince Pie, Apple Pie.
DESSERT.
Coffee, Doughnuts, Ginger-Schnapps,
Sweet Cake, Fruit Cake, Apples, Baldwin.

We have had our second snowstorm. It began yesterday, and continued through a bitter night. Towards nightfall the 13th and 14th Regiments came in from the front at Union Mills (the 15th came in the night before) and marched into their deserted camps, close by us. They brought nothing but their little shelter tents, and the prospect of camping down in the snow, with little food, no fuel, and scanty shelter, was a pretty blank one for them. Our officers went over, however, and offered the hospitalities of the 12th, which were gratefully accepted by hundreds. The absence of most of our men, on picket, left a good deal of vacant room in our tents, which were soon filled with wet and tired men of the other regiments, to whom we were glad to offer the comparative comforts of our camp. They went away this morning warmed, rested and fed.

The weather is clear and very cold today. We hear that our boys on picket are getting along as well as could be expected; but I fear they will suffer tonight, though they will have hard frozen ground instead of muddy slosh, which will be so far an improvement.

The health of the regiment continues pretty good; much better than the average of the Brigade.

I hear that Gen. Stoughton will assume command tomorrow. The Brigade would, however, be entirely satisfied to remain under command of Col. Blunt.

The following promotions have taken place in this regiment: Geo. E. Dimmick, 2d Lieut. Co. B promoted to 1st Lieut. of same Co., vice Lieut. Raymond, resigned. Edwin C. Emmons, Orderly

Serg't Co. B, promoted 2d Lieut., vice Lieut. Dimmick, promoted. Carlos D. Williams Orderly Serg't Co. F, promoted to 2d Lieut., vice Lieut. Howard, deceased.

Yours, G.

SUNDAY MORNING Thermometer 15° above zero today, which is called *cold,* in this region.

At this time, Thanksgiving was not yet a national holiday. It was not until 1863 that President Lincoln declared the fourth Thursday of November a national day of thanksgiving. Until then, Thanksgiving was a state holiday that had started in New England and was slowly making its way south. For the soldiers of the 12th Vermont and her sister regiments, their commanders selected different days to celebrate this holiday because of the duty schedule. The 12th Vermont selected December 4, the day before they went back on the picket line. For the 12th Vermont, the day went off well, with the exception of the Thanksgiving dinner, most of which spent the day at the Alexandria railway station. The regiments did not have their own wagons and teams, so they had to borrow them from the division. With the Army of the Potomac moving south, wagons and teams were hard to come by. As a result, only Company I got their boxes that day. For the rest of the regiment, Thanksgiving dinner consisted of bread, beans, and salt beef. Although the food boxes were moved to Camp Vermont the next day, Benedict and the rest of Company C were on picket duty, so they did not receive their Thanksgiving dinners from home until December 6. That meal was particularly appreciated, as foul weather had made picket duty rough. Fires were not allowed on the picket lines, because they would give away their positions to the Confederates.

Colonel and Mary Blunt joined Major Kingsley at the Thanksgiving dinner party for the regiment's senior staff and invited guests. Mary Blunt had arrived on November 19 and was one of the first officer wives to join her husband at camp for the winter. Other Thanksgiving guests included Lieutenant Colonel Farnham; Q.M. Harry C. Brownson; Adjutant Vaughan; the 12th Vermont's drum major, Perley Downer; the chaplain of the 15th, Ephraim C. Cummings; and Carlton P. Frost from St. Johnsbury, the 15th Vermont's surgeon.

Benedict's "editorial brother" was Q.M. Sgt. George Bigelow of the *Burlington Times*. The Thanksgiving "Bill of Fare" was intended to be humorous. For example, "Chittenden Co. Kohl Slaw" was a reference to the Vermont county from which Company C was recruited. "Pepper *a la contraband*" was black pepper and was a reference to the many escaped slaves and freedmen residing in several "freedmen villages" around Alexandria. Hibernian potatoes was a word play on Irish potatoes.

It started to snow the morning of the fifth, and continued as the 12th Vermont marched into camp and the 16th Vermont marched out for picket duty. The 13th and 14th Vermont then returned from the Union Mills–Cub Run picket line without their tents. The 12th Vermont helped shelter the 13th Vermont, and the 14th Vermont camped in the temporarily vacated stockaded tents of the 16th Vermont.

While Benedict wrote about camp life and duty, he did not write about tourism within his regiment, such as his visit to Mount Vernon and to Washington, D.C. Benedict, for some reason, had a month-long pass to go anywhere in Washington or Alexandria.[7] This was unusual, as most regimental commanders, let alone private soldiers, normally did not get such passes. In addition, each company in the 2nd Vermont Brigade could send two men at a time on a pass to see the sites at Washington, D.C., which was a half day's travel from camp. The Capitol, with its nearly completed dome, and the White House were popular attractions, as was the Smithsonian.

One tourist destination not far from Camp Vermont was Mount Vernon, the home of George and Martha Washington. It was only eight miles away, or a two-hour walk, from Camp Vermont. George Benedict, George Hagar, and four of their comrades from Company C went to Mount Vernon on December 2. They started at 9:30 A.M. and got to Mount Vernon for a lunch of hardtack and salt beef. After paying a quarter apiece for admission, they wandered the grounds, which were slightly overgrown and not well cared for, according to Hagar. After a tour of the grounds, they went into the mansion, which was left as it was when Martha Washington died. Time and weather had taken their toll, as the mansion needed repairs and paint. Inside, the men went from room to room, guided by one of the caretakers of the estate, Benedict Herbert.[8] The mansion's rooms were mostly bare, with worn furniture, but it gave some idea of how the Washingtons lived. Before leaving, the men visited the graves of George and Martha Washington and paid their respects to the first president and the original first lady of the United States.

Brig. Gen. Edwin H. Stoughton did assume command of the brigade the day after Benedict wrote his letter. The men of the 12th Vermont

Brig. Gen. Edwin H. Stoughton.
BRADY COLLECTION, NATIONAL ARCHIVES.

wanted Colonel Blunt to remain as brigade commander. They knew him well but knew Stoughton only by reputation and his time as commander of Camp Lincoln. Blunt's biggest supporter for brigade commander was Farnham, who wanted to command the 12th. Regardless, Stoughton became brigade commander, and things soon changed for everyone in the brigade.

CHAPTER 4

Camp at Fairfax Courthouse

Gen. Ambrose Burnside was an able brigade commander in the first
battle of Bull Run and had done an outstanding job commanding
amphibious assaults on Roanoke Island and New Bern, North Carolina,
during the winter of 1861–62. These accomplishments marked him for
higher commands as the Union army expanded after the summer of 1861.
In time, General Burnside became a popular commander with the officers
and men of his IX Corps as his career approached its zenith. At the battle
of Antietam, however, it was clear that Burnside had been promoted above
his abilities, as evidenced by his actions that caused great carnage in the
battle without accomplishing his corps's mission. On September 17, 1862,
his mission was to cross the Antietam Creek, climb the high ground on the
other side, pushing in General Lee's right flank, and then advance to
Sharpsburg, thus cutting the Confederates off from their line of retreat. One
narrow bridge covered by a Confederate infantry brigade in excellent
defensive terrain was to be the corps's crossing point. Burnside's staff did not
seek other sites to cross the Antietam Creek in the time they had available
before attacking. Instead, Burnside ordered a division to attack what since
became known as "Burnside's Bridge." That division battered itself against
a strongly dug-in enemy, taking heavy losses, yet finally took the high
ground. As Burnside's corps deployed to march on Sharpsburg, Confederate general A. P. Hill's division counterattacked as it arrived on the field
after a thirty-mile forced march at the end of the day. With this unexpected
threat, Burnside withdrew his men back across the Antietam Creek to the
positions they had started from earlier that day, thus wasting the lives and
courage of his men, as well as losing a chance to crush Lee's army. Burnside's failure to find other ways to cross the Antietam or come up with a

better and different plan to accomplish his corps's mission foreshadowed events that occurred a few months later, with a much higher cost in Union lives.

When President Lincoln relieved General McClellan, Burnside was next in line to command the Army of the Potomac and was offered the job. Burnside replied that he did not want the command, as he felt that he was not up to that task and McClellan was his friend. Burnside was given the choice of taking command of the army or serving under his rival, Gen. Joseph Hooker, who was next in line for the job. So with reservations, Burnside took command.

Burnside reorganized the six corps of the Army of the Potomac into three grand divisions to better coordinate moves from three headquarters, rather than six corps headquarters. The Right Grand Division was composed of the II and IX Corps, under the command of Maj. Gen. Edwin "Bull" Sumner; the Center Grand Division was composed of the III and V Corps, under the command of Maj. Gen. Joseph Hooker; and the Left Grand Division was composed of the I and VI Corps, under the command of Maj. Gen. William Franklin. After this reorganization, Burnside marched his army to take Fredericksburg before Lee's army could dig in.

Everything went well for Burnside until he tried to cross the Rappahannock River and found that his army needed boats or pontoons to cross. During the first week of December 1862, Burnside and most of the Army of the Potomac waited near Fredericksburg for bridging material to arrive. When it did, they crossed the river and walked into a trap. Lee with Gen. James Longstreet's corps was dug in on St. Marye's Heights, which dominated the local area. Burnside was unable to outflank this position on December 11 and 12. Rather than withdraw from this bad situation, Burnside decided to attack the strongest part of Lee's defensive position. On December 13, the Army of the Potomac attacked Lee's dug-in army on Marye's Heights, suffering heavy losses with little to show for their efforts. During those six hours of combat, the Army of the Potomac lost most of its 12,653 men killed in the Fredericksburg campaign, which was more than Antietam, whereas the Army of Northern Virginia lost only 5,309 men.[1] While the loss was great, the Army of the Potomac's loss of morale was even more destructive; for the first time, the men in the ranks felt that they were being used as cannon fodder and that their leadership had failed them.

Twenty miles to the northeast, the battle of Fredericksburg had only an indirect effect on the 12th Vermont. On December 11, Benedict and his comrades had been about to spend the night on picket duty, when instead they were called back and told to prepare to leave Camp Vermont. Most of the men did not know what was going on. Some thought that they were finally joining the Army of the Potomac as it marched south. As a result, packing up their gear was almost a festive time.

Camp near Fairfax Court House, Va.
Dec. 15, 1862

Dear Free Press:

More moves on the big chess board, of which States and Counties are the squares, and Divisions and Brigades the men. And as the older troops push to the front and into the smoke of the battle, the Reserve, of which the Vt. 2nd Brigade is a portion, moves up and occupies the more advanced positions of the lines of defenses around Washington, vacated by our predecessors.

You have already been informed that General Sigel's corps marched to the support of Burnside, last week, and that the Vermont 9 months Brigade has stepped to the front into their deserted places. Our five regiments are now in camp round Fairfax Court House and along the line to Centreville, doing picket duty by turns, on the lines near the latter place.

The orders for us to march came on Thursday evening last, while the 12th was out on picket. The boys were ordered in at once and reached camp about ten o'clock. They came in singing "John Brown," in high spirits, and camp was soon humming with the bustle and stir which follow the order to prepare to break camp. Bright fires of the no longer needed packing boxes, which came filled with Thanksgiving from Vermont, were soon blazing in the company streets, and the work of packing knapsacks began. With most of the boys the first thought was for the stores of creature comforts, still remaining from the Thanksgiving supply, and each man proceeded to make sure of *some* of it, by putting himself outside of such a portion as his capacity would admit of, be the same more or less. Many packed into boxes the more valuable and portable articles of luxury, trusting to good luck and the quartermaster to get them transported after us. It was midnight before the camp was still, and after two hours or so of slumber we were aroused again.—A reveille was sounded at 3, the tents were struck at 4, the line of march was formed at 5, and by 6, the whole brigade was on its way. The morning was a magnificent one, clear, rosy, and frosty, and the men stepped light and springy as they filed away. I was detached on special duty and did not accompany the column; of course I cannot describe the incidents of the march. It lasted for ten hours, the 12th halting at their present camping ground at 4 P.M., in which time the Brigade accomplished a march of *twenty miles.*—The pace was moderate and the stops frequent, about a quarter of each hour being allowed for rest; but it was altogether the severest march as yet undergone by our Regiment. It is to be remembered, in estimating the labor of such a march, that the weight of the packed knapsack, about doubles the amount of exertion. Most soldiers would, I think, prefer a march of twice the distance in light marching order, to one of ten or twenty miles with knapsack, haversack, canteen and overcoat. Our boys took it right manfully, however. But *twelve* of the 12th fell to the rear, of whom four were brought in by ambulances, the remaining eight following the column in, on foot, not greatly behind time—a proportion of stragglers much less, if I am correctly informed, than that of any of the other regiments. Of Co. C, one man, just convalescent from a three weeks run of fever, and who should not have attempted to march at all, was taken up by one of the ambulances at midday. Another man who had been off duty, from ill health, came in with the stragglers; the rest, to a man, marched into our present camping ground (about a mile west of Fairfax C. H.) with the colors.

I returned to Camp Vermont the day after regiment left. The 3rd Brigade of Casey's Division were already installed in the winter quarters built and almost completed with so much labor by the Vermont Regiments. The 4th Delaware was in the camp of the 12th, and an altogether new order of things was in force. The men looked and acted not at all like our orderly Vermonters; the quiet and discipline of the Vermont Camps, had disappeared. Muskets were popping about promiscuously all around camps; petty thieving was the principal business on foot, and Mr. Mason, the gray headed "neutral" who owns the manor, was praying for the return of the Vermont Brigade. His fences were lowering with remarkable rapidity; the roofs of some of his outhouses had quite disappeared, and Col. Grimshaw, commanding the Brigade, had his headquarters in the front parlor of his mansion. I could not give him a great deal of sympathy, for I believe him to be a rebel; but I was glad the spoliation was not the work of our Vermont Boys.

I followed the regiment, on Sunday, taking the military railroad train to Fairfax station. Here, and all along the road to the dirty little village of Fairfax Court House, four miles to the north, I struck and watched with great interest, the movement of a great army tide, pushing on to the field of conflict. Here a drove of beef cattle, next, a battery of Parrot guns, there a travel worn regiment, marching with tired lag and frequently hunching up their heavy knapsacks, then one resting by the wayside, then a battery of fine brass 20-pounders, then another regiment and another, and the long white lines of army wagons filling every vacant rod of road, for miles and miles, and miles, as far as the eye could reach. It was the rear guard of the 12th Army Corps, from Harper's Ferry and Frederick, en route for Dumfries and supporting distance of Burnside, on which I had struck, and I learned that for over twenty hours, the stream of men and materiel of war had flowed over the road in the same way.—It is only after seeing such a movement, that one begins to realize something of the size of the business which is now the occupation of the nation.

I turned from the road across the fields to a pine grove; like some of those to the north of Burlington, in which lay the camp of the 12th. The regiment was drawn up in solid square at the edge of the timber. As I drew near, the strains of "Shining Shore," broke the stillness, and as I joined the body, the men were standing with bared heads, as the Chaplain invoked the blessing of God on our cause, on our fellow soldiers now in deadly fight, or our own humble efforts, and on the homes we left to come to the war. It was a transition, in a step, from the strong rush of the tide of war to a quiet eddy of Christian worship, and the contrast was a striking one.

We are at present in our little shelter tents, pitched promiscuously among the pine trees; but there is no hardship. The weather is mild and fine, and the ground as dry as May. We can hardly realize that it is the middle of December. Before a storm comes, we shall hope to have our A tents again. How long we shall remain here, of course we do not know. The position is not a bad one for a considerable stay. The parade ground in front is a broad level stretch of meadow, and the display on Dress parade this afternoon was especially fine.

A new Brigade band of 17 pieces, has been organized under the able leadership of Mr. Clark, of St. Johnsbury, whose Concerts in Burlington you doubtless remember. It already plays like a first class band. With a month more practice, few brigades in the army will have as good music as this. The music for our Dress Parade tonight was furnished by the Band, and was a decidedly attractive feature.

I mentioned in my last, the expected coming of our new Brigadier General Stoughton. He came and took command a week ago yesterday, Col. Blunt has, of course, returned to his own place in command of the 12th, having demonstrated as far as it could be done without a time of active service in the field, his fitness for the command of a Brigade. Consulting only their own interests and feelings, the men of the 12th would never consent to his leaving his place at their head. For his sake, however, and knowing that we would still be under him, as our Brigadier, we should have rejoiced at his appointment to the permanent command of our Brigade. But that, it seems, was not to be. It is but simple justice, also, to say that Lieut. Col. Farnham, during his temporary advancement to the command of the Regiment, has shown every quality of an efficient, careful, courteous, and able commander.

We are waiting with intense interest for news of the results of the combined movements on Richmond. Providence seems to be smiling on us, in this fine weather, and we cannot doubt of a full triumph of our arms. If between Burnside and Banks the rebel capital cannot be taken, who shall attempt the job?

Yours, G.

P. S. The rain has come before our tents have, and a juicy time is in progress.

As the regiments marched out of Camp Vermont for the last time on December 12, they had near-perfect weather for marching, as it was cool and dry. After a few miles of marching, the men in the ranks were warm but not overly hot. The roads on which the 2nd Vermont Brigade marched were in good shape, with little mud, making the soldiers' footing not too difficult. Yet not all the brigade's soldiers marched that morning. The men too ill to march remained at the regimental hospitals at Camp Vermont until they were sent to local general hospitals. A few others, including Benedict, either stayed in camp or were on special duty elsewhere. Why Benedict remained behind is not known, as he returned to Camp Vermont the day after his brigade left it, he may have helped arrange transportation for the sick, since the regiment's ambulance followed the regiments forward. Or he may have been detailed to get the wagons and mule teams to move the regiment's tents and other equipment to Fairfax Courthouse. Benedict took the train from Alexandria and arrived alone at the 12th Vermont's new camp on Sunday, December 15, at the end of church parade, probably near 3:30 P.M., the time that service appears on the regimental schedule. Then he got a chance to settle in and write a letter home during the remainder of this day of rest.

The 12th Vermont and the rest of the 2nd Vermont Brigade marched to the Fairfax Courthouse to replace the XI Corps, under the command of Maj. Gen. Franz Sigel, which had been redeployed out of the area. This put the 12th Vermont and its brigade on the western edge of Washington's defensive perimeter. The 2nd Vermont Brigade's mission was to guard this possible avenue of approach into Washington, D.C. The key terrain features of the area were the Bull Run River and Cub Run, a small river that ran north to south and joined the Bull Run near Blackburn's Ford. In his next letter, Benedict describes Cub Run as a thirty-two-foot-wide river in some places, meaning that it was an obstacle for the Confederates, and control of the river fords, which Benedict and his regiment guarded, was important.

The area's transportation system was equally important and included the Little River Turnpike, which ran through Fairfax Courthouse, and the main road that ran from the Blue Ridge Mountains in the northwest to Alexandria in the southeast. Just outside Fairfax Courthouse, in Germantown, the Warrenton Turnpike, another major highway, forked into this road, adding to its importance. Three miles south of Fairfax Courthouse was Fairfax Station, then a major Union supply base, located on the Orange and Alexandria Railroad. This railroad ran east-west from Alexandria to Manassas and connected with the Manassas Gap Railroad near Manassas Station, about fifteen miles west of Fairfax Courthouse. The fords, the railroad, and the

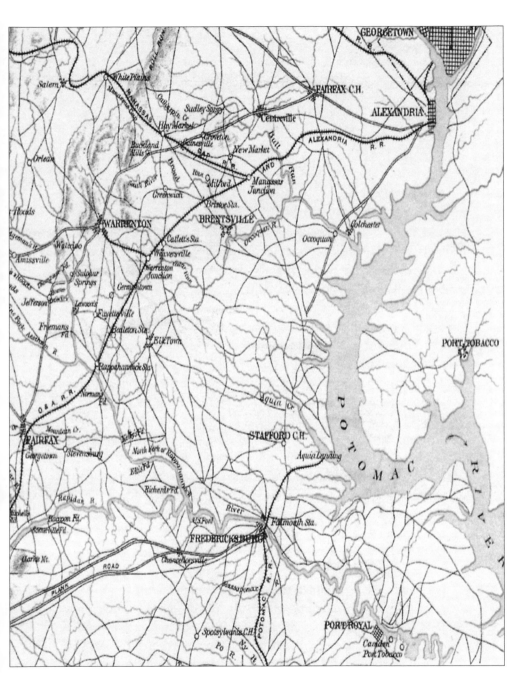

The 2nd Vermont Brigade's operational area 1862–1863. WAR OF THE REBELLION: OFFICIAL RECORDS OF THE UNION AND CONFEDERATE ARMIES, MAP BOOK.

supplies at Fairfax Station all had to be protected, and the three battles fought near where the 12th Vermont and the 2nd Vermont Brigade now stood picket and guard attested to the importance of the area.

Picket Camp, Centreville, Va.
Dec. 19, 1862

Dear Free Press:

The main Camp of our Brigade is at Fairfax Court House, eight miles back of here. From thence a regiment is sent every four days to picket the lines in this vicinity. The turn of the 12th came day before yesterday, before we were fairly warm in our camp at Fairfax C.H. We started at half past 7 A.M. with two days' rations in our haversacks, and were marched briskly hither, making but one halt of 10 minutes on the way. We marched over the Centreville turnpike, which has been so often filled with the columns of the army of the Potomac, in advance or in retreat. The skeletons of horse and mules, left to rot as they fell, were frequent ornaments of the highway, and the remains of knapsacks, bayonet sheaths, and here and there a broken musket, strewed along the road, told the story of panic and disaster, in months and years gone by. Three hours brought us to the highlands of Centreville, covered with forts of which eight, are in sight from this camp, connected by miles of breastworks and rifle pits, the work of the rebels, which kept McClellan so long at bay, during the impatient months of last winter. One of the famous "quaker" guns lies near our camp.

The regiment halted here, and the right wing was at once dispatched to the picket lines, Co. C, under command of Lieut. Wing for this occasion, forming a portion of the detachment. Three miles more of sharp marching across fields, over a surface seamed with ditches, and covered with a little low vine which tries its best to trip up the traveler, brought us, about noon, to the picket lines; and the men were at once distributed to the stations, to relieve the men of the 16th Regiment, who for four days had kept watch and went on the line. The space allotted to Co. C, extended for a mile or more along the turbid stream of Cub Run, from a point near its junction with Bull Run, up to and beyond the ford and bridge, where "Fighting Dick" Richardson opened the fighting, July 18, 1861, of the first battle of Bull Run. Back from the stream a little, are the log hut camps of two Georgia regiments, the 1st Kentucky, and a battery of rebel artillery, which wintered here last winter. The huts are square, of logs plastered with mud, with shed roofs of long split shingles or of poles covered with clay, low door, single small aperture for a window, and capacious fireplace and chimney of stone and mud masonry. They are a portion of the famous hut camps of Beauregard's army, which occupy the desirable camping spots for many a mile around and beyond, in which the rebel army spent a comfortable winter, while our army was shivering in tents. Our reserves are now posted in them [a picket reserve consists of fifteen or twenty men on whom the pickets fall back for support if attacked, and from which men are sent at intervals to relieve the men in the line] and find them still right warm and comfortable shelter on these cold nights.

Let me describe to you a day and night of picket duty. We were stationed within hailing distance of each other, one man at a station for the most part, but sometimes two or three together at posts requiring especial vigilance, along the eastern bank of Cub Run, a small muddy stream, a rod or two wide, which for the present is the boundary of Uncle Sam's absolute control. Beyond its other bank is debatable ground, a cavalry patrol of the 1st Virginia (loyal) Cavalry (the headquarters of which regiment are here at Centreville), and occasional reconnoitering expeditions, alone disputing its procession with the enemy. The Cavalry post a vidette on the Gainesville road, and send a patrol daily out over the road for four or five miles. We took our posts, in a flurry of snow, exactly at noon. Each man's thought was first of his fire and next of his dinner. The nearest fence or brush heap furnishes the means of replenishing the one, the haversack supplies the other. From its depths the picket produces a tin plate, a piece of raw pork, a paper of ground coffee, ditto of sugar, and a supply of "hard tack." If inclined for a warm meal, he cuts a slice or two of his pork, and fries it on his plate or if less fastidious, he takes it raw with his hard bread. His cup is filled from his canteen and placed on the fire, and a cup of coffee is soon steaming under his nose. With such materials, and the appetite gained by a march of a dozen miles, our pickets made a royal meal.

The afternoon passed with but little incident. At my station, I had but a solitary visitor, a gaunt and yellow F.F.V., who came to say that he was particularly anxious to save the rails he had left around his cattle yard, and rather than have them burned, he would draw some wood for the pickets—a suggestion which found favor with our boys, and the old fellow found occupation enough for himself, boy and yoke of oxen, for a good share of the day, hauling wood to the stations. I talked with him some time. He was a Virginian born, owned a farm of 150 acres, had no apples, and no orchard to raise any with, no potatoes either, nothing that a soldier would eat, except corn meal, and couldn't sell any of that, as his supply was small and he could not cross the picket line to mill; had never taken the oath of allegiance nor been asked to take it; was a peaceable man himself, and meant to keep friends with the soldiers the best way he knew how; found some good men and some hard fellows among them on both sides; had lost a great deal by the war; but felt most the loss of his *horses,* which he said were taken from his stable while he was sick, by some Union soldiers; had no slaves or anybody to help him, but his boy; had no gun of any description and never owned one; was glad to believe the war could not last forever, and only hoped it would be over soon, in time to leave him some of his fences and timber.

At our reserve station, in the old rebel artillery camp, some stir was occasioned by a colored individual, one of a family of free negroes who own a fine farm of 400 acres just across the Run, who came in to say that a man who he believed to be a secesh soldier, dressed in citizens clothes, had just been at his house and made numerous inquiries as to the number and character of our pickets. Lieut. Wing at once started out with two or three men, saw the fellow making tracks for the woods, and gave instant chase. He gained the timber, however, in time to make good his escape. As such a search for information might be preliminary to a rebel dash on our picket line, the affair had a tendency to put our men on the alert. Further down the line, the men of another company, while scouting round the premises of another farmhouse, discovered in the barn a suspicious looking box, which, when opened, disclosed within a black walnut box, covering a metallic burial case, containing a corpse, which the family there averred to be the body of a Southern officer, which was left there on the retreat of the rebel army last March, with directions to keep it until it should be sent for. But it has not been sent for and perhaps never will be.

The night settled down clear and very cold. With the darkness came orders to put out the picket fires or keep them smoldering without flame or light. Your humble servant was stationed alone on the bank, some fifty feet above Cub Run, opposite a rude foot bridge thrown across the stream. My turns of duty were from 4 to 8 and 10 to 12 P.M. and from 2 to 4 and 6 to 8 A.M. The stars shone bright; but there was little else to see. The stream rippled away, with constant murmur, and the wind occasionally sighed and rustled through the trees on the bank; but there was little or nothing else to hear, till just before I was relieved at midnight, when three reports of firearms came from the direction of the cavalry vidette, out on the Battlefield, two or three miles away, and shortly after a sound of the clatter of hoofs on the frozen ground. The sound died away and the night was still as before, when I returned to the reserve. The fires were burning brightly in the wide fire places, and seated around within, we told stories and cracked jokes, and discussed the campaign and wondered where Banks had gone. Suddenly a hasty step is heard without, and one of the pickets puts in his head at the door to announce that men are moving on the opposite bank of the stream. While he is talking, bang goes a musket from our line to the left, and then another. *Something* is going on, or else somebody is unnecessarily excited. We seize our pieces, and hurry down to the ford, close by, where if anywhere a rebel party would probably attempt a crossing, and are not quieted by hearing in a hurried whisper from the three trusty men stationed there, that a small party of men had just come stealthily along the opposite bank, stopped at the ford, discussed in a low tone the expediency of crossing, and then, disturbed by the firing and stir down our line to the left, had hastily retired.

Our boys kept quiet for the comers were invisible in the shadow of the opposite bank, but had they stepped into the water they would have fired on them. Of course they might return and more with them, and dropping low, so as to get a sight against the starlit horizon, we watched intently for half an hour or more. The alarm and sudden turn out was a little exciting, but the boys were for the most part pretty cool; and a hostile body attempting the crossing about there would undoubtedly have met the contents of fifteen good rifled muskets, tolerably well aimed. But no more sound was heard, and the men, pickets and reserve, returned to their posts. A sergeant and two men sent down the line, had in the meantime discovered that the shots fired were by two of our sentinels, who hearing a movement in the bushes across the run, had fired at random. I returned to my sentry post, but there was no more alarm. I saw between night and morning, the big Dipper in the North tip up so that its contents, be they water, or milk from the milky way, must have run out over the handle. I saw the triple studded belt of Orion pass across the sky. I saw two meteors shoot along the horizon, and that was all the shooting I saw. I saw the old moon, wasted to a slender crescent, come up in the East; I saw the Sun rise very red in the face at the thought that he had overslept himself till half-past seven, on such a glorious morning; I heard a song bird or two piping sweetly from the woods; but I neither saw or heard any rebels. With daylight, however, a Union cavalry man, on foot, bareheaded, with scratched face and eyes still wild with fright, came to our line just below me, and told a story which explained the alarm of midnight. The vidette, 16 in number, of which he was one, posted out some three or four miles, while carelessly sleeping around their fires, had been charged into by a party of White's rebel cavalry, who captured all their horses and seven or eight of their number; the rest scattered into the bush in all directions, and it was doubtless some of them trying to make their way into Centreville, who created the alarm along our line, and came so near being fired on by our men at the ford.

Such is a night of picket duty at the front.

DECEMBER 20

I hear this morning that our infantry pickets are to be withdrawn from the line along Cub Run, when cavalry will take their places, and that we shall go into the redoubt close by, today, to be relieved, I suppose, tomorrow, by another regiment of the Brigade.

A grand review of the other four regiments by Gen. Stoughton took place yesterday at Fairfax C.H.

The health of the Co. C is good.

Yours, G.

Benedict and his comrades had more than a month's experience on the picket line, but this was the first time they knew they had a serious chance of contact with or danger from the Confederates or their supports, as this area marked the edge of Union control. There was more activity on this picket line than on their previous one because of Confederate cavalry and guerrillas in the area.

The Confederate fortifications and winter quarters served as silent reminders of the Confederate military power and the area's recent history in the war. The Confederate winter quarters Benedict mentions had belonged to Brig. Gen. David R. Jones's brigade, composed of the 7th, 8th, 9th, and 11th Georgia Infantry and the 1st Kentucky Infantry. This brigade, originally composed of the 7th, 8th, and 9th Georgia, with two battalions of the 1st Kentucky under the command of Col. Francis S. Bartow, fought at the first battle of Bull Run. They lost 60 men killed and 293 wounded, as well as Bartow, who was killed there.[2] During the spring of 1862, the two battalions of Kentucky infantry were transferred west and the 1st Georgia Regular Infantry was assigned to the brigade. Jones was promoted to command a division, and Brig. Gen. George Anderson assumed command of the brigade. The brigade had fought in Jones's division as a part of Maj. Gen. John Magruder's command in the Peninsula campaign. At the time of Benedict's letter, this brigade was at Fredericksburg, in Maj. Gen. John B. Hood's division, in General Longstreet's corps.

The area in which Company C was stationed, along with that part of the picket line, was the Confederate defensive area after the first battle of Bull Run through March 1862, when Confederate general Joseph E. Johnston pulled the Confederate army out before General McClellan could strike at it. During the winter of 1861–62, McClellan did not attack the Confederate fortifications or engage in offensive actions, because he thought Johnston outnumbered and outgunned him. This belief was reinforced by a large number of gun emplacements with decoys known as "Quaker guns," logs shaped and blackened to look like cannons. They were so named because Quakers were well-known as pacifists. When the Army of the

Confederate Winter Quarters and Fortifications near Centreville, Virginia.
BRADY COLLECTION, LIBRARY OF CONGRESS.

Potomac advanced on Johnston's works after his retreat in March 1862, they found hundreds of these "Quaker guns," and this did not enhance McClellan's stock with the Federal government. Now Benedict and his comrades got to see these "Quaker guns" up close near their picket posts.

Benedict describes a visitor as a "gaunt and yellow F.F.V.," as he considered any white landowner in the area who refused to take the oath of allegiance to the Federal government to be a member of the First Families of Virginia. Actually, the social elite of Virginia owned more than this farmer, who had a 150-acre farm and only a few slaves. From Benedict's description, this farmer seems to have barely made ends meet and wanted to prevent further damage to his property from either army, which is why he was offering the picket post free firewood. It was easier to cut and carry that than to continually split and mend rails for fences. This farmer's attitude is an interesting contrast to that of George Mason at Camp Vermont. However, he and Mason had one thing in common: They wanted the war to end so they could live in peace.

The account of the line crosser was the only such event Benedict details in which someone escapes them. This man was more than likely a Confederate soldier trying to get home for the holidays and not a spy. It is unlikely that a spy would force the Union picket line during broad daylight, as his chances of getting caught were good. The picket post at which this man almost got caught was manned by Pvt. Dick Irwin, his buddy Charles, and Pvt. Charles Garrick. Garrick spoke with a heavy French Canadian accent, having been born and raised in Montreal, and was called the "French man" by Irwin.[3] These men and Lieutenant Wing tried to capture the intruder but lost him in the woods after a short chase.

Part of the picket's job was to stop anyone who tried to cross the picket line. If it was a Confederate deserter or Union soldier without orders or a pass, he was placed under guard and taken to the divisional provost marshall's office at Fairfax Seminary. Officials would interrogate a Union soldier and inform his commander, then decide whether to send him back and what punishment, if any, to give him. In the case of a Confederate deserter, they would interrogate him, give him the oath of allegiance, and allow him to join the Union army and be shipped west to guard the frontier. If the deserter did not want to join the army, they would let him go and he would find work in the North. Escaped slaves were questioned about Confederate activity in the area and then sent to one of the many freedmen camps near Washington and Alexandria. White civilians without passes had to be cleared into the area by corps headquarters and were held at the picket line until headquarters relayed a decision by telegraph. If these civilians had family in the North or had no plans to return to the South, they were usually allowed to travel north provided they did not remain in the Washington, D.C., area. Civilians associated with the Confederate government or army were arrested and sent to Washington's Capital Prison.

The dead Confederate officer that Company D found in the barn aroused some morbid interest and a sense of mystery. The officer likely was from one of the Georgia regiments whose winter quarters were close by. It is a strange situation, as one would think that if they could get the coffin and shipping container to this barn by wagon, they could have transported the remains on the same wagon to the railway station at Manassas or Gainesville, about ten miles or a half day's travel away, before the Confederate army's retreat that spring. Given the confusion over their withdrawal, more than a dead officer was lost by the Confederates, and the fate of this man's remains, as well as his name, is still a mystery. In contrast, most of the men of the 12th Vermont who died of disease were shipped home for burial. Each company in the 2nd Vermont Brigade had a fund to pay the expenses to have a comrade's body shipped home at the cost of about $90.[4] Of the men who died of disease or accident in the 12th Vermont, 90 percent of them were shipped home for burial.[5]

Camp Near Fairfax C.H.
Dec. 26, 1862

Dear Free Press:

Those who suppose our life in the army an idle one should try it awhile. Yesterday being Christmas, was comparatively a leisure day, but it was almost the only one we have had. Almost every hour of the day has its duty, and we are not allowed the long evenings, in which so much is done at home. Lights must be out in all the tents at 9 o'clock, and we rarely light up in the morning; the consequence is that we make long nights rests of it and spend time in sleeping which oftentimes we would gladly spend in writing, to our friends at home.

New Years day has almost come. If we here are not obliged to celebrate it by marching through sleet and mud I shall be glad. We had a very fair Christmas in camp. The day was as mild as May, as is today also. By hard work the day before, our mess had "stockaded" our tent, that is, raised it up some three or four feet on sides of logs laid like a log house; it is in fact a little log house with a canvas roof. We have in it a very good California stove—a sheet of iron over a square hole in the ground, with a flue leading to a little chimney of brick and stovepipe outside—and as we have been confined of late to rations of hard tack and salt pork, we decided to have a special Christmas dinner.

We got some excellent oysters of the sutler, also some potatoes—very nice ones. Two of the boys went off to a nice, clean, free-negro family, about a mile off, and got two quarts of rich milk, some hickory nuts, and some dried peaches. I officiated as cook, and, as all agreed, got up a capital dinner. I made as good an oyster soup as one often gets, using that tin pail which came with ginger snaps, as a kettle—also fried some oysters with bread crumbs—for we are the fortunate owners of a frying pan in our tent. The potatoes were boiled in a shallow tin pan, and were as mealy as any I ever ate. We had, besides, good Vermont butter, nice boiled pork, good bread; and made a luxurious meal, closing with nuts, raisins and apples, and cocoa-nut cakes just sent to one of our mess from home. For supper we had rice and milk, and stewed plums— unfortunately the last of a nice lot of dried ones sent for Thanksgiving. Now that is not such bad living for poor soldiers, is it? We do not have it every day, though; but we have had many luxuries since our Thanksgiving boxes came.

We have a very pleasant camp ground just now, and if allowed to remain, shall make ourselves quite comfortable.

We had a visit from Dr. Thayer in our tent tonight. It was good for sore eyes to see the Doctor and hear directly from home; and he will tell you when he gets back that he found here a right hearty looking set of fellows.

DEC. 27

I did not get this letter off this morning, and have just time to say that we are in quite a stir tonight. Cannonading has been heard to the South all the afternoon and we are under orders to march at a moment's notice, with one day's cooked rations. It is probably only ordnance practice somewhere, but may be an engagement. It is rumored that we are to be ordered forward in course of a week, but I do not know what foundation there is for the rumor.

Yours, G.

With the war on, the lack of snow on the ground and May-like weather, and the fact that the men were away from home and family, it did not feel like Christmas to most on either side of the picket line or in camp. The 16th Vermont was on the picket line guarding against a Confederate visit that day. For the other regiments General Stoughton ordered that all duties possible be limited on Christmas Day. But when Capt. David F. Cole and Lt. George W. Robinson of the 12th Vermont's Company D, the company from St. Albans, did not conduct guard mount that morning it incurred Stoughton's wrath. He had both officers arrested and sent their names to division headquarters to have them undergo a competence board and be removed if they failed.[6] Christmas on the whole was more somber than Thanksgiving, but the men gave small gifts to their friends, such as a gift of writing paper given to Pvt. Dick Irwin by his friend Charley.[7]

Some members of the 12th Vermont and others of the 2nd Vermont Brigade hiked to the nearby Chantilly battlefield, about three miles up the Little River Turnpike to the northwest, to see what happened there that past summer. One of these men, from the 12th Vermont, Company K, known only as "B," wrote to his hometown paper, the *Rutland Weekly Herald,* about the signs of battle they saw that day: bullet-scarred trees, half-buried bodies, abandoned personal gear, and the remains of torn paper cartridges.[8] They spent some time burying those who had fallen there a few months before and fixing the graves of those already buried. For these men, it was anything but a typical Christmas.

Although Christmas had been mundane for the 12th Vermont, the New Year got off to an eventful start with a visit by Confederate general J. E. B. Stuart and a brigade of Confederate cavalry.

Camp Near Fairfax C.H.—Va.
December 29, 1862

Dear Free Press:

We have been having rather stirring times during the past twenty-four hours. Saturday afternoon the sound of artillery to the south, put our commanders upon the alert, and we had orders to put a day's rations in our haversacks and be prepared to march at a moment's notice. No marching orders came, however, and we spent a quiet night. During the day on Sunday, rumors of a sharp engagement at Dumfries, 25 miles south of us, in which our forces were worsted, of their retreat and the hurrying forward of troops to reinforce and recover the lost ground, reached us, and prepared us for a start. Just at night-fall came a renewal of the order of the night before, followed quickly by the command to fall in. Col. Blunt was absent at Alexandria, in attendance on a court-martial; not an agreeable circumstance either for himself or for the 12th, but his place was efficiently supplied by Lieut. Col. Farnham by whom we were quickly formed in line, and marched hastily a mile to Fairfax Court House. Two other regiments, the 13th and 14th and the 2nd Connecticut battery, attached to our Brigade, moved with us, in the bright moonlight, and filled the turnpike with a long dense column of armed and eager men. We were hurried straight through the village, and it was not till we halted behind a long breastwork, commanding a fine sweep of nearly level plain to the East, that we had time to ask ourselves and our neighbors, what it all meant. The word was soon passed round that a formidable rebel raid was in progress near us—that a large rebel cavalry force was approaching Burke's Station, four or five miles below us on the railroad—that an attack on Fairfax Court House was anticipated, and that the Vermont Brigade must hold the position for tonight at all hazards. Three regiments and three guns of the Battery were to defend that village; the 15th was at Centreville on picket, and the 16th, with three guns, was sent to Fairfax Station.

At our post, the 12th held the centre of the breastwork, extending on both sides of the Alexandria turnpike (along which the enemy was expected to advance) and crossing it at right angles. Two companies of the 13th and a portion of the 14th, were on our right; the remainder of the 13th was disposed on our left, and the balance of the 14th was placed a short distance in our rear, as a support. The battery, a fine brass howitzer and two rifled pieces, was placed on the turnpike. Companies B and G of the 12th, under command of Captain Paul, were sent forward half a mile on the road, as skirmishers, and a cavalry picket of five or six of the 1st Va. Union cavalry, was placed still further out.

So arranged, we waited hour after hour, on a bright and comparatively mild moonlight night. We liked well our position, and longed only for a chance to give the rebels James Island over again, with the odds in our favor. Occasionally an orderly rode down the road to the outposts or dashed up to Gen. Stoughton with fresh dispatches of the rebel advance, but nothing especially exciting took place till about eleven, when suddenly the situation became interesting. First came a courier with a message for Gen. Stoughton, whose reply, distinctly audible to our portion of the line, was, "tell him my communication with Gen. Abercrombie is cut off, but I can hold my own here, and will do it." Then came orders to load, and instructions for the front rank—(your humble servant was fortunate enough to be in the front)—to do all the firing, if occasion for firing should arise, and the rear rank do all the loading, passing forward the loaded pieces to their file leaders. Then came a dash of horsemen down the road, riding helter-skelter, and the "devil take the hindmost." We did not know then what it meant exactly, but found out afterwards that it was the cavalry picket, driven in and frightened half to death by the rebels. The stir among our officers, which followed their arrival, told us, however, that it meant something. Col. Farnham, cool as a cucumber, rode along the line, giving the men their orders and instructions. Major Kingsley in calm and clear voice added some words of caution, and injunctions to fire low, and General Stoughton riding up said, "You are to hold this entrenchment, my men. Keep cool, never flinch, and behave worthy of the good name won for Vermont troops by the 1st Brigade. File closers, do your duty, and if any man attempts to run, use your bayonets." Captains, each in his own way, added their encouragements to good behavior. And the men on their part, either needing no incentive, or catching the spirit of their officers, held themselves in readiness for action, with what seemed to me (my observations being mainly confined to Co. C, but extending to several other companies), almost perfect self possession. If there were cowards in our line they concealed well their apprehensions, and I have no doubt, had its possession been contested, that line of earthworks would have been held against any hostile force in a way which would have brought no disgrace on our Green Mountain State.

We waited in silence a few minutes, when suddenly our ears caught a faint tramp of cavalry, beyond the point of woods half a mile before us, where our skirmishers were posted, then some scattered pistol shots; then the shrill cheers of a cavalry squad of perhaps thirty or forty men on a charge, and then with startling distinctness the bright flash and sharp rattle of the first hostile volley fired by any portion of the 12th in this war. It was a splendid volley, too. Both companies fired at once, and their guns went off like one piece, without a scattering shot. The effects of the volley were not fully learned till daylight; but I may as well anticipate a little my story, and give them here. They were, eight rebel troopers wounded, and removed by their comrades (this our men learned from a man in front of whose house, a little ways on, the rebels rallied); three horses killed, three saddles, a rebel carbine or Sharp's rifle, manufactured in Richmond, and bearing the place, name of maker and date, 1862, on the lock plate, a good Colt's revolver and three secesh hats—these articles captured, and a pretty good horse, with U.S. on his flank, found riderless in the road and thus recaptured. The rebel troops scattered in all directions at the fire, and rallied and formed again further back. Our men expected a second charge, and were ready for it. This time they would have allowed them to come closer and made the fire more deadly; but after a short halt the rebels turned and rapidly retreated.

We at the breastwork knew nothing of these details. We only heard the volley, and taking it for the opening drops of the rain, waited patiently for whatever should come next. Nothing came, however. All was still again. In half an hour or so, lights like camp-fires began to show themselves about a mile in front, and our artillery was ordered to try its hand. Four shells were fired; bang went the guns, almost under our noses (Co. C was posted close to the road), and whiz went the shells, but they drew no response. A reconnaissance was next ordered. Captain Ormsbee of Co. G—one of our very best Captains, and of one of our very best companies— with 30 men of his own and Company B, marched straight up to the fires, a bold act under the circumstances. They were found to be fires of brush built to deceive us. A free Negro whose house was near by, informed Capt. O. that the rebels had just been there, under command of Gens. Fitzhugh Lee and Stuart, both of whom had been in his house an hour before.

They had, they said, two brigades of cavalry and some artillery, and they had pushed on to the *north*. This news was somewhat startling, I fancy, to our officers. It was taken to mean that the rebels were circumventing us and would probably shortly close in on us from the North or West. We were accordingly withdrawn from the breastworks, double-quicked back to Fairfax Court House, and were posted (I speak now only of the 12th) in the fields along the brow of a hill, in good position to receive a charge of Cavalry. Here we waited through the remaining hours of the night. The moon set; the air grew cold; the ground froze under our feet; but we had nothing more to do, but to shiver and nod over our guns, till daylight. There was a little excitement at one time over some fires seen near our camp, which we feared the rebels might be ransacking; but scouts sent out found them to be our own forces, of the 13th I believe. At sunrise we were glad to be marched back to camp, and to throw ourselves into our tents, where most of the men have slept through the day, taking rest while they can get it, for we are still ordered to have arms and rations in readiness for instant marching. I doubt if we shall go out tonight, however. We hear today that the rebel Cavalry having made one of the most daring raids of the war to within a dozen miles of Washington, have pushed on North to Leesburg, and will doubtless make a successful escape through the mountains.

I have given so much space to this hasty sketch of our little skirmish and night's duty, because it is the thing of greatest excitement with us at present, and not of course, for its essential importance. But it has been a very interesting bit of experience to us, and not without value, in its effect upon the discipline of the Brigade. It has added to the confidence of the men in their officers, from Gen. Stoughton down, and I guess the men did not disappoint their commanders. Today our good Colonel is again with us, to our exceeding satisfaction. He started with the Adjutant to join the regiment last night by way of the turnpike, which was then held for two miles or more by the rebels; but was advised by Capt. Erhardt, in command of a squadron of the Vt. Cavalry at Annandale, not to attempt to go through, and wisely took the advice. It would have been sorrow for us had he been taken by Stuart's troopers.

The medical care of the Regiment now rests on Ass't Surgeon Conn, Surgeon Ketchum having been advanced to the Medical Directorship of the Brigade. Commissary Sergeant Derby is promoted to Quartermaster's Sergeant, and will make a first rate one. Private "Charley" Thatcher of Co. C succeeds him as Commissary, and has with considerable experience in the duties, every business and personal qualification to fill the position capably and well.

The men of our Company suffer from colds, as do all the regiment, but are otherwise generally well.

Yours, G.

DEC 30

We have spent an undisturbed night, and I have time this morning to add one or two more particulars of the affair of night before last. Our forces have taken four or five prisoners of the rebel cavalry. One was captured by our own advanced guard at daylight—a hard-looking, butternut-clad trooper, apparently just recovering from a bad spree; he accounted for his used up appearance by averring that they had been six days in the saddle. The others were taken by the Vermont Cavalry, and only go partway towards balancing the loss of Lieut. Cummings of Co. D of the Vermont Cavalry, and three of his men, who were out on picket and were taken by Stuart's men. It is ascertained that the forces of Lee and Stuart made a circuit of a semi-circle around us, passing between us and Washington, and round to Chantilly on the west of us, where a force of 300 Cavalry, including a portion of the Vermont Cavalry, from Drainsville, came upon them and drove in their pickets; but finding themselves in the presence of a greatly superior force, retreated. It was reported in Washington, and fully believed by many, that our whole brigade was taken prisoners.

Heavy reinforcements have now been sent out to our support, and we anticipate no serious danger. Still affairs are in rather feverish state, and we may be marched in any direction, at any moment.

I had hoped to find space to describe our present pleasant camping ground, but must leave it for a future letter.

The weather is remarkable—days very mild, with magnificent sunshine; nights cooler, but still not much like Vermont.

Yours, G.

Although Benedict was a good reporter and does a good job for a soldier in the ranks of describing a nighttime action, there were some details regarding how this action began that he was unaware of. On December 27, three Confederate cavalry brigades crossed the Occoquan River, attacking several picket posts belonging to the 66th Ohio and the 77th Pennsylvania Infantry Regiments between Occoquan Village and Wolf Run Shoals.[9] The 66th Ohio telegraphed its headquarters that the regiments were being attacked by 4,000 cavalry with a battery of four guns and requested reinforcements and ammunition resupply. In the meantime, units in the area, including the 12th Vermont, were alerted around dusk to be ready to move with a day's rations and in light marching order. Things soon quieted down, however, and Union commanders thought that the Confederate raiding force had withdrawn and told the Union forces to stand down. That night, two of the three Confederate cavalry brigades and a four-gun battery of light artillery broke though the Union picket line and began their raid of the area near Dumfries. During the day, rumors filled most of the area's camps that General Stuart and his cavalry or Stonewall Jackson's infantry were headed their way, and in force. Without reliable information, unit commanders, such as Stoughton, did not move their units.

Waiting for the 2nd Vermont Brigade ended at 4:30 P.M., when an aide from Maj. Gen. Henry Slocum's headquarters arrived with telegrams to give Stoughton some idea of what was going on. This information confirmed that Stuart was at Burke Station, well inside the Union defensive perimeter, three miles east of Fairfax Station and about five miles south of Fairfax Courthouse—all too close to Stoughton and his command. Casey's division headquarters ordered Stoughton to protect the stores at Fairfax Station at all costs and, if possible, to hold the Confederate force until superior infantry and cavalry forces arrived to engage and destroy it.

At 8:00 P.M., Stoughton sent the 16th Vermont with a section of artillery from the 2nd Connecticut Light Artillery to bolster the defenses at Fairfax Station. He also telegraphed Col. Frederick D'Utassy of the 1st Provisional Brigade attached to Casey's division to send two more infantry regiments and a full battery of artillery to Fairfax Station. Stoughton then telegraphed Col. Redfield Proctor of the 15th Vermont on the picket line to be on the alert for Confederate cavalry and of the possible need to march his regiment to Fairfax Courthouse if the situation required. At 9:00 P.M., Stoughton's communications with other major units were cut off, which was a sure sign of trouble heading his way. By this time, the whole area was alerted. D'Utassy's and Stoughton's infantry regiments were in position or moving to meet Stuart's command. In addition to Casey's troops, two infantry brigades from General Abercrombie's division had been deployed near Annandale, as well as XII Corps's regiments to the west and southwest of Fairfax Courthouse. While Union forces were on the alert, few knew where Stuart and his command were or what they were doing.

Stuart had captured the telegraph office at Burke Station and knew better than the Union commanders what was going on and what forces stood against him. He wanted to ride into Fairfax Station to capture or destroy what was there, but he now knew that it was too well defended to attack. So he decided to ride north, hoping to spread confusion and perhaps capture an unready Union garrison. But as Benedict recorded, that was not the case. The 12th, 13th, and 14th Vermont Regiments and half of Sterling's battery marched out of camp through Fairfax Courthouse and east on the Little River Turnpike toward Alexandria for half a mile. They then entered a ready-made breastwork on a knoll facing east that commanded that part of the road. Stoughton sent Capt. Ora Paul's Company B and Capt. Ebenezer J. Ormsbee's Company G to a patch of woods about 500 yards in front of the main defensive line as an early-warning and ambush site along the Little River Turnpike.[10] As senior commander, Paul was in charge of this 180-man force, which now waited with loaded muskets for the first sign of the enemy cavalry.

At about 10:00 P.M., the mounted pickets were driven in by the fast-approaching Confederate cavalry. Confederate horsemen could soon be heard and were barely in range when Paul sent a volley into their ranks that stopped them cold. The Confederates quickly wheeled around, getting out of range before these infantrymen could reload their muskets, and took stock of their situation.

For Benedict and the other men in the main defensive position, this thunderclap of musketry got their attention. They were hoping for a chance to fire on the Confederate cavalry and knew they were in a good position to do so. Nothing happened, however, as the Confederate commanders considered their options and made plans. Unknown to Benedict, Stoughton sent one of his staff officers to Paul's position to see what was going on. Paul sent a scouting party to learn the enemy's intentions as bonfires were lit at the Confederate positions. First Sgt. Daniel K. Hall of Company G led a squad composed of three of his men and three men from Company B to the Confederate picket line under an improvised flag of truce to assess the position.[11] Hall told the Confederate pickets that his commander would like to parley with the Confederate commander. After fifteen minutes, the Confederate sergeant of the guard told Hall that his commander would communicate with Hall's commander in the morning and bade him and his men good night. The squad returned to its advanced position, and the staff officer returned to Stoughton with the information that the squad had gathered. Then Stoughton ordered Capt. John Sterling to fire a few rounds of solid shot at the Confederate positions with his battery. All of the guns in the section fired off a round, but there was no reaction or movement from the Confederate position. Stoughton sent a staff officer to the advanced position and ordered a probe of the Confederate position. Ormsbee, with a platoon from his company and another from Company B, advanced and found that the Confederates were no longer there. As Benedict records, a freedman told Ormsbee that the Confederate cavalry had moved north, and Stoughton redeployed the brigade to meet that threat, which, as time went on, did not come.

Lieutenant Colonel Farnham was currently in command of the 12th Vermont, as Colonel Blunt was at Alexandria to attend a court-martial. Upon hearing that the 12th Vermont was alerted to General Stuart, Blunt started for his regiment but was stopped at a Union cavalry picket because the Little River Turnpike was not safe, with the Confederates roaming the road. Blunt did not want to end the day as a guest of the Confederate army in Richmond, so he remained where he was. Col. Francis Randall of the 13th Vermont did not start the day with his command, either, but he got to his command just fifteen minutes before the Confederate cavalry got him. Nevertheless, the men that night saw that their chain of command was ready for action. Stoughton had been with the brigade less than a month and appeared suited for his new position.

Stuart and his troopers bypassed the 2nd Vermont Brigade and avoided contact with Union cavalry for the next few days. On the last day of the year, he and his command returned to Confederate lines with 300 prisoners and 100 wagons of booty from Union sutlers. According to Stuart's report, he lost one man killed, thirteen wounded, and thirteen missing.[12] One of these missing men was captured by the 2nd Vermont Brigade, according to Stoughton's report, in which he credits the brigade with a prisoner, two horses, and two saddles. Though this seems like a meager haul, it was bloodless brigade action that accomplished its mission. Stoughton's command prevented the destruction of the supplies at Fairfax Station, as well as a large amount of materiel that was removed from Burke's Station by wagon and reached his lines.

Stuart's raid added some excitement to a year that was running out, but it was not the only event that caused excitement for the 12th Vermont. On December 30, the brigade mustered for pay and was inspected by Stoughton. But the paymaster either did not come that day or ran out of money, as the men of the 12th Vermont were not paid until January 27.[13] They were paid from November 1 to December 30, so Benedict and other privates in the 12th Vermont received $22 each. This made the soldiers, their families, and sutler Stearns happy, as most soldiers were short of cash at that time.

New Year's Eve lacked the usual celebrations. Yet the war fundamentally changed on New Year's Day. On January 1, 1863, the Emancipation Proclamation took effect, and the Federal government declared all slaves under Confederate control to be free. This proclamation was a compromise between Northern abolitionists and slaveholders in the still-loyal states of Missouri, Maryland, and Kentucky, as it did not free any slaves unless they escaped from Confederate owners and crossed into Union lines after the new year. The Emancipation Proclamation changed the character of the war from a limited one where negotiation could have ended it, to a total one, where one side or the other would have to be destroyed to obtain victory. The proclamation also staved off foreign intervention, as France and England could not support or defend slavery, and that prevented them from intervening in the war from that point forward. Slaves by the thousands heard of the Emancipation Proclamation and headed to Union lines, further disrupting the Confederate economy at a time when it was already near its breaking point.

While the Confederates considered the Emancipation Proclamation Lincoln's pact with the devil, it was not popular with many Union states either. States in the West, as well as New York, which had a large immigrant population, had viewed the war only as necessary to restore the Union. They did not like the concept of freeing the slaves, as they feared that the former slaves would move into the area and compete with immigrants, lowering wages and diluting political influence. The proclamation increased desertion and decreased enlistments and reenlistments from these states, which caused a crisis in a few months' time, when active campaigning resumed in the spring. These issues did not yet affect the lives of men on the front, however.

On New Year's Day in the eastern theater, it was quiet except for the talk of Stuart's latest visit. In the Midwest, it was a different story, as January 1 was the last day of fighting at Stones River, in Murfreesboro, Tennessee. The Union soldiers repulsed Maj. Gen. Braxton Bragg's army and foiled his invasion of Kentucky. Had Kentucky fallen to the Confederates, this would have changed the dynamic of the war in that area. Kentucky could have provided more men and materiel to the Confederates, and this also would have moved the center of the conflict to Ohio, Indiana, and Illinois, thus

drawing troops from those states back to their defenses. Although the battle of Stones River was just as important as the ones fought later that spring
and summer, it was hardly, if ever, mentioned in the letters home from the
soldiers of the 2nd Vermont Brigade, including Benedict, who, in his next
letter, gives some thoughts about the year just ended and what he expects
to happen in the year to come.

Camp near Fairfax C.H., Va.
January 10, 1863

Dear Free Press:

I must alter the 62 I have written by force of a twelve months'
habit, to 63—which reminds me that the old year has been made
into the new since I wrote you last. The Old Year has gone and
taken with him three months of our term of service. We cannot
hope that the coming six will deal with us as gently as have the past
three. Rough as portions of our soldier's life have been, and unlike
as it all has been to the comfort and quiet of our Vermont homes,
we have thus far seen but little of the roughest part of war. But it
must come, though its approach is so gradual that we hardly per-
ceive it. From the security of our camp of instruction on Capitol
Hill, we passed to the more arduous duties of work on entrenchments and picket service, at Camp Vermont. We exchanged that
for our present more exposed position, where picket duty means
active watch for rebel cavalry, and where some of our regiment
have actually met and drawn trigger on the enemy. In time, no
doubt, will come the still harder experience of protracted marches,
of the shock and trial of battle, of wounds and capture and death
for some of us. More than this, the war as a whole, is to be more
desperate and deadly in [the] future, because waged with a foe
maddened by privations and loss of property, and especially by the
Proclamation of Freedom. We have already ceased to hear much
talk about "playing at war." It is owned to be *work* and pretty
earnest work, now; and if it grows hotter as a whole, it will of
course be the harder in its parts. But come what will, I for one—
and I believe I am one of many thousand such—shall "endure

hardness" the more cheerfully, and fight, when called to, more heartily, because Freedom has been *proclaimed* throughout the Land for whose unity and welfare we struggle, though its full accomplishment may cost years of trial and trouble.

I promised once, I think, some little description of our present camp. It is on a pleasant slope, stretching in front to the south-east out to a broad *Campus Martius,* between us and Fairfax Court House, on which take place the brigade drills to which Gen. Stoughton treats the brigade almost daily. In the rear, the lines of tents extend into a fine grove of pines, shaped like three sides of a hollow square, the sides of which extend out beyond the camp on either hand, and kindly protect us from all winds but the East wind. A brook near by on our left, affords us water for washing, and a spring, fifty or sixty rods off, gives water for cooking and drinking A regimental order forbids the cutting of the trees within 200 yards of the camp, and thus ensures to us the ornament and protection of our tall evergreens. The ground has been nicely cleared and leveled, and the underbrush cut away from under the trees near the camp. On the whole, it is the pleasantest spot we have as yet occupied, and if we must spend the winter in this region, we shall be content to spend it here. The Colonel and his staff have had their tents surrounded by sides of split logs, with fire places and chimneys of brick, making very comfortable habitations; and the men have for the most part raised their tents on stockades of logs, adding greatly to their comfort though detracting somewhat from the external appearance of the company streets, for it is impossible to give a row of little log huts, plastered with mud, the neat appearance of a line of simple tents. Still, neatness and cleanliness are scrupulously attended to, and the general good health of the Regiment as contrasted with the average of the army and of this brigade, bears strong testimony to the good care of our Colonel and his subordinate officers, in this particular.

I must not omit to mention that our camp is graced by the constant presence of the amiable and accomplished wives of Colonel Blunt, Lieut. Col. Farnham, and Capt. Ormsbee, who have taken quarters with their husbands, and share camp fare with them, interest themselves in the hospitals and sick men, and give to us all, in a measure, the refining and restraining influence of women's presence, without which any collection of men becomes more or less like a bear garden.

The time of the regiment, at present, is mainly devoted to drill, with occasional episodes of picket duty; and we are on the whole, making marked progress in discipline and drill. Gen. Stoughton, in a general order, issued a day or two since, declares that in these respects, this brigade already presents a favorable contrast to the troops of other States, around us; and I believe it is mentioning only an acknowledged fact, to say that the 12th leads the Brigade, in general good appearance on the parade ground and good order in camp. I might go farther and speak of the position which Capt. Page's company holds in the regiment, in the particulars named, but I modestly refrain. If it is second to any, we of the Company would like to know it, and to learn the reason why.

Not one of the company is at present in hospital. Colds and coughs are pretty prevalent, otherwise the company is in first rate physical condition.

JANUARY 12, 1863

My letter was interrupted by an order which sent the right wing of the 12th out on picket duty at Chantilly. The twenty-four hours did not pass without some incidents, which, if they were the first of their kind, might deserve mention; but having already given you some idea of picket duty here, I let them pass, only saying that Company C, which was posted in the stations at the extreme front, lost none of its reputation for coolness and good judgement, in circumstances which afforded some indication of how the men will behave in pretty trying spots.

We are enjoying, this evening, a visit from our friend, and fellow townsman to most of us, J. A. Shedd. His well-known and beaming face and hearty greetings, bring to us as much of Burlington as we could get in any one man's presence, and have done us good.

Yours, & c., G.

The fact that officers' wives sometimes wintered with their husbands is an interesting and neglected part of Civil War history. Many officers from

Left to Right: Mary Farnham (on Burnie), Lt. Col. Roswell Farnham (on White Face), Lt. George Bigelow, Asa P. Blunt, Maj. Levi Kingsley, and Chaplain Lewis I. Brastow at Wolf Run Shoals. BRADFORD HISTORICAL SOCIETY.

the 12th Vermont and her sister regiments could afford to pay for their wives to travel south, where they either boarded in Washington or stayed with locals who were willing to take them in until their husbands' quarters were ready. Enlisted men's wives came south, too, although even less is known about their experiences in camp, as no accounts from them have been found. Colonel Blunt's wife, Mary, was one of the first officer wives to arrive, on or about November 19. She had been planning to travel with Lieutenant Colonel Farnham's wife, Mary, but, Mrs. Farnham was ill when it came time to leave.

Mary Johnson Farnham had known her husband, Roswell, since he was thirteen and she was ten, as they had grown up together in their hometown of Bradford, Vermont. Roswell graduated from the University of Vermont and studied to be a lawyer. He and Mary married on Christmas Day 1849.[14] Until he started his law practice, they ran a school together in Bradford. In the spring of 1861, Mary Farnham saw her husband leave for Virginia as a first lieutenant in the 1st Vermont Infantry Regiment. He returned to her later that August and became captain of the local militia company, the Bradford Guards. Upon his commissioning as the executive officer of the 12th Vermont a year later, Roswell could afford to send for Mary to winter with him.

When Mary Farnham at last traveled to Virginia on December 11, she was supposed to travel with Captain Ormsbee's wife, Jennie, but Jennie did not meet Mary's train, so Mary continued on without her.[15] After a day's travel, Mary arrived in Washington at 6:00 P.M., where she was met by her husband. He had escorted Mary Blunt from Camp Vermont to Washington and arranged lodging, board, and transportation to and from Washington for the wives when the situation at the Fairfax Courthouse camp permitted. Mary and Roswell Farnham had a day together before he had to return to the 12th Vermont, where he made arrangements for her and Mary Blunt. While the women waited, they visited wives from other Vermont regiments at the same boardinghouse at 434 D Street.[16] While there, they heard a constant parade of ambulances transporting the wounded from Fredericksburg.[17]

Roswell returned on December 19 to complete the details for the women's transportation to and lodging at Fairfax Courthouse. After a late start on December 21, Mary Blunt and Mary Farnham took the ferry to Alexandria. There, sutler Stearns loaded their trunks and other luggage in the back of his covered wagon. The two women rode in the wagon, using the trunks as seats. Although it started to snow on their sixteen-mile journey to Fairfax Courthouse, Mary Farnham decided that she needed some air and walked for several miles behind the wagon. The only other traffic on the road was other supply wagons pulled by horses or mules and driven by Union teamsters who "were frozen as blue as their overcoats."[18] As Mary walked, she also noticed that almost all of the houses and outbuildings along the route had been stripped by Union troops for lumber.

Shortly after dusk, the snowstorm stopped. Stearns and the two women arrived at the 12th Vermont's camp to find it empty, as the regiment had left for picket duty. Chaplain Brastow and Pvt. Nelson Roger, Farnham's orderly and cousin, had remained to ensure that the officers' wives were taken care of. After supper and tea, Nelson took Mary Blunt and Mary Farnham to a house just outside the camp owned by a Mrs. Whitney, where they boarded until Blunt's and Farnham's quarters were ready a few weeks later.

Mary Farnham, Mary Blunt, Jennie Ormsbee, and many other wives from Vermont wintered in the camp near Fairfax Courthouse, and later at the camp at Wolf Run Shoals. Mary Farnham left Virginia on April 13,

1863. A handful of wives remained until the end of their husbands' service. A few joined their husbands on a soon-to-be-famous march north in June 1863. While they were in camp, these wives added a woman's touch. They helped with the sick in the regimental and brigade hospitals, and risked the diseases that were ever present in the camps. Still, no wife is mentioned in the records or in letters home as having died because of her exposure to camp life.

Mary Farnham is the only wife from Vermont whose letters and diary survive from this winter. These writings constitute an important record of a woman's experience of the Civil War.

Though many men in Benedict's company and regiment may have wanted to fight as soon as they were mustered, the gradual approach that Benedict describes in his letter worked better in the long run. Because they had a lot of guard, picket, and fatigue duty, as well as drill, the 12th Vermont and her sister regiments were better trained than most other Union regiments that had been mustered at the same time. The Vermont regiments also had a core of well-trained and seasoned officers, which would pay off in the months to come. Until then, during the frequent interruptions of duty, the men drilled in company, battalion, and occasionally brigade formations, thus practicing the movements they would perform when they went into combat.

CHAPTER 5

Camp at Wolf Run Shoals

O n January 20, 1863, Gen. Ambrose E. Burnside marched the Army of the Potomac out of its camps around Falmouth, Virginia, in another attempt at fighting Lee's army. The troops began their march in good spirits, wondering where they were going and hoping for better results than in their last encounter against the Confederate army. But that afternoon, the rain and their troubles began. It rained for the next four days, turning the roads into impassable muddy tracks. By the time the rain stopped, the infantry had made at most a mile's painful and exhausting march a day. After each day's march, the soldiers halted near the roadside to eat a cold meal and perhaps sleep in the cold mud, and this condition sapped whatever morale the army had left. Though it was bloodless, the "Mud March" caused Burnside's removal as the Army of the Potomac's commander.

George Benedict was not in Virginia while the Army of the Potomac was on the march. He had started a twenty-day furlough on January 18 to take care of important "personal business" in Vermont.[1] Neither his personal papers nor other documents record what business he had in Vermont. Before Benedict had left Vermont for Virginia, his father was running the post office, and his brother took care of his other business interests. Whatever situation occurred that they could not handle, it must have been important, because few men in the brigade got furloughs home. This furlough turned out to be well timed, as the 12th Vermont soon moved, and Benedict's comrades would have been happier if they could have joined him in Vermont. An anonymous soldier from the 12th Vermont, who signed his letter only as "W," described the unpleasant circumstances.

Camp in the Mud
Wolf Run Shoals, Va.
Jan. 22

Dear G:

Monday, on Battalion drill, the ominous orderly with orders from headquarters made a visit. Of course we at once surmised that something was up, and thought sorrowfully of our dear old shanty, built by the toil of our own hands and hallowed by a full month of comfortable occupancy. The drill went on however; but soon after our return from it, the order came to be ready to march in the morning—whither no one could tell. We began packing knapsacks ready for the move, but nothing as to a breaking up came till just as we were going to bed, when word came to have tents struck at six o'clock next morning, and to be in line of march at six and three quarters. That corn meal had not been used and it seemed too bad to lose so much good material, so we went to work and got up some Johnny cake and pancakes, which we surrounded at once and they went capitally.

The next morning was as beautiful as heart could desire, bright, cold, and ground frozen hard. We knew we were to come here, but thought it was only eight or nine miles, and that we should do that bravely. It turned out of course, that the place was much further off than any one expected—instead of three miles beyond Fairfax Station it proved to be a good *seven* miles—and the road here is beyond any power of description. You have seen the road from the Court House to Fairfax Station—that is a Roman viaduct, compared with this. We are located about half a mile from the Occoquan River. The 13th regiment followed us and is now with us. The 15th and 16th are at the station with the 2d Connecticut Battery,—the 14th is still at its old camp. The 12th took the lead on the march, and the Colonel was bound, I take it, to give the 13th a taste of quality of the 12th, for we only rested three time[s] on the march, and then only about ten minutes. We arrived here, making a march of 12 miles over the hardest road to travel on you ever saw, about noon, and turned into the old camp of the 3rd Wisconsin regiment. They had just left, and the fires were still smoking in the fireplaces as we came in and took possession of the few stockades ready for habitation. That regiment was only about 400 strong, and of course there were accommodations for only half of us. However, we doubled up and but few of the shelter tents were called into requisition. That night, one of the fiercest rain storms I ever knew, began, and has lasted without intermission for now 48 hours. Imagine our condition—it is beyond conception to any one but an old soldier. Many of the boys have been about drowned, and have bailed the water out of their shanties by the pailful. As I dragged my boots from under my head this morning, one of them felt heavy, and on investigation, turned out to be half full of water.

Today and yesterday, large fatigue parties have been at work and have cut and laid a new corduroy road half way to Fairfax Station.

We are terribly in the mud; it is all over and under and around us. But we have a new camp laid out already right in the deep woods, with plenty of timber around. The country is broken and hilly, and the wildest I have seen. There is much that is amusing in the incidents of the past two days. I should like to tell you, but I haven't time.

Your friend and fellow sufferer and soldier.

W.

The 12th Vermont now had a new camp at Wolf Run Shoals. This camp was the least liked, yet it turned out to be the one the regiment spent the most time at. Wolf Run Shoals was the key ford on the Occoquan River, which formed the southeastern edge of Washington's defense perimeter. This river was a major natural obstacle for any army that wished to move through the area, as it lacked bridges and had only four fords for crossing points. Wolf Run Shoals was located where Wolf Run, a small stream that flowed due south for several miles, flowed in the Occoquan; three small islands made the river fordable at that point. Running north and south was Wolf Run Road, which went to Fairfax Station four miles north and to Dumfries about seven miles south. Despite the letter writer's low regard of this road, it was an important one, because it cut through the pine forest that covered the north bank of the Occoquan. The terrain near Wolf Run Shoals was rough, with bluffs and ravines cut by several small streams.

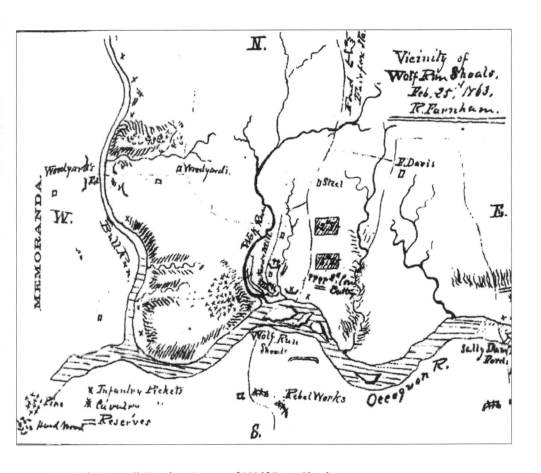

Lt. Col. Roswell Farnham's map of Wolf Run Shoals. FARNHAM PAPERS, UNIVERSITY OF VERMONT.

Clear, level ground was limited, giving the area a claustrophobic feel. The 12th and 13th Vermont's impression of the area was not a good one as they marched down Wolf Run Road for the first time and spent a lot of time working to improve it. This first impression did not improve as the same heavy rain that created the Army of the Potomac's "Mud March" turned the Wolf Run Shoals camp into a mud pit.

The brigade's move was not the only change for the 12th Vermont, as several officers resigned from the service. Up to this time, two officers had resigned because of health reasons, and more now followed, some for reasons other than poor health. In Benedict's division, if a regimental or brigade commander or even General Casey had reason to question an officer's ability, he could have that officer face a board of examination. This board was composed of five higher- or equal-ranking officers, who tested that officer's tactical and administrative knowledge for his position. If the officer failed this examination, he was dismissed from the service and served the rest of his enlistment in the ranks. This possibility motivated the less competent to resign and go home. In the 12th Vermont during January 1863, five company-grade officers in the regiment had to face the competency boards. Capt. David F. Cole and Lt. George W. Robinson were examined by a board after their Christmas Day run-in with General Stoughton, which found both men "fully qualified for the position they now held."[2] But all of the officers of 12th Vermont, Company I, resigned before facing their boards, causing some turnover of company-grade and noncommissioned officers in the regiment. Colonel Blunt selected Company I's new officers instead of having the company elect them. The men of the company were unhappy about this, but they had no say in the matter, as they complained in letters home. Blunt promoted Lt. George E. Dimmick of Company A to command Company I, 2nd Lt. William Loomis of Company C to be Company I's first lieutenant, and Sgt. Edward D. Redington to become the company's second lieutenant.

These promotions led to several changes in Company C as well. To replace Loomis, Blunt selected George Benedict, a good choice, as he had the talent and was clearly underemployed as a private. Whether Benedict found out about his promotion at home or when he returned to camp, he did not say. Since reports of his promotion appeared in the Vermont newspapers, he probably had a chance to get a new uniform. Others were also promoted in the regiment. Pvt. George Hagar, the regimental adjutant's clerk and sometime acting regimental sergeant major, was promoted to regimental sergeant major. Although Hagar's duties did not change too much, he now managed the regiment's first sergeants and supervised the manning of the picket, guard, and fatigue details, keeping him busy and outside, which he liked.[3]

Benedict's furlough ended on or about February 6, and the next day he wrote a letter to the *Burlington Free Press*.

Camp near Wolf Run Shoals, Va.
February 7, 1863

Dear Free Press:

Once more in Camp! For your humble servant, after eighteen days absence on furlough, the change is from the snows of Vermont to the mud of Virginia from the peace and comfort of New England homes to the insecurity and desolation of this border region, from sleeping between sheets and eating at tables, and the various luxuries of civilization, to canvas quarters and camp fare. For the 12th, also, the change within the three weeks past is not a slight one. We have exchanged the broad level stretches and more open and cultivated region of Fairfax Court House, for a rough and broken country, wooded with hardwood groves and second growth pines, sprung up on worn out tobacco-fields, and scantily peopled with scattered secesh farmers. Near us, several hundred feet below the level of our camps, runs the Occoquan, a muddy stream, about as large as the Winooski. Across it, on the heights beyond, are rebel earthworks, thrown up by Beauregard's soldiers last winter, now untenanted.

Our camp is on a knoll from which the men cleared the pine trees some two weeks since. It is much more contracted in its limits than our former fine camp near Fairfax, and sooth to say, less attractive in almost every particular. The company streets are hardly a rod wide; but the tents are well stockaded, almost without exception, and in default of sheet iron and brick for stoves and square chimneys, are supplied with fireplaces of rough stone, and chimneys of sticks and mud. The first battalion drill since the regiment left Camp Fairfax, came off today. The men have had all they could do in digging rifle pits, picket duty, constructing corduroy roads—

of which they have made miles between this and Fairfax Station, and the labor of clearing and making camp; and between rain and snow and mud, have had the roughest time they have as yet known. Their spirits are good, however, in spite of mud and hard work and rough fare; and as I write, the music of guitar and violin and well attuned manly voices, serenading the ladies, whose presence in camp I have heretofore mentioned, and who have accompanied their husbands thus far towards Dixie, reaches me on the evening air, and tells of light hearts and good cheer.

I have one or two changes to add to those you have already noticed in the 12th. Quartermaster Geo. H. Bigelow, has been appointed 1st Lieutenant in Company B, and detailed as Quartermaster of the Regiment. Sergeant S. G. Hammond, has been promoted to be 2nd Lieutenant in Company B, in place of Lieut. Warren, resigned, and private Geo. I. Hagar of Company C, has been made Sergeant Major of the Regiment (in place of Sergeant Major Redington, promoted) a place which, I need not say, he is abundantly capable of filling well.

Yours, G.

Benedict compares the Occoquan to Vermont's Winooski River, which starts in the Green Mountains, flows northwest pass Montpelier, and empties into Lake Champlain just north of Burlington and south of the town of Winooski. The Winooski River is about twenty-five yards wide at Montpelier and about a hundred yards wide at Burlington and rarely fordable at points in between. That is a difficult distance to cross under hostile fire, and thus the Occoquan must have been a major obstacle. However, the rainy weather shut down the campaign season, as the resultant mud made travel for an army nearly impossible except by railroad or on one of the few improved roads in the area.

Camp near Wolf Run Shoals, Va.
February 14, 1863

Dear Free Press:

Little or nothing of startling interest has occurred in the Camps of the Vermont Regiments at "the Shoals" since I wrote you last.

The two (the 12th and 13th) have nearly *ten* miles of picket line to guard, and picket service is the most important and arduous occupation of the men. There have been skirmishes between cavalry outposts, sights of rebel patrols, and rumors of coming attack from rebel cavalry, enough to keep us somewhat on the alert; but the long roll has not sounded, or hostile shot been fired by us. Colonel Blunt has been practicing the men at target firing of late, and they are making sensible progress in proficiency in the modern method of administering the kind of "blue pills" which are the only cure for rebellion. Yesterday and the day before, strong fatigue parties crossed the river and destroyed the rebel earthworks on the heights on the other side, commanding our camps. It was a wise precaution; but while the roads are in their present condition, we can hardly be in great danger from rebel artillery. The mud in the roads, where they are not corduroyed, varies from deep to bottomless, and the rains, without being very constant or heavy, are frequent enough to keep the roads from settling. A week of sunshine, however, would again enable armies to move.

The weather is quite mild. It is raining quietly as I write, with the thermometer at 58° and the mercury has been as high as 70° in the sunshine in our camp during the past week. The backbone of the winter, if not the rebellion, is broken in this region. We shall probably not have more than one more *right* cool spell, and shall henceforth have much warm weather.

The health of the regiment has improved during the past ten days, and may now be called pretty good on the whole, though many of us suffer from the disturbing effect of the water, which is by no means as good here as we have found in our former camps. Co. C is called the healthiest Company in the regiment, and is so I think.

The Vermont 2nd Brigade is you know a portion of the 22nd Army Corps (heretofore called the Reserve Corps, Defences of Washington) under command of Maj. Gen. Heintzelman, and the 12th and 13th are on the extreme outmost boundary of the new "Department of Washington."

Yours, G.

Lt. George G. Benedict.
BENEDICT PAPERS, UNIVERSITY OF VERMONT.

For the men of Company C, the routines of camp life, with picket, guard, and fatigue details, remained the same in their new location and had long lost their novelty. Such was probably not the case for Benedict, who, as a new officer, was now in charge of the details instead of performing the work. That is not to say that he now had it easy. There was a big difference between giving commands and following them in the ranks. As the officer of the guard, he was busier than a private, and because he was in charge, if something went wrong, he was considered responsible for it. He checked his company's picket stations twice a day, which involved a lot of foot travel. In addition, the guard called him to the picket post whenever something unusual happened. Benedict also trained with the other officers in tactics and with sword and pistol drill while the privates were off duty.

The "blue pills" Benedict refers to as a cure for rebellion were bullets that, when taken out of their paper cartridges, were bluish gray. Target practice was slowly becoming part of the training program for new regiments in the Union army. At the beginning of the war, it was uncommon on both sides, and few regiments fired their muskets before going into battle. But the 2nd Vermont Brigade eventually received permission to fire forty rounds of ammunition for target practice. The soldiers in these regiments also fired their muskets after picket duty, which gave them additional practice and emptied their rifles, thus preventing injuries while off duty. This training gave the 12th Vermont and her sister regiments a proficiency with weapons that few new regiments possessed, unless they had seen combat. In the 13th Vermont, the best shot earned two weeks off picket, guard, and fatigue duty, which was a strong incentive to shoot well.[4] Benedict does not mention whether the 12th Vermont had a similar reward.

Benedict does not record in his letters his February trip to Washington, D.C. Lieutenant Colonel and Mrs. Farnham invited him to accompany them to the capital as a guide.[5] Benedict knew Washington better than most in the regiment, and it would give him a chance to see his fiancée, Katherine Pease, who was visiting friends and family there at the time. Benedict and the Farnhams left Wolf Run Shoals at about 3:00 P.M. on February 11. They had an uncomfortable trip north in the regimental ambulance during a snow shower. The road was in poor condition, pitted and rutted from weeks of wet weather and heavy supply wagon traffic, and the ambulance ride was jolting. The trio arrived after dark at Fairfax Station, where Quartermaster Brownson's wife, Sarah, gave them supper and lodging.

The next morning, they took the train to Alexandria, then the ferry to Washington. They arrived at about 11:00 A.M., and after brunch at the National Hotel, they visited the Capitol, with its nearly finished dome, and watched the Senate in session. Mary was sick the next day, so they returned to camp on Saturday the fourteenth.[6] Katherine spent nearly three weeks in Washington and visited the 12th Vermont's camp at Wolf Run Shoals. Before she left for home, Benedict probably saw her a few times, as he was resourceful and had connections. Other events also kept him busy.

Camp Near Wolf Run Shoals, Va.
February 22, 1863

Dear Free Press:

I believe I ventured, in my last, the statement that the backbone of the Winter if not the Rebellion was broken, in this region. I beg leave now to take back the assertion. The time is coming, undoubtedly, when both will be shattered, but at present the dorsal columns of the season and of secession are *not* fractured—distinctly not. I am writing in the midst of the hardest snowstorm we have seen in Virginia, and one that would not disgrace today the bleakest hillside in Old Vermont. The diary of the weather for six days past is about as follows, and may be interesting as a sample of Virginia winter and weather: Tuesday a fall from ten to twelve inches of heavy snow. Wednesday snow on the ground, but settling fast, and affording material for some tall snow-balling in the afternoon. (*Mem.* The left wing led by Co. C, after a hot battle with the right wing, rallied for a desperate charge, engaged them at half pop-gun range and drove them handsomely into their entrenchments behind their company quarters—casualties, two bloody noses and three or four contused eyes or ears from percussion snow balls. N. B.—Wounded all doing well). Thursday pouring rain which carried off the remainder of the snow. Friday, high wind, drying the mud rapidly. Saturday, warm bright sunshine, air like May—Bluebirds and robins singing. Men all out "policing" up the quarters and camp, and enjoying the sweet breath of Spring. Sunday, opens dark and cold, with a heavy storm of fine dry snow, falling at the rate of an inch an hour through the day, drifted as it falls by a cutting East wind, and closes at nightfall with not much short of eighteen inches of snow on a level [ground], and promise of a cold snap of several days duration.

Picket service is decidedly "rough," at such a time, and some mothers' hearts I know of, would ache to give shelter and relief could they see their brave boys out on the picket line, cowering under their booths of pine branches, through which the snow and wind find frequent entrance, and holding their wet and chilled hands and feet to the fires which struggle for mastery with the snow, and which at best can only avail to surround themselves with circles of "sposh" and mud. But we keep up good heart and cheer, mid sun or storm, and before this reaches the eyes of our friends, sunshine and mild weather will have returned to us, and snowstorms be over I trust for the season. In camp our stockaded tents afford comfortable shelter; our supplies of food and fuel are abundant, and we have on days like this nothing to do but make ourselves comfortable.

It may be thought, perhaps, that there is no need of keeping men out on picket at such a time; but our surroundings here have taught us that constant vigilance by night and day, in all weathers, is the price of safety. We realize constantly that we are in the enemy's country, if it is but 25 miles from Washington. The inhabitants of this region are all secesh. As usual wherever we have been in Virginia, the young and able bodied men are all gone. The old men are just quiet and civil enough when in the presence of our soldiers to keep themselves from arrest; but render what aid and comfort they give to anyone, to the other side. The women are secesh without exception; the little girls sing rebel songs, and the hoopless, dirty and illiterate young ladies of these F.F.V.'s boast that their brothers and sweethearts are in the rebel army, and chuckle over the time coming, when the roads settle, when Stonewall Jackson will rout us out of here in a hurry. One or two sharp skirmishes of the Michigan Cavalry with White's rebel cavalry have occurred near us recently in one of which our side lost fifteen men, and a cavalry picket was cut off but two days ago within three miles of our camp. Our position is however a tolerably strong one; we have here with our two regiments, the 2nd Conn. Battery, Capt. Sterling, six brass guns manned by a fine set of fellows recruited mainly from the big manufactory of the Wheeler & Wilson Sewing Machine Manufacturing Company at Bridgeport; and we are now connected by telegraph with Fairfax Station and Washington, so that reinforcements could be quickly called out if we should be attacked. I think we could make a stout fight by ourselves if necessary, and hold the post against a much superior force.

I was about to submit some patriotic considerations in view of the fact that this is the anniversary of Washington's birth; but I must cut my letter short and spare you.

The Regiment has sustained a serious loss in the resignation of Capt. Landon, of Co. K (the Rutland Company), who has been compelled by business complications to retire from the service. He was an excellent officer and will be much missed by his Company and brother officers.

Our new Assistant Surgeon Ross, has arrived and entered upon his duties.

Yours, G.

Benedict correctly surmised that he had been overly optimistic regarding the ends of both the winter and the Confederacy. He and the North

Winter Quarters for I Company, 12th Vermont, at Wolf Run Shoals.
Left to Right: Cpl. George Witherell, Sgt. Albert E. Metcalf, Pvt. Robert D.
Farr, and Sgt. Joel H. Holton. HOUGHTON COLLECTION, UNIVERSITY OF VERMONT.

saw later that year, in the Virginia Wilderness, that the staying power and strength of the Army of Northern Virginia were better than they had imagined. Winter was a more familiar opponent to these Vermonters, but unlike the winters they were used to, the Virginia weather was fickle, switching from cold and snowy to almost summerlike with sunshine and balmy tempertures, only to change again a few days later. This caused the Wolf Run Shoals camp to be perpetually damp and muddy.

The snowball fight allowed the men to blow off steam and was a good change of pace from camp's dull routine. And the 12th Vermont was not the only regiment to team up against its neighbors and let the snow fly. It was better than waiting for the weather to change and the snow to clear and for drill to take up the time between guard and picket duty. The 12th Vermont and the 2nd Vermont Brigade were sick of both.

In his letters, Benedict does not write about the local inhabitants in a favorable light. He refers to Virginians as F.F.V.'s if they owned property or slaves; the rest, if they were white, he calls "secesh," short for secessionist. Vermonters viewed anyone who had not taken the oath of allegiance with suspicion.

As 1863 went on, events proved the 12th Vermont was in the enemy's territory, despite the lack of Confederate troops in the area. Benedict and his comrades soon learned that Union control ended where the Union's picket and guard lines did. The locals, for the most part, were secessionists, and it did not help that Union troops camped on their land, burned their fence rails, foraged their livestock, and caused immeasurable damage to their livelihood. This destruction tried the patience of even the most loyal Unionists causing a lot of ill will against the Federal government. These disgruntled civilians soon began providing food, shelter, and information to Confederate guerrillas, or at least looked the other way.

Both sides in this war celebrated George Washington's birthday and claimed his legacy as their own. The Confederates considered themselves the natural heirs to Washington's legacy, as he was a Virginian and they believed they were fighting the second American Revolution, another War of Independence. The Union men considered themselves the defenders of the American Revolution and believed that if Washington were still alive, he would have led their army. At the beginning of the war, Washington's birthday was celebrated as a holiday on both sides, usually with parades and special formations, and with Washington's farewell address read aloud to the troops. There were no such festivities in the 2nd Vermont Brigade or the XXII Corps in 1863, however. The Fourth of July was another holiday that was claimed by both sides. Each celebrated it in a similar manner, especially this year.

As the weather finally began to warm up, so did Confederate activity near the 12th Vermont and her sister regiments.

Camp near Wolf Run Shoals, Va.
March 8, 1863.

Dear Free Press:

The 12th is now in the seventh week of its occupancy of its present camp—a longer stay in one spot than it has yet made, if my memory serves me rightly. Six weeks has hitherto been about the limit of our abiding in any one place, and when that time is up, the boys begin to expect the order to break camp and march. We have formed no such intense attachment to our camp at the Shoals, that we shall not be pretty well content to leave, wherever we may be ordered, and little matter how soon the order comes. The region about us is a dreary and forbidding one; the camp is more contracted and less pleasant than two or three of our former ones; the time we have thus far spent in it has been the most trying season of the year; the alternations of snow, rain, frost and mud, have told on the health of the regiment, and we have, I suppose, somewhat more sickness than ever before, among both officers and men; our picket duty—in pleasant weather, the pleasantest duty of the soldier—has been severe and rough, and take it all in all, though our situation here might be worse in a thousand particulars, we should all, I think, be satisfied to run our risks of bettering our condition by a move.

You are not to understand from what I say that we are especially dissatisfied, "down in the dumps," or disheartened, even for a moment—not at all. The men of the 12th are wont to carry a stiff upper lip, under all circumstances. The "red, white, and blue," sung by an extemporized Quartette club, with a still chorus of manly voices, comes to my ear as I write, from one of company streets, with a sound of hearty cheer, which tells a different story from that. About a tenth of the Regiment are off duty, from measles, fevers, and ailments of one sort and another. The balance are, I think, more plucky, and resolute in the great purpose of the war than ever, and grow still more so daily. "There is more fight in me," said one of our men of Co. C, yesterday, "than when I came out, or ever before. I supposed when I enlisted that nine months in the service would give me enough of War, and I remained of that opinion till quite lately. Now I am *in for the war,* be it long or short." The man who said this had no *lack* of fight in him at the start, mind you, and I believe he represents a majority of the regiment. The *Regiment* has more fight in it today than ever before. Fuller acquaintance with the temper and purposes of the rebels, discussion of the issues involved, and especially the news we get from home of the sayings and doings of the miserable "copperhead" journals and their followers at the North, have stirred to the bottom the fountains of honest indignation, and given strength to the purpose and patriotism of us all. The army is unanimous in this feeling so far as I can judge. Having enlisted to fight traitors, the soldiers as a mass propose to fight them *through,* and would give those at home the same treatment they do those at the South.

MARCH 9, 1863

I was going to complain of lack of incident here, of which to write; but since I began my letter, we have been supplied with some of that missing article. You will have heard by telegraph, before this reaches you, of the dash of rebel cavalry into Fairfax Court House last night, and the capture in his bed of Brigadier Gen. E. H. Stoughton, commanding this Brigade. The camp is humming with the news, but in the uncertainty as to how much that is told of the attending circumstances is truth, I shall not attempt to describe this very creditable (to the *rebels*) occurrence. I beg leave to say, however, that none of the disgrace of the affair belongs to the regiments of the Brigade. It should be understood that Gen. Stoughton was not taken from the midst of his Brigade. The Vermont regiments nearest to the comfortable brick house which Gen. Stoughton occupied as his headquarters, were at Fairfax Station, *four miles south* of him, while the 12th and 13th are a dozen miles away. The risk of exactly such an operation, has been apparent even to the privates, and has been a matter of frequent remark among officers and men, for weeks past. How could they protect him as long as he kept his quarters at such a distance from them? That's the question.

The moral of the transaction is too obvious to need suggestion.

Col. Blunt has just been ordered to take command of the Brigade, and is consequently removing his headquarters to Fairfax *Station.* When *he* is pulled out of bed by a single company of rebel cavalry, fifty or sixty miles from their nearest support, I will let you know.

I alluded to the general health of the Regiment above; I am glad to add that Co. C is among the healthiest companies in the Regiment, if not *the* healthiest. We have but four or five men excused from duty, and none of them dangerously ill. The pine forest in the rear of our camp has been cut away lately to let in air and light, and permit the ground to dry, and every precaution is taken by the Surgeon and officers to prevent sickness among the men, as far as possible. The ground is settling now rapidly, between the showers, and in fact in spite of them, and we trust the season of deep mud will soon be over.

Yours, G.

Few men of the 12th and 13th Vermont Infantry Regiments wanted to remain at Wolf Run Shoals by this time, despite Benedict's reassuring reports home, as the number of sick and dying soldiers was climbing, and the area was depressing. While the men waited for better weather and the return of the active campaigning season, a chain of events caused much excitement in the camps of the 2nd Vermont Brigade. It was Capt. John S. Mosby who initiated these events, and his actions made him a growing problem for Union troops in the area.

Mosby started the war by enlisting in the 1st Virginia Cavalry and became its adjutant within a year. However, because of a personality clash with Fitzhugh Lee, who took command of the 1st Virginia cavalry when General Stuart was promoted, and Mosby's talents, he was attached to Stuart's headquarters as a scout. In this position, Mosby reconnoitered the route for Stuart's ride around General McClellan's army during the Peninsula campaign and showed a talent for working behind Union lines. Mosby rode with Stuart during the Dumfries raid, and in the confusion, he stayed behind to start what was officially known as the 43rd Partisan Ranger Battalion. In the months to come, Mosby and his men gathered intelligence, harassed Union communications, and forced the Union to pull manpower from the front to guard its rear in what was soon called "Mosby's Confederacy."

At the end of February 1863, Mosby and his command began flexing their operational muscles and were noticed by the cavalry commander Col. (Sir) Percy Wyndham. Wyndham, a British soldier of fortune serving with the Union army, soon grew tired of Mosby's hit-and-run tactics and threatened to burn down any town or house that offered Mosby and his men assistance. That threat offended Mosby, and Wyndham became his next target.

On the night of March 8–9, Mosby and a handpicked force of twenty-eight men left for Fairfax Courthouse to visit Wyndham. These men were the core of Mosby's command and had detailed knowledge of the area, as most had grown up and still had family there. This knowledge assisted Mosby in getting in and out of the area undetected, as they were able to use the local terrain better than the Union cavalry. Mosby's men slipped past Union pickets on that moonless, rainy night. A deserter from the 5th New

York Cavalry, Big Yankee Ames, had joined Mosby's group a month before and now assisted them. Ames knew the location of picket posts and could bluff his way through them if necessary, but the ride to Fairfax Courthouse proved uneventful. Arriving at Fairfax Courthouse around 2 A.M. on Monday, March 9, Mosby conferred with a local or two to determine the situation of the town and his target. To his disappointment, Wyndham had left for Washington the day before. However, Mosby and his men did not leave empty-handed.

He and his men broke up into three groups. Mosby went with five men to Dr. Gunnell's house where General Stoughton and his staff were quartered, while the other two groups went to secure horses and supplies for their use in the town. Mosby posed as a messenger and gained entry into the house when Stoughton's aide-de-camp, Lt. Samuel Prentice, opened the door. Mosby pulled a pistol on him. While the rest of his men secured the bottom floor of the house, Mosby and two men went up to see Stoughton. Mosby woke up Stoughton and asked him if he had ever heard of Mosby. Stoughton, slowly coming to his senses, said, "Yes, have you captured him?" Mosby answered, "No, he has captured you!" With the assistance of two Confederate soldiers, Stoughton was dressed and ready to ride.

Twenty minutes after leaving Stoughton's headquarters, Mosby took stock of his haul. He had captured Stoughton, a large number of his staff, some of the staff of the 5th New York Cavalry quartered in another building, and fifty-nine horses. Although Mosby was disappointed that he had not captured Wyndham, this haul made up for it. The group then mounted up and started to ride west. As they were moving, Lt. Col. Robert Johnson, who commanded the 5th New York Cavalry, opened his second-floor window and challenged the group on riding at that hour. Three of Mosby's men dismounted to capture Johnson, yet they were not enough to overcome the colonel's wife, who held them off long enough that he could escape. Mosby's men returned to the group without him.

Mosby, feeling that he was pushing his luck, ordered the group west into a pine forest and over rough ground to cross the Union picket lines before dawn. As it was dark and the Union prisoners outnumbered the Confederate raiders, several captives took the opportunity to escape. One of them was Prentice, who slowly maneuvered his horse to the edge of the group. When he thought the raiders were not looking, he stopped his horse in the woods. After he could no longer hear the group, he slowly rode in the other direction out of the woods. But before Prentice found Union troops to raise the alarm, Mosby and his command were across Confederate lines. About half of the Union prisoners had escaped, but Stoughton was not among them, as Mosby rode next to him until they arrived at Stuart's headquarters at Culpeper Courthouse.

This was one of his most famous raids of the war and made Mosby a household name in both the North and South. On the other hand, it was the end of Stoughton's military career. The circumstances of his capture were embarrassing, and when it hit the press, it killed his future in the Union army. Stoughton became a laughingstock when Lincoln said that he could make a brigadier general in five minutes, but horses cost $125 apiece. Stoughton's situation was not helped by the fact that Gen. Silas Casey and his regimental commanders had warned him about his personal safety in this exposed position. The 12th and 13th Vermont Regiments were at Wolf Run Shoals, and the 14th, 15th, and 16th Vermont Regiments were at Fairfax Station, too far away to have protected or helped him.

Why did Stoughton stay at Fairfax Courthouse at such risk? He and a lot of other Union commanders did not appreciate the threat that Mosby and other guerrillas posed, and it was Stoughton's bad luck to be the one who was captured. In addition, his mother and sister were wintering with him at the time, which made him reluctant to move closer to his regiments. Stoughton had placed his creature comforts above his safety, and he paid the price. Stoughton's living arrangements had also fueled his unpopularity with his men, who lived in the mud while he enjoyed himself in a good house removed from danger—or so he thought. The 12th Vermont was not sorry that Stoughton was gone, because they did not like his command style or the heavy-handed way he had gone after Cole and Robinson at Christmas. The 12th Vermont also felt that Colonel Blunt should have been the brigade commander instead of Stoughton, and there was some resentment when Blunt was not given command. The most interesting comment on Stoughton's capture was from the 16th Vermont's adjutant's clerk, who wrote in the personnel actions section of his records that day that Stoughton had "transferred to Mosby's Command."[7]

The world first found out about Stoughton's capture when Blunt telegraphed Casey's headquarters in Washington to inform him of Stoughton's and the brigade's telegraph operator's capture. Casey had Blunt assume command of the 2nd Vermont Brigade and come to the divisional headquarters for new orders. These included moving the brigade's headquarters to Fairfax Station, which was done shortly thereafter. In the following months, Mosby visited the 2nd Vermont Brigade a few more times. However, these regiments faced a more dangerous foe than either Mosby or Robert E. Lee at that time.

Camp near Wolf Run Shoals, Va.
March 21, 1863

Dear Free Press:

I am glad to be able to announce an improvement in the health of the Regiment since I wrote you last. The existence of some sixty cases of pneumonia and typhoid fever, of which eight proved fatal in quick succession, alarmed us all, at one time. But a change has taken place for the better—due, apparently, to the increased care and precautions taken for the health of the men, for the weather has continued as trying as heretofore—we had snow and sharp cold weather yesterday and last night, and have a drizzling rain today. There have been no more deaths within a week past; the number on the sick list has decreased considerably, and the new cases of fever are of a milder and more manageable type. The suddenness with which death gave the final discharge, in several of the fatal cases, was startling. In one case, the man was taken sick one day, went into the hospital the next, and died the next. In another, the poor fellow had just sent a message to his friends saying that he was pretty sick, but hoped he should get along with it, when he fell into a dreamy wandering state, complained of the weight of his knapsack, and did not see how he *could* carry it across the river. Suddenly his breath stopped; the soldier was over the river, without his knapsack and never again to be trouble by its weight.

There is now, I believe, but one man (a member of Co. K) in hospital, who is considered dangerously ill; and a week of sunshine, such as we *must* have soon, it would seem, will bring the regiment back to its usual average of health.

Our esteemed Colonel, as I believe I wrote you, is now commanding the Brigade during the absence of Gen. Stoughton at the front, leaving the regiment under the watchful and capable care of Lieut. Col. Farnham. Col. Blunt has been making his presence felt at Fairfax Station, in the right way. The Station, as you may know, is the point of supply for all the troops in this region, in Camp at Centreville, Union Mills, Fairfax Court House, Fairfax Station, and Wolf Run Shoals. The quantity of Quartermaster and Commissary's stores here, is of course, very large—and the position is one which is ordered to be held at all hazards. It is now, I am happy to say, in a very much better condition for defence than ever before. Within the past week, rifle pits have been dug and breast-works by the mile thrown up, by the men of the 14th, 15th, and 16th Regiments, along the high ground surrounding the Station on every side, from behind which they will be happy to meet any force likely to be sent against them very shortly. The picket lines have also been closely looked after by Col. Blunt in person; the various departments of supply, for the Brigade, have received attention; and the Brigade and Regimental hospitals have had the benefit of the Colonel's occasional and unannounced presence and quick eye for defects in management and care. One learns to value energy and attention to his business in a commanding officer, after seeing how the influence of such qualities is felt throughout down to the last private in the Brigade.

How long the rebels will leave our infantry regiments unmolested, of course I cannot say; but the way in which our cavalry suffer of late, is a caution to us all. You have heard of the late capture of Major Wells, a captain, two lieutenants and twenty men of the Vermont Cavalry, at Drainsville. This was followed up night before last, by the gobbling up of a picket reserve of the Pennsylvania Cavalry, numbering some twenty men, a short distance to the right of our own picket line on the Occoquan. These surprises, I must say, are getting to be altogether too frequent, and are anything but creditable to the branch of the service, which seems to have the monopoly of them.

I have, by the way, recently met one or two of the men who were present at the surprise of our Vermont Cavalry at Aldie, two or three weeks since, and can add some incidents not heretofore published. The statement that no pickets were thrown out by Capt. Huntoon is I am assured, incorrect. Pickets were sent out about a mile, on three roads. The whole party, pickets doubtless included, were, however, thrown off their guard by a body of the 18th Pennsylvania Cavalry which met them on its way in from the outside, and reported no rebel anywhere in the region. The men and horses were most of them hemmed in by the rebels in the yard of a mill, from which the men had got grain to feed their horses, which accounts for the large number captured. The rebel force under Capt. Mosby numbered, according to his own statement, but 27 men. Capt. Woodward's horse was killed instantly, while in full gallop towards the foe, by a ball in the spine and fell upon Capt. Woodward pinning him to the ground. While lying thus, almost crushed by the weight of the animal, a rebel ruffian rode up and commenced firing at the prostrate Captain, who would probably have thus been murdered in cold blood, had he not had strength enough left to draw a small pistol from his breast pocket, with which after once or twice trying he was lucky enough to send a ball through his assailant's body. One man of his Company defended himself for some time from two rebels who were trying to seize his horse, which he held by the halter, by striking at them with the *bridle and bits.* Gurtin or Curtin, the brave Rutland boy who was so severely wounded, was seen to stop with the balls flying around him and after he had two *through* him, and deliberately load his revolver, which he had emptied, and discharge it at the rebels, after which he put spurs to his horse and made his escape. He now lies in the hospital at Fairfax Court House, and I am sorry to say in a critical condition, a rebel ball having passed through the bone of the pelvis, into the groin, where it cannot be extracted.

Several of the men who were captured with Gen. Stoughton and accompanied him to Richmond, have been paroled and have returned. They say that they were taken to Culpeper that night and next morning, and remained there over one day, a delay which would probably have ensured the re-capture of the prisoners, had a sufficient cavalry force followed upon their tracks. Gen. Stoughton was well treated at Culpeper by Gen. Fitzhugh Lee, who was a classmate of the General's at West Point; but after his arrival in Richmond he was taken to the Libby Prison, where he now lies in company with 108 officers of our army, who are all confined in one room. A lady acquaintance of the General's in Richmond had furnished him with some blankets; but he was kept on the same scanty fare as that allowed to the other prisoners—a third of a loaf of bread and a small piece of poor meat *per diem*. The General and his friends are hoping, as I hear, for his speedy release on parole.

Yours truly, G.

As with most soldiers in their first winter quarters, everyone got sick with something because the men were living so closely together. The wet weather saturated the ground, and after eight weeks of encampment at Wolf Run Shoals, there were sewage and runoff problems. The 12th and 13th Vermont's camps were on high ground, and eventually the contaminated water ran off into the Occoquan River and Wolf Run. These rivers were also the regiments' sources of water, and drinking the water caused a high number of cases of typhoid fever, the camp's biggest killer.

The 12th Vermont's 1863 records show that during this round of disease, eight men were discharged for disability and eight died of disease in March, and thirteen were discharged and fourteen died in April.[8] These numbers do not include the hundreds who were not dangerously ill but incapacitated.

On March 21, Colonel Blunt assigned Benedict to be one of the brigade's aides-de-camp and moved him from the 12th Vermont to brigade headquarters at Fairfax Station. This is why Benedict was so knowledgeable about Blunt's activities while the 12th Vermont was stationed at Wolf Run Shoals. It was a good move for both Benedict and the brigade, as the brigade staff benefited from his talents. After Benedict was removed from Company C, he wrote fewer letters to the *Burlington Free Press,* but when he did write, he now had a more informed view of the brigade's situation and a different perspective.

As an aide-de-camp, Benedict's new job was to gather and transmit information to the brigade commander. While in garrison, he assisted the brigade commander in drafting reports, orders, letters, and other paperwork of a command nature to the regiment and division headquarters. While in the field, he performed reconnaissance of the local area and march routes for the brigade commander when needed. He also acted as the commander's representative to the regimental and divisional commanders and staff to coordinate brigade operations. While he was learning his new job, he was probably assisted by Lt. George Hooker, who had been in the army for two years and had been an aide-de-camp since Stoughton took command of the brigade the past December and brought Hooker over from the 4th Vermont Infantry Regiment. Hooker was a battle-hardened veteran from the 1st Vermont Brigade, who had earned the Medal of Honor for single-handedly capturing the colors of the 16th Virginia Infantry, its commander, and 160 soldiers by bluffing them into thinking that he was a part of large force about to arrive at the battle of South Mountain.[9]

Benedict probably hoped that the brigade headquarters would stay at Fairfax Station, which was a better place to live than Wolf Run Shoals, but the headquarters soon moved. On March 23, 1863, General Casey ordered the brigade to redeploy the three regiments that guarded Fairfax Station. The 12th and 13th Vermont remained in place and were joined by the 14th Vermont on the afternoon of March 24. That same day the 15th and 16th Vermont marched to Union Mills, some ten miles down the Orange and Alexandria Railroad from Fairfax Station. These two regiments were familiar with the area, having spent several weeks there on picket duty the preceding November when the brigade was stationed at Camp Vermont. This time, however, Col. Redfield Proctor was in command of the detachment. His orders were to protect the railroad bridge that crossed the Bull Run and resist Confederate attacks as long as practical, then fall back under pressure to Fairfax Station to bolster the troops at this depot should the Confederates attack in force.[10] The 15th and 16th Vermont also provided a picket force from Island Ford to Yates Ford on the Bull Run River and guarded the Orange and Alexandria railroad bridge at Union Mills. As the 14th, 15th, and 16th Vermont Regiments marched, the weather was foremost in everyone's mind. With the spring, active army operations would resume. The question for the soldiers of the 2nd Vermont Brigade was whether they would be a part of it.

Camp at Wolf Run Shoals, Va.
April 9, 1863

Dear Free Press:

If I sometimes begin my letters with talk about the weather, it is because it is a subject of prime importance in every camp. Upon the weather, as all have learned, depend to a great extent the movements of armies; for field artillery and supply trains are dependent on the roads, which are dependent on the weather. The connec-

Lt. Col. Roswell Farnham, Maj. Levi Kinsley, and the 12th Vermont at Dress Parade. Houghton Collection, University of Vermont.

tion, too, is immediate between the weather, and the health of the troops, a matter the full importance of which can hardly be realized by anyone not connected with the army. The risks the soldier thinks most about when he first enlists, are commonly those of the battlefield. After he has been out awhile, not wounds or death upon the field, or capture, or hard marches or privation—not these, but *sickness,* is the great dread of the soldier. As long as he is *well,* if he is a true man, he cares nothing about the rest. For a month past we have encouraged ourselves with the thought, that the season of snows and mud was now about over. The inhabitants hereabouts told us that they frequently commenced ploughing in February, and that their gardens, such as they have, were always made or making by the middle of March. I suppose this is so; but we have no evidence of the fact, this year, beyond their say so. If you could have heard the storm howl here, last Saturday night, or seen the pickets wading to their posts next day through snow which fre-quently in the hollows was over boot tops, you would have come to the conclusion that winter was not "rotting in the sky" in Virginia, however, it may be elsewhere. Today, which is the finest day we have had for two weeks, the snow lies still upon the shadier hillslopes, and the air is chilly in spite of the sunshine, as in any April day in Vermont. We have now done counting on the speedy return of mild and pleasant weather. It may come, when it pleases the kind Ruler of the sunshine and storm; but our boys declare that they shall not be surprised to leave Virginia in a snow storm when our time is out next July.

The sick list of the 12th continues large—is larger now, I am sorry to say, than ever before numbering not less than 120, besides a number who suffer from severe colds, &c, but are not sick enough to require the surgeon's care. This diminution from the effective force of the regiment, while the details for picket duty are increased rather than diminished, tells sensibly upon the labors of the well and strong. But while there is some complaining, of course, all are ready to own that they had far rather do the work of the sick and feeble ones, than to take their places in the hospitals. There have been one or two more deaths since I wrote you last, but on the whole, the attacks of fever and pneumonia are less severe and fatal than before. The Twelfth, heretofore the healthiest, seems to be now the sickliest regiment in the Brigade. Why this is so, it is hard to explain satisfactorily. Partly perhaps, because the other regiments had their "sick spells,"and got through the process of acclimation sooner; partly because the measles had a run in the winter and left many men in poor condition to resist the exposures of the spring; partly, perhaps mainly, owing to unhealthy location of the camps and water not of the best quality. The last two reasons will not hold after this. This week the regiment has moved camp to a hardwood knoll, a quarter of a mile from the old one. The location is higher and more airy, the company streets much wider, and the whole ground much better than the old one. The men have taken their time, erected their new stockades before they left the old ones, and when the mud dries will be *very* comfortable in their new quarters. I wish you could look in to some of the new shanties, and see *how* comfortable. I have one of Co. C's in my eye, as I write—stockade of logs, uniform in size, split in halves, laid flat side in and hewed smooth, a good five feet high, and nearly and closely covered by the canvas roof; door of board in one side, rather low and small to be sure but big enough for all practical purposes; good floor of hardtack boxes; bunks, or berths rather, at one end, each wide enough for two men, one over the other, made of smooth poles, which answer every purpose of a spring bedstead, sheet iron stove, monitor pattern, at the other end; sofa of split white wood, without end or back; gun rack, filled with its shining arms—the principal ornament of the room; shelves to put things on, pegs to hang things on, and other luxuries and conveniences too numerous to mention—why, it is good enough for the honey-moon palace of the Princess and Prince of Wales, good enough even for a soldier of the Army of the Union. How long the men will occupy their new quarters of course no one can tell. The way in which the Brigade is strung out along the front of this Depart-ment would seem to indicate that the intention of the military authorities is to keep us here for some little time; but the exigen-cies of the service disarrange all minor plans continually.

This Brigade is now picketing some twenty odd miles of line, as the river runs. The 14th guards the lower Occoquan from the low-est ford at Colchester to Davis' ford, three miles below the Shoals. The 12th and 13th picket from there to Yates' Ford, a couple of miles below Union Mills. The 15th and 16th take care of the rest of the line up to Blackburn's Ford, on Bull Run, where the pick-ets of Gen. Hay's Brigade meet our own, and continue on the line to the North. It is understood that Gen. Stahl is withdrawing the cavalry for the most part from picket service, throughout the lines around Washington, and concentrating them for reorganization and re-equipment, in and about Fairfax Court House. He has fifteen regiments, numbering some seven thousand sabres, in camp there, now. Infantry supply their places, and will more than make them good, for such service.

The men of the 12th have been greatly gratified by the recent removal of the headquarters of the Brigade to the vicinity of the Shoals, thus bringing Col. Blunt in a measure back to them. With all due confidence in and respect for their other officers, the boys feel safest when near their own Colonel, and under his experienced eye, and I believe the Colonel is as glad to be near his regiment as they to have him there.

Our pickets and patrols have been repeatedly fired on at night of late by bushwhackers. The natural consequence is a closer supervision and stricter measures with the inhabitants within and near our lines. Brigade Provost Marshal, Capt. Wm. Munson, has been for a week or two past engaged in visiting all the houses in this region, searching for and confiscating all arms and property contraband of war, and registering the names and standing as to loyalty of the citizens. Some of this sort of work has been done before; but never I suppose as thoroughly as now. It goes hard with some of these F.F.V.'s to give up the old fowling pieces (of which quite a collection is accumulating at headquarters, some of them as long as Long Bridge nearly, and old as the invention of gunpowder apparently) which have been handed down from father to son for several generations; but they have to come.

It is one of the most difficult and embarrassing portions of the duty of a commanding officer, in such a region as this, to deal properly with the non-combatant inhabitants. The innocent, in numberless cases *must* suffer with the guilty, from the nature of the case. Col. Blunt is kind to the sincerely loyal, of whom there are a *very* few, and to the really inoffensive, of whom there are more, within our lines, and is looked up to by them as a protector and friend; but the men, whose influence contributed to bring about the present state of things, whose sons are in the rebel army, and whose sympathies are with that side now, get little consolation when they come to Col. Blunt to complain. They are informed that as they *would have* secession and war, and have sown the wind, they must take the consequences and reap the whirlwind. Such dialogues as the following are not infrequent: *Citizen,* "Good morning, Colonel," *Colonel,* "Good morning Sir." *Citizen,* "My name is ———— ———— your troops are stealing my rails, I'd like to save what I've got left, and wish you'd order them brought back that ain't burnt, and stop them taking any more." *Colonel,* "H'm, did you vote for secession?" *Citizen,* "Well"—hesitating, "Well I did, Colonel, but it is too late to talk about that now." *Colonel,* "Too late to talk about rails, too, sir. Good day sir." Exit Citizen with a large flea in his ear, and rage in his heart at the d—— Yankees.

But to return to the Provost Marshal's operations, I was going to say that enough of information and arms had been obtained to fully warrant the search. Muskets have been found hid in the closets, and cartridges and percussion caps by the thousand hid away in the women's bureau drawers, the possession of which they relinquished with extreme reluctance. Some citizens have been sent in to Washington for safe custody, and it is hoped that this playing peaceful citizen by day and bushwhacker by night is measurably stopped, for the present. Capt. Munson has performed his delicate duties, so far as I can learn, with great good judgment and efficiency, and I may add that he is in all respects an excellent and active officer.

We turn back now from our lines remorselessly, all fugitives from Dixie, except contrabands, who do not come this way often, and deserters from the rebel army who drop along occasionally. Three came in today, one of them a pretty intelligent young man of 25, the other two bright-eyed and good looking boys of 17, all members of the 5th Va. Cavalry. They are clothed in the coarse cotton or cotton and wool butternut colored jackets and trousers which commonly form the uniform of a rebel soldier, when he has one; and tell the often repeated story of scanty rations, hard treatment, and poor pay. The twelve dollars a month which they are paid barely cover the cost of their clothing, at the rates at which they are charged to them, so that the rebel soldier in fact works for the food and clothing, and not over much of either. One of these was a Baltimore boy who joined the rebel army on its invasion of Maryland seven months ago, in a hurry, and has repented at his leisure. They brought their carbines with them, tell straight stories, and if cleaned up and dressed in Uncle Sam's uniform would be pronounced by anyone three nice looking soldiers. They say that an impression that the war is to continue indefinitely prevails now, in the south, and is disheartening many who have hitherto held out strongly for the rebel cause.

This being a fast day in Vermont, a general order from the Col. commanding directed the relief of the men from all unnecessary duties, and the observance of religious exercises appropriate to the occasion.

The unsettled state of the camp of the 12th prevented our good Chaplain from preaching a sermon. I attended divine service in the camp of the 14th and heard a patriotic and excellent sermon by Chaplain Smart of that regiment.

Yours, G.

In the time between Benedict's March 21 and April 9 letters, the brigade prepared for a possible Confederate attack on their positions. The 12th Vermont and her sister regiments were issued extra ammunition and ten days' marching rations on March 29. The 13th Vermont was ordered five miles down the river to cover a ferry crossing opposite Occoquan Village that same day and made its camp on the estate of a local woman known as Widow Violet. While the 2nd Vermont Brigade prepared for Confederate attacks in its front, the brigade provost marshal took measures to prevent trouble in its rear.

Capt. William Munson, the 13th Vermont's D Company commander, had the additional duty of brigade provost marshal. As provost marshal, Munson was the brigade's acting law enforcement officer. This was why he and a detachment searched the local houses and confiscated any weapons of military value to counter the growing threat of Confederate guerrillas in the area. Munson, an 1854 graduate of Norwich University, was promoted a month later to executive officer of the 13th Vermont, becoming the highest-ranking graduate of this military school in the 2nd Vermont Brigade. While Munson and his men searched for weapons, a detachment of about a hundred men under the command of Maj. Levi Kingsley destroyed the fortifications that the Confederates had left the spring before in the front of Wolf Run Shoals, so that they could not use them again to threaten this river crossing.

Benedict's account of the three Confederate deserters surrendering to the pickets was just one example of increased activity as the weather improved. A few days later, on March 30, the 15th and 16th Vermont caught a Confederate deserter, and on April 9, they caught three more. As the number of line crossers increased, it became clear that active operations were beginning. On April 12, the 2nd Vermont Brigade received the following telegram from Division Headquarters.

Headquarters, Casey's Division—Washington—April 12th, 1863

Colonel Blunt:

General Casey directs that your brigade be prepared to take the field tomorrow morning. Each regiment will carry 40 rounds of ammunition in their cartridge boxes and 60 rounds in their wagons. Each battery will have its ammunition boxes filled and 200 rounds in wagons. The troops will carry 7 days rations—3 of which cooked will be carried in haversacks. The men are to be provided with shelter tents.

This telegram set events in motion that affected the brigade for the rest of the month. Benedict records those effects in his letter of April 26.

Camp at Wolf Run Shoals, Va.
April 26, 1863

Dear Free Press:

It is more than two weeks now since orders came for the 2nd Brigade to be in readiness to take the field; but we still linger on the banks of the muddy Occoquan. The order to make ready was promptly and energetically complied with. The extra baggage of officers and men (wives included in some cases) was sent into Alexandria or Washington, or back to Vermont; the tents of the troops were turned back to the Quartermasters, and shipped to Alexandria; the men overhauled their "cotton bureaus," and discarded superfluities with Spartan rigor; supplies of food and ammunition were duly provided and distributed; and the feeble men were sent into the City Hospitals. This last, by the way, was an unfortunate proceeding, as it has turned out. Over a hundred men were thus sent in from this regiment, of whom many would, probably, *today* be on duty, if they had stayed in camp, and many more in a very few days more, who will now, probably, have to go through the circumlocution office of the hospitals and convalescent camp; and some will hardly more than rejoin their regiment, if at all, before their term of service will be out. But the orders of the

Medical authorities were peremptory, and there was no help for the thing. The Brigade was to be "cleared for action," reduced to fighting trim and it *was done*—we have been ready any day since, to sail in, but the order to move does not come. We trust that we are not to be kept here any longer, in the doubtless important, but inactive and inglorious duty of the "Defence of Washington." We have "stood guard" long enough. If there is anything to be *done,* and they will only allow us to have a hand in, while our time lasts, it is all the favor we ask of our military rulers.

The ranks of Co. C have been sadly depleted by the prevailing maladies, and two more of our number have passed away, where they will never more be required to answer to earthly roll call. The Company and the cause has lost two good soldiers, in the deaths of Corporal Pope and Private Sutton. Pope was one of those *perfectly trusty men,* on whom their officers rely with absolute confidence. Always ready, when in health, industrious, earnest, faithful, judicious, obliging, a true patriot and a good man—no soldier in the Brigade had a better record to point to, than that of Corporal John Pope. We had all learned to respect and esteem him, and we mourn for him as for a brother. Sutton, too, was a faithful and excellent soldier—such as we can ill spare. I fear that there are more to follow them. A season of steady dry and warm weather, however, such as I trust we are about to have, will do wonders for the health of the command.

Brigadier General Stannard arrived last week, and assumed command. He is right welcome to all the Brigade, for the soldiers know his sterling qualities, and to none more so than to the 12th, to whom his coming also restores their own good Colonel.

I must close this hurried letter, without mention of some other matters of more or less interest.

The Paymaster is paying the Brigade four months pay, much to the satisfaction of all, of course.

Yours, G.

On April 13, the brigade received a telegram ordering that those who were in the regimental and brigade hospital and who could not move in ten days be shipped to hospitals in Alexandria and Washington, D.C.[11] That was a standard indicator that the brigade would move. Benedict mentions more than a hundred sick soldiers being sent to these hospitals, but his number was a tad high, as regimental records show that fifty-four men from the 12th Vermont and twenty-two men from the 13th Vermont were sent to these hospitals between April 13 and 18.[12] At the same time, Company C of the 12th Vermont lost Cpl. John Pope, a twenty-six-year-old mechanic, to typhoid fever on April 17, and Pvt. John H. Sutton, a twenty-eight-year-old farmer, to the same disease on April 25.

Many of the officers' wives now left for home, as it looked as though the brigade would be going into active service. Mary Blunt and Jennie Ormsbee left in March. Sarah Brownson left for Vermont on April 14. Mary Farnham spent a week sight-seeing in Washington, D.C., then left for Vermont on April 20. Mary Farnham was sad to leave, as she ended her diary of her time in the South, but she was comforted that Roswell and his regiment would be home in three months.

The 12th Vermont and her sister regiments did not move at this time, however. Why the 2nd Vermont Brigade did not move on or about April 13 is not known. The roads were in poor condition, but another reason may have been that Gen. Silas Casey was relieved from his command on April 15.[13] Why he was relieved was not published, but George Hagar and others thought Casey was relieved to work on training programs for the numerous black regiments the Union was fielding. This turned out to be the case, and Casey also became the president of the board that examined all the officer candidates for these new black regiments.

Brig. Gen. John J. Abercrombie assumed command of Benedict's division on April 15.[14] He was an 1822 graduate of West Point and a veteran of the Black Hawk, Seminole, and Mexican Wars, in which he was wounded and breveted for bravery. In the Civil War, Abercrombie saw action in the Shenandoah Valley with Gen. Nathaniel Banks in the spring of 1862. He also commanded troops in the Peninsula campaign and was wounded at the battle of Fair Oaks. Since October 1862, Abercrombie had commanded a division with the XXII Corps, the one north of Casey's. In this service, Abercrombie proved himself an effective and experienced officer who commanded a division well.

The 2nd Vermont Brigade also got a new brigade commander at this time. It was not Colonel Blunt, but George J. Stannard, whose name was advanced by Casey and Governor Holbrook to the Senate to become a brigadier general. Stannard assumed command of the 2nd Vermont Brigade

Brig. Gen. George J. Stannard.
BRADY COLLECTION, NATIONAL ARCHIVES.

on April 21, after the Senate confirmed his nomination. He was a forty-two-year-old self-made businessman from St. Albans, Vermont, who before the war was a partner in a local foundry. Stannard had joined the Vermont militia in the 1850s and was considered by some the Vermonter to volunteer for service in Lincoln's call for seventy-five thousand troops. But political considerations sidelined him from service in the 1st Vermont Infantry, though not the war. In a few months' time, Stannard became the executive officer of the 2nd Vermont Infantry Regiment. He served with the 2nd Vermont for a little more than a year before being called by Holbrook to raise and command the 9th Vermont Infantry in July 1862. This regiment was mustered in and sent to Washington in August 1862, then to the Harpers Ferry Garrison just before it surrendered to General Jackson's forces in the Antietam campaign. Stannard and his new command became prisoners of the Confederate government for a few days before being paroled. Stannard and the 9th Vermont were then sent to Fort Douglas, Illinois, to guard Confederate prisoners of war and wait for their exchange, which occurred in March 1863. Holbrook's selection of Stannard was excellent, as he knew most of the brigade's senior staff and commanders from their service in the 1st Vermont Brigade and was well known and respected by them.

Stannard's arrival at the 2nd Vermont Brigade on April 21 was one more sign that army operations were about to begin. Another sign was Paymaster Halsey also visiting the 12th Vermont that same day. The men of the 12th Vermont were very happy to receive four months' pay. The weather was growing warmer and the mud had dried, and General Hooker's plans to defeat General Lee in a few weeks were almost ready. In a few days, the Army of the Potomac would march into the Virginia Wilderness to fight the Army of Northern Virginia. This event would indirectly affect the 12th Vermont and the other regiments of the 2nd Vermont Brigade.

CHAPTER 6

Camp at Union Mills

When Gen. Joseph Hooker was assigned to command the Army of the Potomac, the army's morale was at rock bottom. Making his job harder, he did not have Lincoln's confidence, and the Union high command let it be known that they had considered Hooker the least undesirable general available to command the army. However, Hooker slowly gained the confidence of both the soldiers and officers in the army and in the Union high command.

Hooker boosted the army's overall morale when he reorganized the Commissary Department and weeded out incompetent or dishonest officers. The quality and quantity of the soldiers' rations were improved, reducing disease caused by poor diet and lifting the soldiers' spirits. Hooker then took on the army's desertion problem by offering an amnesty to deserters, granting more furloughs for soldiers to visit home while the army was in winter quarters, and executing several deserters who had been caught. The general's most lasting change was the authorization of corps patches, which changed the army from a blue mass to one with identifiable brigades, divisions, and corps. Now men and officers had a greater sense of belonging to these larger units. This increased both morale and army effectiveness, as divisional and corps staffs and commanders now had some idea of whose troops were around them in the field, thus reducing confusion among commands.

Hooker reorganized the Army of the Potomac by abolishing Burnside's grand divisions, cutting a layer of army bureaucracy and the confusion it created. The most important of Hooker's organizational changes was his consolidation of the Union cavalry into its own corps, rather than being spread among the infantry brigades and divisions. This allowed the cavalry to capitalize on their assets of speed and firepower. Now, led by a number of up-and-coming officers who had the ability and experience to command regiments, brigades, and divisions of cavalry, the Union cavalry was on a tactical parity with its Confederate counterpart. With the army reorganized, morale restored, and the weather improved in the spring of 1863, Hooker was ready to fight the Confederate army.

Hooker's plan for his spring campaign was simple. Using the I, III, and VI Corps as a holding force near Fredericksburg, he took the II, V, and XI Corps and maneuvered through the Wilderness to catch General Lee's army unaware and out of position to defend itself against this attack. The plan was that when Lee and his army moved to counter these maneuvering elements, the holding corps would advance and attack a much weakened defensive line near Fredericksburg, thus putting more pressure on the Army of Northern Virginia and crushing it between two pincers. At the same time, the cavalry corps would raid the Confederate army's rear area to disrupt its communication and supply lines, further diminishing Lee's ability to react to Hooker's main attack.

While Hooker's plan seemed perfect on paper, Lee graphically demonstrated Napoleon's maxim that "in a plan, everything is in its execution," at a little-known town in the Wilderness called Chancellorsville. As Hooker's units moved to their assembly points during the last few weeks of April, rumors began in the camps of the 2nd Vermont Brigade that something was going on. Sergeant Major Hagar wrote his family on April 22 that the Army of the Potomac had moved to Warrenton, some twenty-four miles from Wolf Run Shoals, with 140,000 troops.[1] The improved weather in the spring always brought rumors of something about to happen. This time, from the vast movement of troops and their supplies, it was clear that something big was going on. From the officers on down to the men in the ranks, all wondered how it would affect them. The experience of these Vermont troops was that every time the Army of the Potomac moved south, they too moved south to protect the army's communication and supply lines. But this time these Union troops were closer to that action than they realized.

Union Mills, Va.
May 4, 1863

Dear Free Press:

On Friday morning last, the 12th broke camp and moved towards the front. The orders of the General Commanding the

2nd Vermont Infantry Brigade's Headquarters at Union Mills, Virginia, May 1863. Houghton Collection, University of Vermont.

Division, called for a regiment to go out to Warrenton Junction, for the protection of the Railroad, which has lately been re-opened to the Rappahannock, and is likely soon to be an important channel of supplies for the army; and the 12th was selected for the duty. The regiment, officers and men were glad enough to leave Wolf Run Shoals, and to go where there was a prospect of more active service, and took up the line of march in high spirits. The sick men were, of course, left behind; in the camp hospital, and will be removed as soon as practicable to the hospitals in Alexandria. The regiment reached Union Mills at about eleven o'clock, and shortly after took cars for Warrenton Junction. The main portion of it now lies in camp about 3 miles beyond Warrenton Junction, two companies being stationed at Catlett's Station, this side.

I am on detached service at present, and did not accompany the regiment on the march; but was glad to improve the opportunity to visit them yesterday. Taking a seat on the engine of a supply train, in company with Col. Blunt and several officers of the brigade, we whirled away. We soon reached the historic ground of

Manassas Junction, its plains seamed with rifle-pits, and its low hills crowned with earthworks, almost by the score. Thence to Catlett's our iron horse picked his way more carefully over rails which were torn up and bent on fires of the ties by the rebels last summer, and have since been straightened after a fashion and relaid, and along a track which is strewed on each side for miles with car trucks by the hundred and other burnt and blackened remains of the trains destroyed by Gen. Banks, and by the rebels in the famous raid on Gen. Pope's headquarters before the last Bull Run battles. The surrounding country from Bristoe's on to Warrenton Junction and beyond, is a fine, high, open and comparatively level region, in strong contrast with the barren hills along the Occoquan. The scattered planters' houses showing evidences of more prosperity, and the fields under cultivation to a greater extent than in any portion of Virginia where we have hitherto been stationed.

Near Bristoe's we were stopped by a frightened telegraph operator, on horseback, who said he had just escaped from Warrenton Junction, which place he reported in the hands of the rebel cavalry—who according to his account had come in and captured the whole of Union cavalry there. We heard his story and pushed on to Catlett's where we learned a different one, and hastening on to Warrenton Junction we soon had the evidence of our own eyes upon the true state of the case. A force of cavalry in the blue uniforms of Uncle Sam's boys held the Junction, and the bodies of a dozen dead horses strewed around the solitary house at the station told of a sharp skirmish on that spot. Springing from the train, I had taken hardly twenty steps before I came upon the body of a dead rebel—stretched stark and cold, face upward, in coat of rusty brown and pantaloons of butternut. They showed me papers taken from his pockets, showing him to be one Templeman, a well known scout and spy of the noted Mosby's command. Passing on to the house I found lying around it seventeen wounded "butternuts," of all ages, from boys of sixteen to shaggy and grizzled men of fifty years. They lay in their blood, with wounds as yet undressed, for the skirmish ended but a little while before we arrived, some with gaping sabre cuts, some with terrible bullet wounds, through the face, body or limbs. It was a rough sight. Four or five rebel prisoners, unhurt, stood by, with downcast faces, but willing to answer readily all civil questions. Close by, covered decently with a blanket, lay the body of a Union cavalry man, shot in cold blood, after he had surrendered and given up his arms, by a young long haired rebel, who had received his reward for the dastardly act, and lay near his victim, with a severe bullet wound in his stomach. The floor of the house was strewed with wounded Union cavalry men, among them Maj. Steele of the 1st Virginia, mortally wounded, and two of Mosby's officers. Their wounds had just been dressed, and the surgeons began to give attention to the wounded rebels outside.

From men engaged on both sides, I soon learned that Mosby, who has recently been made a Major for his activity in the rebel service, with 125 men, made a dash upon the outpost of the 1st Virginia Union Cavalry, at the Junction, about nine o'clock that morning. The men of the 1st Virginia were taken by surprise, dismounted and with their horses unsaddled, and after a short fight surrendered. They account for their surprise by averring that the front rank of the rebels were clothed in U.S. uniform, and they supposed them to be a friendly force. Mosby was, however, a little too fast for once. He was not aware of the presence of a portion of the 5th N.Y. Cavalry, in camp in a piece of wood near by, a squadron or two of which made their appearance on the scene, while the rebels were securing their prisoners, and charged in on them at once, hot foot. A running fight followed in which the prisoners were all retaken, and twenty-three of their captors killed, wounded and made prisoners. Mosby was chased for ten miles, his force for the most part scattered, himself, as it is reported, wounded in the shoulder, and a number of his men wounded who made out to get into the woods and escaped capture. The 1st Virginia lost their Major, mortally wounded, 1 man killed and nine men wounded, and the 5th N.Y. a Captain and two Lieuts. wounded not very badly. The result of the operation was, you see, altogether in our favor. Three men of the 12th Vt. were taken near the camp, by Mosby's men, but escaped in the skirmish, one of them bringing in a rebel horse with him. The pickets of the 12th took a straggler from Mosby's force. A party of the 1st Vt. Cavalry, which is in camp just beyond the 12th, joined in the pursuit of the rebels, but was not in at skirmish.

Going on to the camp of the 12th Vt. I found the regiment encamped on a pleasant piece of level ground, the men making themselves as comfortable as possible under their little shelter tents; all considerably stirred up by the events of the morning, which took place so nearly under their noses, and feeling as if they were pretty well out into the enemy's country. The regiment is in a rather exposed position; but such risks are part of the soldier's allotted portion. If attacked I know that the 12th will not disgrace the state.

The health of the regiment is improving, and will be still better now that they are on the move. Co. C, has, as you know, lost another man, in the death of private Stoughton. He was apparently one of our hardiest men, often enduring exposures which many men would sink under, and besides doing his own full share of duty, often did that of other men, being always ready to take the place of an ailing comrade. He ran right down, when taken with Pneumonia, gave up all hope, from the start, and gave his life to his country without a murmur.

We are waiting with intense anxiety for news from Gen. Hooker's Army.

Yours, G.

P.S. There are but eight men left in hospital at the Shoals as too sick to be moved.

The season here is from all accounts little or no earlier than in Vermont. The fields are just beginning to look pretty well covered with green but the leaves of the forest trees are not yet started.

The Brigade has orders to be ready to march at an hour's notice. We look for lively work here if disaster overtakes Hooker.

G.

Although the news of Mosby's setback was good, Benedict soon learned that the news about the Army of the Potomac was not. The men learned of Hooker's defeat first by rumor, and later by newspaper. Hooker's plan had worked well until, for some reason, he stopped his army in the Wilderness near Chancellorsville to wait for Lee. This was a fatal mistake, as giving up the battlefield initiative to Lee proved costly. Before crossing the Rappahannock River, the Army of the Potomac had outnumbered the

Army of Northern Virginia almost two to one and achieved the element of tactical surprise against it. In the Wilderness, however, the Union army was road-bound until it cleared the woods, and it could not deploy its troops and artillery to make its numbers felt against the Confederates. Failure to clear this poor ground laid the foundation of Hooker's defeat. Lee seized the initiative, using a small part of his army to slow the Union troops advancing from Fredericksburg and another to hold Hooker's advancing column in the Wilderness near Chancellorsville. Then Lee ordered General Jackson to take his corps and attack the Union's right flank. Jackson attacked at dusk on May 2 and drove in the Union's right flank, causing a panic that turned the battle against Hooker and ended the threat against Lee's army.

Hooker's loss had two positive results for the Union. The first was that during his flank attack, Jackson was severely wounded, losing his left arm, which knocked him out of the battle. On May 10, he died of pneumonia. This cost the Confederacy an irreplaceable general and created serious implications in the months to come. The other result was that Hooker saved his army to fight another day by pulling it across the Rappahannock before Lee could defeat either part of it in detail. Both sides ended up where they had started only a few weeks before, with 16,845 casualties for the Army of the Potomac and 12,764 for the Army of Northern Virginia.[2] The 2nd Vermont Brigade did not learn about the details of the battle of Chancellorsville for several weeks, but their minor role in Mosby's May 4 attack showed why they were in the area.

On the same day that Jackson died, three runaway slaves entered the camp of the 12th Vermont with their master in hot pursuit. That man was John Minor Botts, a sixty-one-year-old politician from Richmond. Botts had spent the last thirty years of his life in the state legislature and the House of Representatives and was well known in Virginia politics. Unlike most Virginia politicians, however, Botts was against secession and did not remain silent when Virginia left the Union, saying that states did not have that right.[3] When Confederate president Jefferson Davis suspended the "Writ of Habeas Corpus" (the Constitutional protection from being jailed without charge) in the spring of 1862, Botts was arrested and jailed without charge for six weeks in Richmond. After his release, he moved to an estate named Auburn, near Brandy Station, Virginia, in January 1863.[4] Four months later and five miles from this estate, he and his three slaves stood in front of Colonel Blunt, who would decide the slaves' fate.

Botts demanded his "property" back, being "a good Union man," and told Blunt that the Emancipation Proclamation only affected slaves who were outside of Union control, unlike his three slaves now. For the men of the 12th Vermont, the situation was all the more interesting in that the leader of these escaped slaves was Botts's son, born to a slave mother and named after his father. Farnham described him as being whiter than Farnham was, with blue eyes and brown hair, and probably could have escaped again if he was returned to his father's estate.[5] Blunt pondered Botts's request and said he believed that the Emancipation Proclamation affected states that were loyal to the Union. Since most of Virginia was not, and Botts and his "property" were in the Confederate-controlled part of the state, his slaves were free in the eyes of the Union government. Blunt did allow Botts a chance to talk his slaves into freely returning, but they would not. Botts, in frustration, then requested to have the colonel's decision overturned by a higher authority, and this was sent through the chain of command by telegram.[6] No response to Botts's request has been found, although these escaped men stayed with the 2nd Vermont Brigade for the rest of its service and returned to Vermont with the troops. Therefore, the answer must have been to allow these men to go free. Botts remained at his estate, and when the area reverted to Confederate control, Stuart arrested, then released him on October 12, 1863. After this encounter with Confederate authorities, neither side bothered him or his estate again.

As May continued, the 2nd Vermont Brigade provided the manpower to protect work crews and bridges on the Orange and Alexandria Railroad, from Rappahannock Bridge to Bristoe Station. Each regiment had to watch for the enemy in the front and rear and was spread over miles, which concerned General Stannard, who felt that each regiment was overextended and vulnerable. On May 19, the 12th Vermont came in contact with the Confederate army for the first time since December 29. This meeting differed from the previous one in that these soldiers were not raiders or cavalry, but Confederate infantry from the Army of Northern Virginia. While Confederate pickets took position on the other side of the river, the only action taken by either side was to talk with each other. Both sides agreed not to fire on one another, and the Confederates tried to trade their whiskey for Yankee coffee. Blunt permitted the truce, provided the Confederates did not cross their side of the bridge, but not the whiskey trade. The two sides shouted questions at each other. The Confederates identified themselves as the 14th Georgia Regiment, a part of Thomas's brigade, Pender's division,

Railroad Station at Union Mills, March 1863. Houghton Collection, University of Vermont.

in A. P. Hill's corps after a reorganization of the Army of Northern Virginia a few weeks later. The pickets from the 12th Vermont identified themselves as members of the 112th Vermont Regiment.[7]

When Company C took its turn to picket the Union end of the Rappahannock bridge, one of the soldiers who came in contact with the Confederates was Pvt. Richard Irwin. Of the encounter with the Confederates, he said, "I can say that I have seen the grey back Reb in his untamed glory roaming in perfect freedom on the southern bank of the Rappahannock River."[8] Irwin volunteered for picket duty that day, something he did not have to do, as he was still attached as a clerk in the Quartermaster Department of the 12th Vermont. He got his office job during the winter, which was more his style. As a quartermaster clerk, his work consisted of preparing paperwork to order and account for government supplies for the 12th Vermont from the depot at Fairfax Station, then move them to the regiment at Wolf Run Shoals. His life was easier and he received better rations and quarters than when he was with the company in the field. He did not have to drill and usually did not have to do picket or guard duty.

The truce between the 12th Vermont and the 14th Georgia did not extend to Mosby and his command. Although Mosby had suffered a defeat a few weeks earlier, it had not slowed him down, and he captured a wagon train from the 13th Vermont just outside its camp at Widow Violet's on May 17. These guerrillas also took five prisoners from the 13th Vermont, who were soon paroled and rode off with the five mule teams and supply wagons.[9] Two weeks later, Mosby and his command of about a hundred guerrillas took out an iron horse. On May 30, they ambushed the first train headed to Catlett's Station that morning. The train was loaded with fodder, other dry goods, and passengers, including twenty-five train guards from the 15th Vermont, under the command of Lt. Elden Hartshorn of Company E.[10] As the train headed southwest down the tracks between Bristoe and Catlett's Stations, Mosby and his command, whose weapons included a six-pound mountain howitzer, began the ambush by pulling a rail from the track bed, derailing the moving train. Mosby's cannon fired as the train came off the tracks, putting a hole in the engine's smokestack. This scared the train's passengers and crew and told them the derailment was no accident. As the Confederates reloaded the howitzer, the passengers and crew jumped off the train and headed for the nearby woods and safety. The howitzer fired solid shot again, which this time went through the engine's boiler, destroying it.

After they had secured the area, Mosby's men broke open the locks of the ten cars, taking what they could carry and then burning the rest. Seeing the rising smoke of the burning train, the Union army dispatched a cavalry patrol, which chased Mosby's command and captured his cannon. Among the train's passengers was Chaplain Brastow, whose October 1862 brush with Confederate cavalry in Maryland had been recounted by Benedict in his October 14 letter. Brastow had now seen more action than any other member of the 12th Vermont, except Colonel Blunt. Fortunately, neither he nor anyone else on the train was harmed in the attack. The train's crew and passengers walked through the woods to the nearest Union outpost.

The Union cavalry arrested Hartshorn and his men as stragglers. He was placed under arrest and court-martialed for not defending the train against Mosby and his troops. Lieutenant Colonel Farnham presided over this board composed of Capt. George Woodward of the 15th Vermont; Capt. Asa Foster, now the brigade's assistant adjutant general; and 1st Lt. William Loomis of Company I, 12th Vermont. After the board of officers heard evidence on Hartshorn's actions from June 5 to 11, they determined that Hartshorn and his command had faced an untenable position against an enemy that outnumbered and outgunned them and had the element of surprise, and they cleared him of the charges against him. Running had probably been the wisest decision as it spared his command to fight another day.

As spring turned into early summer, men of the 12th Vermont and her sister regiments were still dying from disease, including two soldiers of Company C in May and June. Benedict records only the death of Guy Stoughton, an eighteen-year-old mason from Burlington, on May 3 of pneumonia. Perhaps in the rush of events in June, Benedict did not get a chance to write of the death of Pvt. Isaac J. Sorrell, a twenty-eight-year-old farmer from Shelburne, on June 20. The 12th Vermont's term now had only a few weeks left before it expired on July 4, and the tempo of army operations was increasing.

Union Mills, Va.
June 15, 1863

Dear Free Press:

The recent movements of Gen. Lee's Army up the Rappahannock, and of Gen. Hooker's forces to meet the enemy thus threatening his right, seem to bid fair to bring the theatre of active conflict close to us. It has been approaching us sensibly of late. The battle of last Tuesday was hottest at and near Rappahannock Bridge and Beverly's Ford, where the 12th Vt. was stationed but a few days ago. Since then the outposts of Gen. Hooker's army and of this Brigade, have been in daily contact for a week. This morning we see the dust and hear the distant roll of drums of two army corps, falling back to this line. The impression is pretty general that the next big fight may take place in this vicinity, perhaps rendering again and *thrice* memorable the historic ground of the two great Bull Run battles.

I had the pleasure of visiting that battleground on Saturday last. The troops of our Brigade have long guarded Blackburn's Ford, where Gen. Richardson opened the first battle of Bull Run, and have picketed upon the outskirts of the first battleground; but the actual battlefield has always been outside of our lines, and is traversed so frequently by rebel scouting parties, that it has not been safe to visit it at all times, or at any time except with a party of size and strength enough to take care of any small squad of "bush-whackers," or Mosby's cavalry.

A very fair party collected for our excursion. We had Col. Blunt, Lieut. Col. Farnham, Major Kingsley, Captains Ormsbee and Paul, Adjutant Vaughan, Lieut. Cloyes, Drum-Major Downer, and Hospital Steward Hard, of the 12th; Col. Randall and Surgeon Nichols of the 13th; Adjutant Peabody, Quartermaster Henry, and several other officers of the 16th, whose names I do not now recall; Dr. Ketchum, Medical Director, Quartermaster Brownson, Lieut. Prentiss, Lieut. Thompson and your humble servant, of Gen. Stannard's Staff, with orderlies and attendants enough to make a cavalcade of twenty-five, armed of course, and well mounted. It was a party, whose capture would make something of a hole in the 2nd Vt. Brigade; but we saw no armed enemy and were seen of none so far as we were aware.

At ten o'clock we started from Union Mills, crossed Bull Run at McLean's Ford, and struck off into a second growth of low pines towards the battlefield. It was some five or six miles thence in a direct line; but, not familiar with all the windings of the interminable bridle paths, which there as elsewhere in Virginia intersect every piece of forest and traverse every valley and field with a complete network, we made a longer distance of it. Still we could not well lose the main direction. For a while we kept near the bank of the Run, edged with trench and breastwork for mile after mile continuously on the southern side. These were Beauregard's works, and are well constructed as the rebel works generally are in this region. Leaving these on the right we bore off to the West and came out in time to a more open and cultivated, or cultivatable country. Col. Randall and Adjutant Peabody were members of the old Vt. 2nd, and at once recognized the neighborhood of their first battle. Down thro' a hollow we dashed, then over a ridge, and soon were gathered on the spot where Rickett's battery was taken, and the victorious advance of our army changed to panic and disgraceful flight. The ruins of the house around which the battle raged fiercely and in which a woman was killed, were near us. The rose bushes still grow in the rank grass which covers what was once the dooryard or flower garden, and blossom as freely as if the storm of battle had never swept over them. A grave, protected and almost hidden by some rails thrown around it, close by the ruined chimney stack, we conjectured to be possibly the resting place of the hapless occupant, whose fate gave her a place in the history of the first great battle of the great War for the Union. The grave of Lieut. Ramsay, and the spot where Col. Bartow, of Georgia fell (once marked by a small marble monument, which for some reason was removed to Manassas Junction by the rebels last summer) are also right there. Plucking some roses to be pressed and sent home as mementoes of the battleground, we passed on and over the field. Guided by Col. Randall we saw where the fighting opened on the right and centre; where the old Vt 2nd, then a regiment of a month old, first went into action; where its line of battle was formed; where it advanced to the support of Rickett's battery; where, upon the attack of Johnston's fresh forces, upon our right, it was ordered to fall back; and where its dead were collected and buried. Many of the dead, who fell in both the first and the last battles of Bull Run, were not buried, but simply covered with earth as they lay, and the skulls and bones frequently protruding from the little mounds show how ineffectual was the process; but the Vermonters, it seems, were decently interred in a row. There are no headboards to mark the graves, and the grass grows thick and green over them. We passed by Dogan's house, still standing, though unoccupied, over to the field of the last battle; we saw of course, "the stone house," windowless and deserted, and marked by cannon shot; and we took our homeward way, by the Turnpike, fording Bull Run at the famous stone bridge, now a bridge no longer.

The battleground is a wide and spacious clearing—not a level field, but a rolling one of hollow and rounded ridges. I saw on it not a trace of rifle-pit or earthwork of any description, and the fighting must have been in the main open stand-up work. The ground is almost covered in one or two spots with skeletons of horses. Its surface is ridged with graves, and strewed (tho' not very thickly) with cartridge-boxes, remnants of uniforms and knapsacks, and here and there a rusty bayonet or unexploded shell. I saw but two or three round shot—six pound balls. Many of the marks of the conflict are doubtless hidden by the grass, which grows probably thicker than before on soil enriched by the blood and bones of fallen patriots and rebels. It is now entirely uncultivated and deserted; but several of the farms around and near it are in a pretty good state of cultivation for Virginia, and in time (perhaps before the close of the war, if not again made the scene of conflict) the plough-share will be driven over its slopes, through grave and cannon rut, and the traces of the great battles will become obliterated.

We reached camp safely after a ride, taken all together, of from 20 to 25 miles, without casualties, save the using up of one or two horses, all of which, however, save one, made out to come in with their riders. The beautiful and spirited black, which I rode for the day, carried me like a bird, hardly turning a hair while other horses were dripping with sweat and foam, and was apparently just as good for 35 miles more at the close of our ride, as at the beginning.

The weather is dry to actual drought. It is over a month, I think, since we have had more than a passing shower, and the grass and crops, such as they are, are suffering. The days are generally clear and hot and the nights uniformly cool. It is good weather for the health of our troops, and this brigade is generally in a fine state of health.

The regiments have been taking turns of late, at the outpost and guard duty out at Bristoe's and Catlett's. The 12th was drawn back to Union Mills a fortnight since, and remains here. The 16th succeeded it out on the Railroad, and was succeeded in turn by the 15th. You understand of course, that if I have heretofore mainly written of the 12th, it is because the mass of your readers are mainly interested in it, and because it is my own regiment, and not because the others are not as well worth notice. All are good regiments. The 13th, Col. Randall, I have not seen in line lately; but I hear that it is in a fine state of efficiency and drill. The 14th, Col. Nichols, I saw on review recently, and was agreeably surprised by the precision with which they marched, and the general good appearance of the men. The 15th and 16th, Cols. Proctor and Veazey, were reviewed here a while since, by Gen. Abercrombie, who had, apparently, heard but little about the Vermont troops during the short time he had been in command of the Division, and who did not attempt to conceal his surprise and gratification at their fine condition as to discipline and efficiency and superior appearance. The following order, issued upon the occasion, is official testimony to this:

HEADQUARTERS, 2D BRIGADE
ABERCROMBIE'S DIVISION
UNION MILLS, VA May 26th, 1863.
SPECIAL ORDER NO. 19.
  The General Commanding desires to express to the regiments inspected today his congratulations on their soldierlike appearance, and to convey to them the approbation of the Division General.
  Gen. Abercrombie speaks in high terms of the Review and Inspection, especially of the manner in which both regiments passed through the manual of arms, and noticed with pleasure the attention that has been paid to drill and discipline by both officers and men.
                By order of Brig. Gen. G. J. STANNARD,
                WM. H. Hill, A. A. G.

It is but simple justice to say, as I do, without any disparagement to the 15th, that the 16th is entitled to the larger share of this high praise. It is a "splendid" regiment, and splendidly drilled, especially in the manual of arms. Good judges say the Regulars do not do it any better, on an average.

It will not be a very satisfactory sight, in some aspects of it, to see these fine regiments, each over 800 strong today; going home at this critical period of the war. But then half of the men, at least, and perhaps more, will re-enlist before the summer is over.

Yours, G.

While Benedict and the others in his brigade considered the end of their Federal service, signs of a large military operation were becoming apparent. Rumors that Lee's army was heading north increased, and clashes between cavalry grew more common. On June 8 and 9, it was not, as Benedict wrote, two infantry corps that were locked in combat, but two corps of cavalry, one Confederate and one Union. Brandy Station saw the largest cavalry battle of the Civil War. On the morning of the eighth, Union cavalry surprised General Stuart and his command for the first time, after his corps had a review the day before. Stuart fought the Union to a draw the next day, yet this battle marked the turning point for the Union cavalry, who had demonstrated that they now could hold their own against Confederate cavalry. From this point on, the Confederate cavalry's ability to

battle its Union counterpart declined, as the increase in Union cavalry leaders, skill, remounts, and forage surpassed the Confederates' ability to replace
the same.

June 8 was also a memorable day for the 12th Vermont, despite the
sounds of heavy combat about ten miles from their camp: the paymaster
paid the men for two months of service. Benedict received $102, Sergeant
Major Hagar received $58, and Private Irwin received $40. The men were
happy to receive their pay, yet most wondered when and where the next
payday would be. Most thought of home and civilian life as their term of
service drew to a close. But the regiment's leadership and the routine of
camp life kept the men busy from sunup to sundown.

On June 13, a group from the 2nd Vermont Brigade visited the Bull
Run battlefield, where the 2nd Vermont Infantry Regiment had fought on
July 21, 1861. This was not only sight-seeing, but it was also training for
the officers, as they saw the ground where untried troops had been sent into
combat, and discussed the lessons learned in this action. The 2nd Vermont
Infantry was Vermont's first three-year regiment, and it served in the Army
of the Potomac from Bull Run to Appomattox. This regiment was raised in
May 1861, mustered into Federal service on June 20, then sent to Washington, D.C., where it was brigaded with the 3rd, 4th, and 5th Maine
Infantry Regiments under the command of Col. O. O. Howard. Howard's
brigade was assigned to Brig. Gen. Samuel Heintzelman's division before
the Union army marched into northern Virginia in July 1861. At about
3:00 P.M. on the afternoon of July 21, after a long day's fighting, Howard's
brigade tried to attack Confederate troops on Chinn Ridge but were
pushed back. The Confederate troops counterattacked soon after and
caused the Union troops to rout, thus winning the day and the field. The
2nd Vermont Infantry's losses were two men killed, thirty-four wounded,
and thirty captured.[11] Of the men who were captured, three died of their
wounds in Richmond.

In this visit to the battlefield, the officers of the 2nd Vermont Brigade
benefited from Col. Francis Randall's experience and knowledge of the battle. Randall had commanded Company F of the 2nd Vermont Infantry,
which suffered one man killed and four wounded, one of whom was captured by the Confederates. Adj. Harland Peabody shared his experiences
about the events of July 21, 1861, from his perspective as a corporal in
Company I of the 2nd Vermont Infantry Regiment. Peabody was promoted to sergeant on November 1, 1861, and was discharged for disability

on May 1, 1862. He recovered his health during the summer of 1862 and enlisted in the 16th Vermont that fall. Another officer who was not with this group yet could have told these visiting officers more about the battle was General Stannard, who was the 2nd Vermont Infantry's executive officer at that time. The two men of the 2nd Vermont Infantry who were killed received a decent burial. Often when the losing army left the battlefield, their dead were simply thrown into a mass grave or covered with dirt where they fell. It is likely that some of the captured Vermonters buried their fallen comrades before being marched to Richmond.

What Benedict did not know that day was that Lee's army was on the march north. On the day that he and the other officers went to Bull Run, Richard Ewell's corps, the vanguard of the Army of Northern Virginia, overran Maj. Gen. Robert Milroy's troops at Winchester, Virginia. This action cleared the Shenandoah Valley for Lee's army, as Maj. Gen. James Longstreet's corps started to disengage from the Army of the Potomac. The overrunning of Milroy was the first sign of trouble for Washington and General Hooker. On June 15, Robert Rodes's division of Ewell's corps crossed the Potomac into Maryland, beginning another invasion of the North in less than a year.

Hooker's reaction to Lee's movements was to march after him to protect Washington, D.C., and Baltimore. For the march, Hooker organized the Army of the Potomac into two wings: one composed of the I, III, and IX Corps, under the nominal command of Maj. Gen. John Reynolds and concentrating near Manassas Junction; the other, composed of the II, V, VI, and XII Corps, under the nominal command of Maj. Gen. Winfield Scott Hancock and concentrating at Fairfax Station. All of this movement was noticed by the men of the 2nd Vermont Brigade, especially those on the picket line, who saw the large dust clouds from the columns of marching men. At night, thousands of campfires lit the area, giving the sky an unnatural glow.[12] Thousands of troops crossed the fords near Bull Run and the Occoquan, as the men of the 2nd Vermont Brigade watched them moving north. At Wolf Run Shoals, the men also saw Hooker and his staff on June 14.[13]

By June 15, the Army of the Potomac, except for the VI Corps and John Buford's cavalry division, had crossed the Occoquan River on their way north. On this day, Gen. Alfred Pleasanton, commander of the Army of the Potomac's cavalry corps, made his headquarters at Union Mills near the 2nd Vermont Brigade's headquarters. That night, Pleasanton and his staff had dinner with Stannard and his staff.[14] The conversation during this dinner more than likely revolved around what Lee was doing and where he was going. The next day, the Army of the Potomac's rear guard, the VI Corps, crossed Wolf Run Shoals on its way to Fairfax Station. That night, many of the men of the 1st Vermont Brigade had a chance to meet and talk with their friends and family members in the 2nd Vermont Brigade. The following day, the VI Corps continued its march north. The movement of the VI Corps meant that the 2nd Vermont Brigade was now by itself, except for Buford's division of Union cavalry, which had orders to move out soon. For the men of the 2nd Vermont Brigade, the brigade's next mission was still a mystery as their time remaining in the army grew shorter.

CHAPTER 7

On the Field of Gettysburg

By June 16, General Hooker and the Army of the Potomac were north of the Occoquan River and east of Bull Run. At this point, the army stopped between the Little River Turnpike and the Leesburg and Alexandria Turnpike for almost a week, until Hooker found out Lee's intentions. Hooker's mission at that moment was to protect Washington, D.C., and he did not want to cross the Potomac River and head north until he had reliable information that Lee and his army had done the same. In those few days, the Army of the Potomac resupplied itself and got ready to move again. At the same time, Hooker and his staff planned for the upcoming campaign. One thing he had to consider was that the Army of the Potomac had significantly fewer men in the ranks than when he had started active operations a month before. With the Army of the Potomac's losses at Chancellorsville and the expiration of Union enlistments that summer, Hooker had about 23,000 fewer men. In response to this problem, Washington provided men by cutting its garrison strength. The forts that surrounded Washington remained manned, but two infantry brigades and one cavalry brigade assigned to the outer defensive perimeter were transferred to Hooker's army.

In the last two weeks of June, the men of the 12th Vermont wondered whether they would stay with the defenses of Washington or be transferred to the Army of the Potomac. Sgt. Maj. George Hagar wrote on June 24: "As our time will be out before the ten days, I hardly think we shall go. We hope for orders from the War Department to start in another direction before the 'moment's notice' comes."[1] Later that day, brigade headquarters received a telegram from divisional headquarters ordering the 2nd Vermont Brigade to be ready to march the next day at a moment's notice. They had

183

been reassigned to the I Corps of the Army of the Potomac and soon would be marching north to join them.

At 7:00 A.M. on June 25, 1863, the 12th Vermont got into column formation at its camp at Wolf Run Shoals. Then Colonel Blunt ordered, "Forward, Route step—March!" and the 12th Vermont left Wolf Run Shoals for the last time. Under a cloudy sky, the 12th Vermont, followed by the 14th Vermont, took two hours to reach the brigade's assembly area at Union Mills, where they joined the 15th and 16th Vermont Regiments. On June 21, the 12th Vermont had marched from Union Mills to Wolf Run Shoals, and now the men were marching back. The last regiment to reach the assembly point was the 13th Vermont, which arrived at 2:00 P.M., having marched almost twenty miles from Camp Widow Violet. The 13th Vermont and the other regiments were given an hour's rest. During that time, brigade and regimental staffs finalized their plans and coordination for the march. Also during this time, company commanders performed final checks of their soldiers' weapons and equipment. The brigade moved out of Union Mills for the last time at 3:00 P.M.. With the exception of the army's cavalry screen, the 2nd Vermont Brigade formed the rear of the Army of the Potomac. The Bull Run–Occoquan picket line was abandoned, and Union control for the next few months extended only to the fortifications of Washington.

It began to rain about 4:00 P.M., as the brigade marched to Centreville. After dark, the brigade camped about two miles north of Centreville, and the men tried to sleep as the rain poured down on them. The men had only their shelter tents, so most buddied up and placed one rubber blanket on the ground to act as a ground cloth, using the woolen blankets for mattresses or pillows and the other rubber blanket for a cover sheet. Thus two men slept as dry as they could in the field.

The next morning, the brigade began its march at 9:00 A.M. after the VI Corps passed, clearing the road. Once on the march, the 2nd Vermont Brigade experienced its first of several traffic jams as it caught up to the VI Corps, which congested the road ahead of them. The Vermont regiments left a trail of items the soldiers discarded to lighten their load. As the miles mounted, the men discarded more and more "nonessential" equipment and personal items, until a few days later, most had only their muskets, cartridge and cap boxes, bayonets, canteens, rubber and woolen blankets, haversacks, and a few personal items. The men went into camp at 8:00 P.M. that night

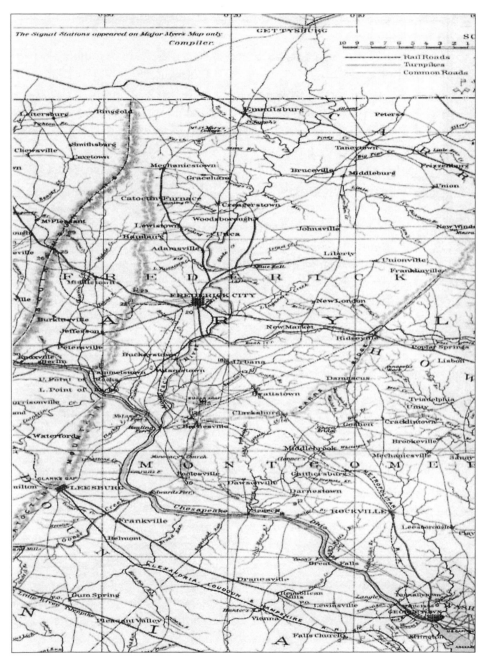

The Union roads to Gettysburg. WAR OF THE REBELLION: OFFICIAL RECORDS OF THE UNION AND CONFEDERATE ARMIES, MAP BOOK.

near Herndon Station on the Loudon and Hampshire Railroad after their first full day's march.

On June 27, the march started at 5:00 A.M. on the road to Guilford Station, where the brigade was to join the I Corps. They reached Guilford Station later that morning, but the I Corps had received new orders to march to Frederick, Maryland, and already had a two-day head start on them. The 12th Vermont and her sister regiments continued north, crossing the Potomac River into Maryland at Edward's Ferry around noon. Although most of the men did not consider it, as they were having enough trouble putting one sore foot in front of another, they had left Virginia with their regiments for the last time. Soon after they crossed the Potomac, the brigade found itself stuck in another traffic jam, which held them up for about three hours. The rest was good for the troops, but it did not cut the miles they had to march when the roads cleared. That night, the 2nd Vermont Brigade camped near the 1st Vermont Brigade a few miles from Poolesville, giving them another chance to visit with friends and relatives.

The 12th Vermont and her sister regiments broke camp and were again on the march at 8:00 A.M. on June 28. By this time, the march had a mind-numbing routine: The men arose sore for roll call in the morning and packed their gear. Then they ate whatever rations they still had or had bought along the way, and rested until first the companies, then the regiments formed up for that day's march. Then they waited for the brigade to form up in the order of march, which changed each day. One regimental commander after another ordered, "Forward, route step, march." Everyone was tired and dirty, and the men wondered where they would stop, as most of their shoes were worn out or close to it. When the march began for the day, the men talked in the ranks. Conversation gradually died out as the mileage and the men's weariness grew. For the most part, the roads were in bad shape. The wet weather and thousands of men's feet, horses' and cattle's hooves, and wagon wheels had turned them into muddy tracks. If they could, the men marched alongside the road, where it was drier and less slippery. At noon, the regiments stopped for lunch and rested for an hour. After another roll call, they were off for the afternoon march in the heat of the day, which added to their misery. At 5:00 P.M., the men stopped for supper and rested for another hour. Afterward they marched until close to sundown then found a campsite for the night. The next day, the process started all over again.

No one in the ranks knew where they were headed, just that it was somewhere north. Most noticed a change between Virginia and Maryland when they crossed the Potomac River. The land was not as careworn as in Virginia. That part of Maryland had not been garrisoned as Virginia had, and the natives seemed more friendly the farther north they marched. By midmorning on June 28, the 2nd Vermont Brigade crossed the Monocacy River, entering western Maryland before marching north to Frederick. They ended their day's march a few miles north of Adamstown.

One man who was not in the ranks of the 12th Vermont or with the 2nd Vermont Brigade staff since the march began was George Benedict. For the first four days of the march north, he was in Washington on detached service, probably coordinating the brigade's transportation home. On June 27, Benedict received a telegram from General Stannard to join him at Frederick the next day with any men from the brigade who were fit to return to active service from the local hospitals.[2] Frederick at that time was the Army of the Potomac's base of supply as it chased Lee's army north. It was also a crossroads as Gen. John Reynolds's wing of the Army of the Potomac marched due north and Gen. Winfield Hancock's wing marched northeast, thus easing the traffic on the main road north.

Benedict arrived at Frederick late on the afternoon of June 28 by military railroad. It was too late for him to find the brigade; without a horse, there was no way he could rejoin it as it grew dark. He managed to find a place to spend the night, though it was difficult, as rooms and beds were hard to come by in a city full of soldiers. The next morning, he had breakfast with Charles Coffin of the *Boston Journal* and Mr. Croanse of the *New York Times* to learn what they knew about the current situation.[3] Then he went to the Army of the Potomac's headquarters to see if anyone knew where Stannard's brigade was located or heading. After getting any other information that could be useful to the general, Benedict hired a horse from a farmer, who went along with Benedict to protect his horse, as, with two armies in the area, it might have been stolen or killed. They traveled through heavy rain and were relieved when they reached the 2nd Vermont Brigade later that morning, just south of Frederick. Benedict then released the horse to the farmer and marched with the brigade for Frederick, which they reached about noon on June 29.

The brigade spent the next three hours resupplying, waiting for the traffic to clear, and taking care of other administrative duties before continuing north. While doing these tasks, the men heard that Gen. George Meade had replaced General Hooker as commander of the Army of the Potomac. Most in the ranks did not know who Meade was, and Stannard and his staff went to the Army of the Potomac's headquarters to learn more and to find out where the I Corps was located. They found out that Lee's army was a day or two ahead of them and that the I Corps had marched due north to the Gettysburg area. As the men waited, the regimental surgeons looked over the men in the regimental ambulances to determine who would recover in the next day or two. The majority, about ninety men, were diagnosed as too ill to continue the march and were left at the hospital in Frederick.[4]

After a three-hour stopover, the brigade pushed on, ending that day's march south of Adamsville, Maryland. The brigade was up and moving by 5:00 A.M. on June 30. The day was very hot, muggy, and overcast. By the end of it, rain added to the misery of the men in the ranks, making it the hardest day of marching yet, as they moved through the Catoctin Mountains. That day's march ended about two miles south of Emmitsburg, Maryland, where they finally caught up to I Corps. That night, Benedict was sent to I Corps headquarters to report to General Reynolds and receive orders for the brigade. I Corps headquarters was located at Moritz Tavern, and it took some time for Benedict to find it.[5] He gave his report to Reynolds, who assigned Stannard's brigade to the corps's 3rd Division, under the command of Maj. Gen. Abner Doubleday, and ordered Stannard to join the corps at its encampment at Marsh Creek on the Emmitsburg Road about five miles south of Gettysburg that morning.

On July 1, the 2nd Vermont Brigade started its march at 9:00 A.M. It was thought that they had only two hours left to march before joining the I Corps's 3rd Division. However, the brigade had to march through two infantry corps—the III and XI—to the camp of the 3rd Division, which put them behind schedule. At about noon, the brigade arrived at the corps camp at Marsh Creek, which was empty except for the supply, ammunition, and baggage trains and their crews, and other personnel who had stayed behind. Stannard learned that the corps had marched at dawn after Gen. John Buford reported that his cavalry had engaged Confederate infantry in force just outside Gettysburg, and this had changed Reynolds's plans. The brigade's new orders were to leave two regiments to guard the corps trains and march the remaining regiments along the 3rd Division's route of march down Fairfield Road to Hagerstown Pike and then to

Gettysburg. Stannard selected the 12th and 15th Vermont to remain with the corps trains, as they were his smallest regiments. He then took the 13th, 14th, and 16th Vermont to Gettysburg and marched northwest on this circuitous route, which allowed them to avoid the traffic of other units marching north. This march took time, however, and it was not hard to hear the sounds of battle and see the large columns of smoke rising just outside of Gettysburg.

The march prevented Benedict and the 2nd Vermont Brigade from taking part in the first day's fight. This probably saved many lives in the 2nd Vermont Brigade, as the I Corps was badly mauled on McPherson's Ridge and later Seminary Ridge in the late morning and afternoon of July 1, by Hill's corps from the northwest and Ewell's corps from the north. Had the 2nd Vermont Brigade been with the I Corps that afternoon, there was a good chance that the brigade would not have survived the encounter and would have done little to affect its outcome.

As night fell, the 2nd Vermont Brigade joined the remnants of the I Corps on Cemetery Hill and went to sleep with their arms. The brigade had about 1,800 men, larger than the average brigade, but they were as yet unproven in battle.[6] Many divisional and corps commanders had seen large, unproven units fall apart on first contact with the enemy, so the 2nd Vermont Brigade was seen as a questionable asset. Most on the battlefield at Gettysburg knew that they were in a battle that could change the course of the war. Since the battle, much has been written about it. One of the first published accounts was Benedict's next letter.

Camp of the 2nd Vermont Brigade
Battlefield of Gettysburg, July 4, 1863

Dear Free Press:

I date from our "Camp" because this is the present abiding place of our Brigade; but it has really little of the camp about it, except the men. We have no tents—the blue canopy above is our only shelter—we have no fires, and nothing to cook, if we had. The men stand or sit in knots near their stacked arms, worn, hungry and battle stained; but a better feeling set of men one does not often see. The big battle is over and every man is proud to have been in it and that he is a member of the Vermont 2nd Brigade.

The scene has shifted since I wrote you last from the shores of the Occoquan to the fields of Pennsylvania. I can give but little space to the march which brought us here. It lasted a week—seven weary days of continuous marching through the mud. The men, you know, were not inured to marching. Some were poorly shod, for in view of the speedy termination of their service they had neglected to exchange old shoes for new, but they marched well. With sore and blistered and often bleeding feet, in some cases bare-footed, they pushed along and made their twenty miles, or nearly that, a day. There was some murmuring the last day or two, at the rate at which they were urged along, but they understood the reason why, when, on Wednesday as we neared Gettysburg, the sound of cannon was heard in front, and an orderly dashed up to say that the 1st corps, to which we were assigned under Major Gen. Doubleday, was fighting the whole rebel army, and needed every man that could be brought up. It was cheering to see the effect of the sound of battle on the tired troops. The ranks closed up, the stragglers took their places, and the men pressed forward with a freer step. But the afternoon was a very hot one, and with our utmost effort we only reached the battleground in time to take position before dark in rear of the line of battle of the 1st corps. The artillery fire ceased at dark, and the men stretched themselves upon their arms in a wheat field, and sank into the deep and reckless sleep of the weary soldier. There was rest for the men; but not for our General. Gen. Stannard was notified, upon his arrival, of his appointment as General Field Officer of the Day, or of the night rather, and that he would be expected to see to the effective posting of the pickets of several other corps besides our own. The duty called for a night in the saddle, upon the army lines, and those who know the General knew that they could sleep in quiet behind the sentinels posted and watched by his experienced eye.

The day opened on Thursday without firing, save now and then a shot from the pickets, but there was a considerable moving of troops on our side behind the hills and low ridges which concealed us from the enemy, and doubtless the same process was going on, on their side, unseen by us. The batteries alone on the hilltops and crests of the ridges menaced each other, like grim bulldogs, in silence.

The three regiments present of our Brigade (12th and 15th had been sent to guard the ammunition and supply trains in the rear—an important duty) were placed behind Cemetery Hill—a round hill crowned by a beautiful Cemetery laid out with an amount of taste and expense very unusual in a place of the size of Gettysburg—and Gen. Stannard was notified that he was in command upon the hill, and would be held responsible for its safety. The position was a central and all important one, and once lost by us could hardly have been recovered, while to relinquish it would have been to relinquish the whole field.

Our batteries were planted, not indeed actually upon the graves, but close to them within the cemetery—such are the necessities of war. We lay behind the hill through the forenoon, the men lounging on the grass, and orderlies, with the horses for officers, hanging around, till about 3 o'clock, when the ball opened by the discharge of artillery and the whizzing of shell around our ears. The very first thrown exploded exactly over the 13th regiment, and two or three men of it were wounded by the fragments. A sudden scampering to the rear, of orderlies, ambulances, and all whose duties did not hold them to the spot, followed. The troops were moved a little closer under the hill, and made to lie down, our own batteries opened sharply and the fight for several hours was an artillery duel. The shells came screaming through the air with not altogether agreeable frequency, mingled, for those of us whose duties called us to the top of the hill, with the occasional humming of minie balls, but there was very little loss of life. Occasionally a battery horse, would plunge and rear for a moment and then drop. As I passed one of the guns, I noticed a fine looking Sergeant of the battery, watching eagerly the effect of the shot he had just aimed; as I came back again, two minutes later, he was lying dead by his gun. Perhaps a dozen men came by us from the skirmish line in front, with gunshot wounds of arm or leg or head. A company was called for as support to the skirmishers. Capt. Foster, of General Stannard's staff, was sent out to station them, and was brought back in a few minutes shot through both legs. With these exceptions I saw no bloodshed for hours. General Stannard moved around among the men assuring them by calling attention to the fact of how little actual danger there was in even a heavy artillery fire, under such circumstances, and the terrified ones gained courage fast. But we were told by the old warriors that this thundering of cannon was only the prelude to a charge upon our lines, and all watched to see when it would come. About six, the sudden opening of musketry firing to our left indicated the spot, and in a few minutes we heard, above the din, the wild yell with which the rebels charge. There was no time to think what it meant, before orders came for our brigade to hurry to the left, where the lines were now being borne back by the enemy. Two regiments had broken for the rear; a battery had been taken, and our brigade, as the nearest reserve, was called to fill the gap. Five companies of the 13th, under Col. Randall, led the advance (the left wing of the regiment under Lieutenant Col. Munson, had been supporting a battery to the right and brought up the rear of the column) and came up on the double-quick. "Can you retake that battery, Colonel?" was the question of Gen. Hancock, as they came up. "Forward boys" was the reply, and in they went. Capt. Lonergan's company of "bould soldier boys" took the lead and rushed at the battery with their Irish yell. Col. Randall's grey horse fell under him, shot through the shoulder, and he went on, on foot. The guns were reached, wheeled round and passed to the rear and pressing on, the boys of the 13th took two more guns, rebel pieces just brought forward, with some 80 odd of the "grey-backs" who were supporting them. This ended the fighting for the night. The 13th fell back to the original line, which thus restored by the Vermonters was held by our brigade to the close of the battle, and held, too, in spite of two desperate charges of the enemy.

With the darkness the firing ceased, and we heard then from our front that sound which, once heard, will not be forgotten by anyone—a low, steady indescribable moan—the groans of the wounded, lying by hundreds on the battlefield. As the moon was rising I rode out upon the field in front of our lines. My horse started aside at every rod from the bodies of dead men or horses, and wounded men. U.S. soldiers and rebels, in about equal proportions, were making their way slowly within our lines. Some of the latter said that Gen. Barksdale of Miss. lay mortally wounded out beyond, and begged to be brought in. A party from the 14th was sent to search for him, but he was not found till near morning.

I saw his body soon after the life had left it, in the morning, and having seen him on the floor of Congress, recognized it at once. He was dressed in a suit of the light bluish-gray mixture of cotton and wool, worn commonly by the rebel officers, with gold lace upon the coat sleeves and down the seams of the trousers. His vest thrown open disclosed a ball hole through the breast, and his legs were bandaged and bloody from gunshots through both of them. He fought apparently without the wig which Speaker Grow once knocked off in the Hall of Representatives, and his bald head and broad face were uncovered in the sunshine.

Our troops dropped in their places and slept again upon their arms. I obtained an hour or two of grateful rest, and then was roused to go in search of an ammunition train. No one knew its exact whereabouts, and for the remainder of the night I rode to and fro through the region in the rear of our army in a fruitless search. The ride, however, gave me an idea of the extent of the bloodshed thus far of the fight, which as the evidences of it accumulated became absolutely appalling. Every barn—and the barns are unusually large and expansive in this region—was a hospital, its floors covered with mutilated soldiers, piles of amputated arms and legs lying outside, and the fields around strewed with unfortunates, awaiting their turn under the operating knife. Trains of ambulances filled with groaning inmates, covered the roads. The wounded men whom I met, sometimes assisted by a comrade, but quite as often wandering alone, who would ask me in faint tones to direct them to the hospital of their corps or division, were I am sure hundreds in number, and of course I met but a fraction of those who were thus searching by night for relief. It seemed to me that every square yard on a stretch of many miles must have its blood stain.

I returned to the brigade at daybreak, and was saluted as I came up with a shell which exploded a few feet off. Its successor maimed the horse of one of the General's orderlies, another still took off the hoof of another horse, close by us, when we took the hint and removed the horses below the ridge. The artillery fire was quite sharp for a while from the rebel batteries opposite us, but died away in an hour or so. It was only a feint to attract attention while the enemy was preparing a desperate attack upon the extreme right. About six o'clock the musketry firing became tremendous about a mile to our right. We could see nothing of it but the white smoke rising above the treetops; but the volleys rolled in one continuous crash of thunder for *seven hours.* The sound did not recede at all, and we knew therefore that our side held its ground.

While this was going on, as it turned out, the enemy was collecting his batteries below the crest of the ridge over against us. The battleground here was a broad open stretch of meadowland, the ground sloping away from the low rounded ridge on which our batteries were placed and just below the brow of which our infantry lay in a double line of battle, perhaps 50 yards apart, and rising to a similar rounded ridge over against us, from half to three fourths of a mile away, which was held by the enemy. Our men used the lull to make a little protection by collecting the rails from the fences, and piling them in a low breastwork perhaps two feet high. This would of course be a very slight protection for men standing erect; but for men lying prostrate they proved a valuable cover, and we found we needed every such assistance before night.

About two o'clock a couple of guns from the enemy gave the signal, from seventy-five to a *hundred* guns were run out upon the ridge over against us, and for an hour and a half, what old veterans pronounced to be the severest cannonade of the war in the East was opened directly upon us. The air seemed to be literally filled with flying missiles. Shells whizzed and popped on every side. Spherical case shot exploded over our heads and rained iron bullets upon us: the Whitworth solid shot, easily distinguished by their clear musical ring, flew singing by, grape hurtled around us or rattled in an iron storm against the low protections of rails, and round shot ploughed up the ground before and behind us. The men needed no caution to hug the ground closely. All lay motionless, heads to the front and faces to the ground. Occasionally a man would be struck but I saw none killed outright, and the loss from the artillery was on the whole wonderfully small. The wounded men invariably received their injuries without outcry, and lay and bled quietly in their places. They understood that for their comrades to attempt to remove them would be almost certain death, and waited patiently till the close of the fight should allow them to be cared for. The general and his staff alone when orders were to be given and carried, stood erect or passed up and down the lines, and kept a close watch to the front for the first indication of the expected charge. Of course our Batteries were not silent. They fired rapidly and well. Suddenly with a loud explosion a caisson of the battery just on our left blew up, struck by a round shot. The smoke rolled up in a tall column, from under which the frightened horses, one or two minus a leg, dashed wildly to the rear. The rebels on the crest cheered at the sound, and poured in their shot still faster. Ten minutes later and a whole battery blew up on our right. For a moment there was a scene of great confusion around it, but a fresh battery dashed up into its place, and our fire reopened with fresh vigor from the spot. A minute afterwards and a rebel caisson opposite us exploded, and it was our turn to cheer.

About three o'clock, the shout, "there they come," from our watchful general, brought every man's arms into his hands, and many a man's heart to his mouth. The head of a heavy gray column came over the ridge and advanced directly upon us. Down they came to about half the distance between our lines and their batteries, when our regiments were ordered up, and rose in a close and steady line. At the sight the rebel columns halted for an instant, then turned at a right angle, and marched for a hundred yards or so to the right, and then turning again at a right angle, came in on the charge, in column by regiments, just to the right of *our* brigade. The regiments holding the lines there maintained their position, and met the rebels with the line of fire; but the grey column still came on with unearthly yells, led by an officer on horseback who rode back and forth along the column waving a red battle flag and cheering on his men. The front of the rebel column had reached within perhaps a dozen yards of the Union bayonets, and it began to be a question how our lines, but two men deep, could stand the onset of a massed column, when a new and unlooked for arrangement changed the appearance of things. The point of attack had no sooner become evident, then Gen. Stannard ordered forward the 13th and 16th regiments to take the enemy on the flank. Their line of battle advanced a few paces, and then changing front, the line swung out at right angles to the main line of our army, directly upon the flank of the charging column, and opened fire. This was more than the rebels had counted on. Their column began to break and scatter from the rear, in less than three minutes, and in three more it was an utter rout. A portion made their way back to their own side; but fully two thirds, I should think, of their column, dropped their arms and came in as prisoners. Of course they suffered terribly in killed and wounded. The 14th, opposite whose line the enemy's column came out from cover, had kept up a constant fire upon them, and a lie of dead bodies marked the line of march, while, where their column came in on the charge, their dead literally strewed the ground. It was a savage onset and a glorious repulse; but it did not end the fight in the center. The 13th and 16th were still in position on the enemy's flank, occupied with the agreeable duty of receiving colonels' and majors' swords, when the order came to about face and meet another charge. Another rebel column was coming down to the left of us, aiming directly at the 14th. The same mode of treatment was applied to their case, with the happiest results. The 14th met them with a hot fire in front, and the 16th hurrying down on the double quick took them on the flank, and bagged about the whole brigade of them. The 16th took in this charge the colors of the 2nd Florida—a beautiful silk flag inscribed with "Williamsburg" and "Seven Pines"—the colors of the 8th Virginia (which were however foolishly thrown away by the sergeant to whom they were given to carry, who pitched them into the bushes declaring that he could not fight with that flag in his hands) and the battle flag of another regiment.

How many prisoners we took in these operations I cannot say precisely. There was a "pile" of them—from 2,000 to 3,000—and if we credit one third of them to the Vermont troops, it is no more than their fair share.

With these repulses of the enemy the big fight in effect closed. There was sharp skirmishing on our left, but no more hard fighting. At dark our pickets were extended out beyond the battlefield, and at nine o'clock our brigade worn and weary was relieved of its position in the front, and allowed to find rest and comparative relief from care in the rear of our army lines.

The length of this hurried letter compels me to leave undescribed many an interesting incident of the fight. One, however, must not be passed over.

During the last sharp shower of grape and shell, with which the enemy strove to cover their retreat, Gen. Stannard was wounded in the right leg by a shrapnel ball. The wound was exceedingly painful until a surgeon came, which was not for an hour or more, and removed the ball, but the general refused to leave the field. He was urged to go by Gen. Doubleday but resolutely declined. He had been for two days in the front line, with his men, and he would not leave them now. Nor did he. He kept up till the regiments had marched back, till the wounded had been removed in ambulances, and arrangements were made for burying the dead, and then at last sank fainting and almost lifeless on the ground.

He was the coolest man I saw on that battlefield, exposing himself in a way that would have been rashness, were it not for the need he felt of animating his men by his example, and of ensuring their good behavior by letting every man see that his eye was on him. He was a constant mark for the enemy's sharpshooters, received a ball through the brim of his hat, another through his coat, and was once whirled off his feet by the concussion of a shell, but nothing daunted or disconcerted him. To his presence and timely orders in a great degree is due the glorious success of yesterday. The General is proud of his troops and they of him, and Vermont may well be proud of both.

Yours, G.

July 4, 1863, opened on the Gettysburg battlefield as a gray, subdued day. After three days of fighting, neither army wanted to attack the other. Thousands of men lay dead, dying, and wounded between them. Both sides watched in case the other did launch an attack, but another attack did not come that day. In the meantime, hundreds of men rested, searched for missing buddies, or waited for treatment at overcrowded field hospitals. The 2nd Vermont Brigade started that day about a hundred yards east and behind the positions they had held the day before. Some men ate whatever rations they had scrounged, some slept, and some wrote letters home. Others looked for friends, relatives, or comrades who were missing after the Confederates' grand charge the previous day. If found alive, they carried them back to a field hospital for treatment. More often than not, they were dead, and the men carried them back to camp for burial, except for a mixed squad from the 14th and 16th Vermont, which they buried close to where the men fell under an oak tree along the Emmitsburg Road.[7]

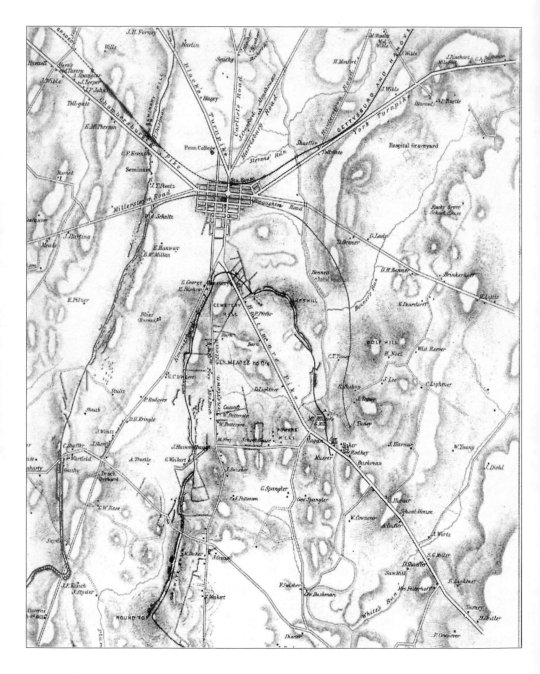

The 2nd Vermont Brigade's operational area 1862–1863. War of the Rebellion: Official Records of the Union and Confederate Armies, Map Book.

While the brigade recovered, General Stannard took stock of his command and considered what would happen next. Stannard's wound was a painful reminder of the actions of the day before, yet it was not too bad in the morning. He had Benedict write the brigade's official report of the battle and talked with his staff and regimental commanders. But by noon, the general's wound had made him weak and ill to the point where he decided to turn over the brigade's command to Colonel Randall the next day.[8] Then Stannard took the advice of Surgeon Ketchum, the medical director of the brigade, and retired to a small, private room close to the hospital that Ketchum oversaw to recover from his wound. More than likely, that is where Benedict wrote his July 4 letter, as a hard rain had begun early that afternoon, and without some type of shelter, letter writing would have been impossible. If Stannard needed something while the doctor was out, Benedict would be there to assist him.

This battle changed Benedict's life. He had faced death but survived three close calls. Now he penned one of the first eyewitness accounts published of this battle, while its memories were fresh. The 2nd Vermont Brigade had awoken on July 2 in the midst of a gathering Union army located along the western side of Cemetery Ridge. The Army of the Potomac's position by then can best be described as a fishhook, with the barb located on Culp's Hill east of Cemetery Hill, and the shank running south and ending at the Round Tops. That morning, they could not see much of the Confederate army, which was located about a mile west of the Union troops on Seminary Ridge. Things were quiet, as Lee and Meade planned what their armies would do to each other that day. In the meantime, Stannard was given the mission of providing infantry support to the I and XI Corps' artillery batteries, located on the north and west sides of Cemetery Hill.

As the day wore on, there was noticeable army activity, and the 2nd Vermont Brigade was more active too. At noon, the left wing of the 13th Vermont was sent to support a battery of the XI Corps on the north side of Cemetery Hill. While an uneasy peace held between the two armies, Benedict learned of the risks of being a staff officer that afternoon, when the brigade headquarters drew sniper fire.

Although no one was harmed, there were a few close calls, as when snipers' bullets put holes in Stanndard's coat and Hooker's hat. However, both men were luckier that day than Capt. Asa Foster, who positioned the

16th Vermont's Companies B and G on the picket line that afternoon. As he did this, a Confederate bullet passed through Foster's right thigh and lodged itself in his left leg.[9] Foster was carried off to a field hospital, where the bullet was removed. Luckily he kept both of his legs and recovered completely in time.

At 3:00 P.M. on July 2, Longstreet's corps' artillery opened fire before Hood's and McLaw's divisions assaulted the Union left. Several shells wounded a few of the men from the 13th Vermont, the first wounded by fire in the brigade. Everyone in the ranks could hear the volume of small-arms fire building to the south of them, as the Confederates advanced upon Sickles's III Corps's defensive positions. This Union corps was soon joined by elements of the V Corps, as the bloodiest fighting of the battle of Gettysburg took place west and south of the Round Tops on the Union's left flank. Toward sundown, the Vermonters played a small part on the northern end of this battle.

By sundown, General Sickles's corps was smashed and starting to give way, and Weir's battery had been overrun close to the 2nd Vermont Brigade. The Union's center was breached; something had to be done to prevent a strong Confederate attack from splitting the Union army or they would lose the battle. General Hancock, who was trying to stabilize the situation, looked for any regiment available to order it forward to form a new defense line and stem the Confederate advance before it broke the Union center. He ordered the 13th Vermont to retake Weir's battery as the Confederates tried to drag it off the field. After giving Colonel Randall his orders, Hancock and his staff rode off to find the rest of the 2nd Vermont Brigade to fill the gap.

Randall himself, astride his gray charger, led his regiment's right wing in an attack on the enemy, making him the target of every Confederate within range. He had not gone far when his horse was shot and fell, pinning him to the ground. Two of his men hurried to move the horse off him, and they continued on. The 13th Vermont recaptured Weir's battery and helped move the cannons behind the new defensive line. Then the regiment advanced to the Emmitsburg Road. Capt. John Longeran's Company A captured eighty-three Confederates at the Rogers house, which was on the west side of the road and the north end of the Peach Orchard. The troops also said they had taken two guns. However, according to Harry W. Pfanz's book *Gettysburg: The Second Day,* the Confederates lost no guns at Gettysburg, meaning that the 13th Vermont retook captured Union cannons or this claim was not true. Benedict is mistaken about all of the 13th Vermont being at this charge. Lt. Col. William Munson and the 13th Vermont's left wing were still on the north side of Cemetery Hill, protecting the batteries there. They rejoined the right wing shortly after dark and after the fighting had stopped.

Soon after sunset, the 13th Vermont returned to its new position, as the 14th and 16th Vermont had established a new defensive line and helped plug the gap that had been created by Gen. LaFayette McLaw's division. As the day ended, so did the fighting. Things started to settle down, but it did not mean that the armies were inactive. In the early-morning hours, Benedict went to look for a lost ammunition train that had not arrived from the rear. After a few hours of fruitless searching, he left Rock Creek Church and headed back to brigade headquarters. On his way, he got lost, and instead of taking the Taneytown Road, he took the Baltimore Pike. He got as far as the gatehouse of Cemetery Hill, where he was stopped by a watchful artilleryman, who asked where he was going. The artilleryman told him that the only people ahead of his position were the Confederate army. With this news, Benedict turned around and found his way back to the brigade.[10] He was not the only person looking for something that night; many were searching for buddies in the dark by candle and lantern light, and others were caring for the thousands of wounded whose bodies littered the battlefield. The next day, these wounded were joined by thousands more of their comrades and enemies.

Confederate brigadier general William Barksdale was a rabid secessionist, the kind of Southerner a Vermont reader would have detested and blamed for starting the war. Barksdale was a former Mississippi congressman and newspaper editor, which gave him some connection with Benedict. Barksdale was a Mexican War veteran, and his political connections gave him command of the 13th Mississippi Infantry at the beginning of the war. Barksdale and the 13th Mississippi saw action in almost every battle of the war in the East up to Gettysburg. He was famous for his temper and aggressiveness, which were demonstrated at Fredericksburg when he wanted to fight the entire Army of the Potomac with his brigade at the edge of the Rappahannock River and had to be called off by Lee. Barksdale was mortally wounded while leading what was considered by some the grandest charge of the war, when his brigade finally overran Union forces in the Peach Orchard at about 7:30 P.M. on July 2. Early the next morning, a squad under the command of 1st Sgt. Henry Vaughan of Company B of the

14th Vermont recovered Barksdale while he was still barely alive. Barksdale asked Vaughan to tell his wife, "I fought like a man and will die like one."[11] Vaughan had also brought in Barksdale's hat and gloves and gave them to Col. William Nichols, who put them in his personal baggage and returned them to Barksdale's widow after the war. Vaughan also did not survive the battle; he was killed later that day.

As July 3 dawned, Confederate artillery opened fire on the Union lines, causing several casualties among the Vermonters. Benedict was lucky again, as a Confederate shell landed several feet from him and his horse but failed to explode. This early-morning shelling caused the brigade to move forward 45 to 75 yards from their previous positions to get out of the line of fire. The 14th Vermont was on the left on broken ground and brush. The 13th Vermont was on the right on a small rise about 200 yards behind the Codori barn and about 50 yards in front of the main Union defensive line. The 16th Vermont was on picket in front of the brigade in the Codori orchard and along the Emmitsburg Road. In the lull that morning, the 13th and 14th Vermont improved their position with fence rails and dirt that they scraped up using tin plates, bayonets, and their bare hands. By noon, they had a two-foot-high breastwork that protected the troops when they were lying on the ground. The brigade command post was on a knoll behind and between the 13th and 14th Vermont.

Benedict and the rest of the 2nd Vermont Brigade waited for the Confederates' next move, which turned out to be a bombardment that started at 1:00 P.M. In his July 4 letter, Benedict has the time as 2:00 P.M., an understandable mistake, as he was unlikely to have consulted his pocket watch during the battle.

As the Confederates started to fire, the breastwork protected the majority of men in the brigade until the enemy fire lifted as their gunners failed to adjust their fire. After each round fired, the cannons' trails began digging into the ground because of the recoil, thus slowly elevating the cannons' muzzles. Benedict, Hooker, Stannard, and the other staff continued to duck shells as they watched and waited to see where the Confederates would advance on the Union lines. The fire died down ninety minutes later and the smoke began to lift. The men on the west side of Cemetery Ridge wondered how many Confederate soldiers were heading their way.

Lee's plan was that this fire would disrupt and demoralize the Union troops on Cemetery Ridge, and then three divisions, around 10,000 men,

Site of the 2nd Vermont Brigade's Headquarters during Picketts Charge (modern view). The small obelisk marks the spot where Maj. Gen. Winfield Scott Hancock was wounded on the afternoon of July 3, 1863. THE WARD COLLECTION.

would assault and break the Union center and win the battle. Gen. James Longstreet sent Henry Heth's and Pender's divisions from A. P. Hill's corps and Pickett's division from his corps at the Union center after the artillery fire stopped. At that moment, the 2nd Vermont Brigade was concerned about Pickett's division, which was marching toward them. Pickett's division at Gettysburg was composed of James Kemper's, Lewis Armistead's, and Richard Garnett's brigades, totaling about 4,000 men. General Armistead's brigade was the largest of the three, and it marched northeast, clearing the woods near the Spangler farm. Garnett's brigade was posted on their left, and it advanced northeast crossing north of Codori farm and marching parallel with the Emmitsburg Road. Kemper's brigade was posted on their right and had the farthest march of the Pickett's division brigades. It marched northeast, crossed the Emmitsburg Road near the Roger's house, and continued toward the Codori farm. This advancing mass of troops had the full attention of Benedict and the entire 2nd Vermont Brigade at that moment. Kemper's brigade was the Confederate unit Benedict describes in his July 4 letter as coming straight at them, and the officer on horseback was forty-year-old Brig. Gen. James L. Kemper.[12]

*Site of Kemper Brigade's advance on July 3, 1863, as viewed from the 2nd
Vermont Brigade Headquarters (modern view).* THE WARD COLLECTION.

A lawyer and state politician, Kemper was one of the rare political generals who were good field commanders. Kemper served as a captain in the
Virginia volunteers during the Mexican War, and his political connections
got him the command of the 7th Virginia Infantry Regiment in the next
one. He fought well at the first battle of Bull Run and in the Peninsula
campaign. In addition, in an odd touch of fate, the 2nd Vermont Brigade
had a picket post on Kemper's plantation at the beginning of their service.
Before the day was over, he was badly wounded and captured. He was
exchanged a few months later, but his wound ended his active-duty career,
although he was promoted to major general and assigned to command Virginia's reserve forces for the rest of the war.

At first, Kemper's brigade appeared to be heading for the 2nd Vermont
Brigade's position, which was concealed from Confederate view by the terrain. At about this time, the 16th Vermont regrouped from picket behind
the 13th and 14th Vermont, as more Union artillery started to engage the
advancing Confederates. Benedict soon relayed orders to Colonel Randall
of the 13th Vermont. These orders were passed on to the regimental commanders, then to company commanders, and their men moved. This movement revealed these Vermonters to the Confederate commanders, who

Site of the 13th and 16th Vermont's attack on Kemper's Brigade flank at Gettysburg (modern view). THE WARD COLLECTION.

shifted their units more northwesterly to avoid these Union troops and aim closer to their objective, as well as to close up with the other Confederate divisions. As the men marched north, Kemper's right flank brushed within twenty-five yards of the 2nd Vermont Brigade's position, and in the next moment, the order to fire was given. During the firing, Stannard saw that his forces were in a perfect position to flank this Confederate assault, as Kemper's brigade advanced for its final attack under this withering fire. Stannard ordered the 13th and 16th Vermont to wheel right and then advance north, thus attacking Kemper's brigade on its right flank as Pickett's division closed with the main Union defensive line. Benedict rushed to give these instructions to Randall.[13]

When the fire slackened, Stannard sent Benedict back to Randall and his regiment, who were still on the Confederate flank, to have the 13th Vermont return to its starting position in case Lee sent another Confederate charge to relieve the pressure on Pickett's division. Benedict's activity put him at more of a risk than he expected. When the 13th Vermont finally broke off its attack, Pickett's division was crushed, and its surviving members either surrendered or retreated. Benedict headed back with the 13th Vermont, pulling ahead of this regiment to join the brigade's headquarters group. He was about ten yards from the command section of 13th Vermont's left wing when he heard a whiz, then a boom, and turned around. The man with whom Benedict had just been talking, Sgt. Maj. Henry H. Smith, was killed. The same shell dismembered another soldier, killed three others, and wounded several others in the ranks. That was his third close call.

When Benedict got back to Stannard, the general ordered him to go to Colonel Veazey and recall the 16th Vermont, because an enemy force composed of Perry's and Wilcox's brigades now advanced unsupported in the open at the 2nd Vermont Brigade's position. The 16th Vermont, with the left wing of the 14th Vermont, flanked this force and knocked it out in a mostly one-sided fight. As Benedict headed to Veazey with the orders, a spent minié ball hit his cartridge box on his belt and bent several pistol cartridges, leaving him surprised yet unhurt. At about the same time, at brigade headquarters about a hundred yards away, a piece of shrapnel hit Stannard in the thigh. Although he was not in danger, this wound was painful. After the firing had ceased, Stannard, ignoring his wound, visited his regimental commanders on horseback.[14] This probably aggravated his wound, which grew worse over the next few days and knocked him out of the war until September. After the sun had gone down and the fighting was over, commanders in the 2nd Vermont Brigade counted their losses: 40 men killed, 248 wounded, and 58 men missing.[15] Twenty-one of these wounded men died of their wounds, and two of the fifty-eight missing in action had been captured. These were Pvt. Edward Farmer of Company H of the 14th Vermont, who died at Andersonville in May 1864, and Pvt. Samuel B. Lincoln of Newfane, Vermont, serving in Company I of the 16th Vermont, who died in captivity at a prison camp near Richmond on November 20, 1863.[16] This was the experience of the 13th, 14th, and 16th Vermont Infantry Regiments at Gettysburg; that of the 12th and 15th Vermont was quite different.

As Benedict writes in his July 4 letter, the 12th Vermont was located at Westminster, Maryland, about twenty-five miles southeast of Gettysburg. On the afternoon of July 1, the 12th and 15th Vermont escorted the corps trains to Rock Creek Church, where they encamped to supply the I Corps in the upcoming battle. Gen. Dan Sickles, the commander of the III Corps, arrived at the I Corps's trains a few hours later. He was unhappy that such a large detachment had been left to guard the trains when a battle was raging and every man was going to be needed. Sickles thought this detachment was the entire 2nd Vermont Brigade, but learning it was two regiments, he

ordered the larger of the two to march behind the III Corps to police stragglers and then rejoin the I Corps. Adj. Roswell Vaughan of the 12th Vermont and Adj. J. Monroe Poland of the 15th Vermont then went through
their books and did a head count: The 15th Vermont had 529 men and the
12th Vermont had 514.[17] Therefore, it was the 15th Vermont that marched
to Gettysburg policing stragglers from Sickles's corps.

On July 2, General Meade ordered the army's ammunition wagons forward to supply the army and sent the remaining supply and baggage trains
to Westminster. Companies B and G stayed with a part of the I Corps's
ammunition train at Rock Creek Church. The 12th Vermont's eight other
companies started for Westminster at 8:00 A.M. and arrived around midnight. Despite the orders of General Sickles and the protests of General
Stannard, Colonel Proctor and the 15th Vermont Regiment were again
sent back by General Meade to guard the trains with the 12th Vermont. For
Farnham, Hagar, Irwin, and the rest of these two Vermont regiments, the
marching ended for a few days. Pvt. Richard Irwin wrote that the march to
Gettysburg "was the most fearful thing I have ever done."[18] He also felt
grateful that he would not risk death or injury at the end of his service,
which had been a possibility until the 12th Vermont's detachment to guard
the trains. The most interesting thing that happened after their march to
Westminster was watching an ammunition wagon catch fire and blow up,
and they heard the battle sounds carried on the breeze from Gettysburg
from time to time.[19]

The 12th and 15th Vermont's guard duty became more interesting on
July 3, as 900 Confederate prisoners marched in from Gettysburg and
became the charges of these two Vermont regiments. By this time, Westminster had become a small city, as seven corps' worth of supply and baggage wagons and their escorts were located near this town. Since the
average corps train had around 400 wagons, there were more than 2,800
wagons, along with the supplies they carried, the horses and mules to pull
them, and the teamsters who cared for and drove these animals. In addition,
Westminster was the closest railroad depot to the battlefield and ensured that
the Army of the Potomac could resupply itself easily, and supplies from this
source began to make their presence felt.

On July 4, the 12th and 15th Vermont heard of the Army of the
Potomac's victory and the news of the other regiments that fought. They
also celebrated the fact that they were soon going home, as it was the last
day of their enlistment. They elected to stay in the army until the battle was

over and, with the army's victory, their services were no longer needed.[20] That day, the 12th Vermont guarded 2,700 Confederate prisoners of war who were being shipped to Baltimore. That night, Colonel Blunt and three companies from the regiment guarded the Confederates and their train at the depot, yet for some reason they did not leave until noon the next day.[21] Lieutenant Colonel Farnham was in charge of the five remaining companies and waited for Companies B and G to arrive from Rock Creek Church, which they did that afternoon. Farnham had 465 prisoners loaded onto the train, and they left Westminster at 3:00 A.M. on July 6 and arrived at Baltimore at 8:00 A.M. The companies then marched with their prisoners to the provost marshal at Fort McHenry and dropped them off. With the prisoners taken care of, Farnham and the rest of the regiment took the train to Philadelphia and started their journey home at 10:00 A.M. They reached the city that evening, got supper, and then took the train to Amboy, New Jersey. From there, they took a steamer to New York City. Farnham and the six companies of the 12th Vermont arrived at New York City at 5:00 A.M. on Wednesday, July 8. Waiting for them were Chaplain Lewis Brastow and Maj. Levi Kingsley, and they and the regiment had breakfast and lunch in the city. This section of the 12th Vermont left on a steamer at 3:00 P.M. and arrived at New Haven, Connecticut, at 9:00 P.M. They reached Brattleboro, Vermont, around 6:00 A.M. the next morning and went into the barracks to rest from the trip. The next day, the 12th started its mustering out of Federal service.

Camp of the 12th Vt.
Brattleboro, Vt.—July 14, 1863

Dear Free Press:

If I recollect alright, my last letter from the battlefield of Gettysburg, contained an intimation that in a subsequent epistle I might attempt to set down some additional incidents of the great battle. I take the first opportunity to fulfill the promise—finding it only here, ten days after the fight, and many hundred miles from the field. As hitherto, I write only of what passed under my own eye, leaving to the correspondents of the city press the description of the battle as a whole.

When I spoke as I believe I did, of the comparative harmlessness of the terrific cannonade to which the Vermont regiments, together with the other forces holding the centre of General Meade's line, were subjected, it was understood, I trust, that the ineffectiveness was only *comparative* and that only in the case of men kept prostrate on the ground. The casualties in the Vt. Brigade were almost entirely from artillery fire, and the aggregate of loss from the enemy's artillery was very large. There were few spots either upon our lines or in the rear of them, free from danger from the thickly flying shells. While thousands of them struck and exploded upon or over our lines, perhaps an equal number passed either by ricochet or directly over to the rear, and caused the loss of many valuable lives and hundreds of valuable horses, many of which had been taken to the rear for safety. Their attentions in the shape of grape and canister were of course confined to the front lines, and there was not the slightest occasion to complain of any *want* of attention on that score. The artillery fire as our boys rose in line and advanced upon the flank of the charging column of the enemy on Friday afternoon, was tremendous, and the *three hundred* killed and wounded of our three regiments, almost all struck during the movements and within the space of half an hour, show that it was not ineffective. The most destructive shot I noticed took effect in the 13th regiment, as it was marching back by the flank, to resume its place in line, after the surrender of the greater portion of the main rebel column. I was hurrying past with an order, when a *thud* and cry of horror close behind me attracted my attention above the whistling of grape and din of exploding shell. I turned to find a cruel gap in the column. Of a file of four, three had been prostrated by a shell together with two officers marching by their side. The outer man was whirled on the ground but I believe not much injured; the second was hit and killed by the passing missile; the third was struck in the centre of the body and literally dismembered, one leg, bared of all but shoe and stocking, being thrown several feet from the body, exploding at the same moment the fragments of the shell [that] killed the Sergeant-Major of the regiment, Smith, to whom I had just spoken a cheering word, while the explosion threw bruised and senseless to the ground Lieut. Col.

Munson, who was walking at the moment at the Sergeant Major's elbow. For a moment the men in the rear of the file which had thus been swept away halted and drew back aghast; but discipline prevailed in another moment, and stepping over their mangled comrades, they closed up the gap and marched on.

But one instance of unmanly want of fortitude attracted my notice, among our Vermont troops. One young man, struck down by a shot which disabled one leg, as the regiment was hurrying forward to meet the enemy, burst forth into loud entreaties to his comrades not to leave him, and rising on one knee he even tried to stop them by catching at the skirts of their coats as they passed him. They could not stay, of course, and it may have been the next day possibly before he was cared for. Such was the case with some of our wounded. The rule which forbids the well ones of the rank and file leaving the ranks to attend to the wounded, hard as it seems, is one of absolute necessity, and if more rigidly enforced and obeyed in all our battles would have saved a hundred lives for every one lost by it.

The drummers and fifers, whose duty it is to man the stretchers and carry the wounded from the field, showed, as a general rule, great absence of body, if not presence of mind, throughout the battle and the tremendous accumulation of wounded men of both sides so far exceeded the means of relief that thousands remained almost uncared for, for many hours. Our Surgeons worked nobly. The capture of a number of Surgeons of the 1st Corps, when our forces withdrew from the town on Wednesday, leaving the hospitals in the town in the hands of the enemy, created a great scarcity of Surgeons. Surgeon Ketchum, the Medical Director of our Brigade, found himself the ranking medical officer, and had charge of all the hospitals of the Corps. Dr. Nichols of the 13th had an extensive division hospital under his capable care, and Drs. Park and Woodward of the 14th and 16th, were placed in similar laborious and responsible positions. All labored night and day over the wounded, until compelled to stop from sheer exhaustion. I was told by one who was present, that as Dr. Woodward was waiting a moment on Friday night, for a shattered limb to be made ready for amputation, his eyes closed in utter weariness, and he fell forward, operating knife in hand, over the wounded soldier before him. It is worth mentioning perhaps, that the medical supplies of our brigade were the only ones approaching sufficiency, and that from them were furnished almost all that was required for the hospitals of the entire Corps on Wednesday night and Thursday, and until additional supplies were brought on Friday from the army depot.

That I have made no mention of individual cases of bravery and good conduct on the field is simply because such were altogether too numerous to mention. The troops of the 2nd Vt. Brigade, being nine month men, the time of some just expiring, and on their first battlefield, were not greatly counted on at the outset by our Corps and Division Generals; they were, in fact, expected to break at the first attack, and as we afterwards learned, strong supports were placed back of us to take our places when we should fall to the rear. But the supports were not needed. Our men endured that fearful cannonade as steadily as the oldest veteran regiment on the field. They rose into the cast-iron tornado that was sweeping over them, as promptly as if they had been on dress parade, and when their line moved, it was to the *front* instead of to the rear. They took the only two guns, so far as I can learn, taken from the enemy during the battle, and probably lessened Mr. Lee's army, in killed and wounded and prisoners, at the rate of about a man for every one of our own engaged. Our friends of the 1st Brigade have been wont to call the 2d Brigade "the picnic party." I am sorry they were not present to see the picnic party go in July 2nd and 3rd.

I rode over the ground on Sunday, from right to left, but can give but little space to the horrors of the battlefield. I had seen nothing with which to compare them, except Brady's photographic views of the field of Antietam, after the fight—and there is nothing in them of evidences of carnage, at all equalling what I saw in twenty places on the field of Gettysburg. In the open ground in front of our lines on the center and left, the dead of both armies lay by hundreds still unburied, though strong burial parties had been at work for 10 or 12 hours. They had died from almost every conceivable form of mutilation and shot-wound. When not killed outright by a ball through the head or heart, the dead lay for the most part on their backs, with clothes commonly thrown open in front, and breast and stomach exposed. The faces, as a general rule, had turned black—not a purplish discoloration such as I had imagined in reading of the "blackened corpses" so often mentioned in descriptions of battlegrounds but a deep bluish *black* giving to a corpse with black hair the appearance of a negro, and to one with light or red hair and whiskers a strange and revolting aspect. In the woods on our right, where the long musketry fight of Friday forenoon raged, I found the rebel dead (our own had been mostly buried) literally covering the ground. In a circle of 50 feet radius, as near as I could estimate, I counted 47 dead rebels. The number of the enemy's dead in two acres of that oak grove, was estimated at 2,000, and I cannot say that I think it exaggerated. On the knoll just on the right of the position of our brigade, occupied by our batteries on Friday, I counted the dead bodies of *twenty-nine* horses. As late as Sunday noon, wounded men were still being brought into the hospitals, some of whom had lain (in out of the way nooks) on the field since Thursday.

But time and space are failing me. The 2nd Brigade is broken up. The 12th regiment having remained on arduous duty in the Army of the Potomac a week beyond the utmost limit of its time (for which it received the thanks of Gen. Newton commanding, the 1st Corps, in a highly complimentary order) took its leave with the hearty good wishes and Godspeed of all with whom they have been associated—has now been mustered out of service, and has ceased to exist as a military body. The 13th has also arrived here covered with dust and laurels, and in a few days will be no more as a regiment. Two weeks more will see the other regiments on their way home.

The service of the nine months brigade has not been exactly what most of us expected, for we counted on sharp active campaigns in the field, and hoped to be in at the death of the rebellion, and to share in the final triumphs of the Great War for the Union. But if less glorious than that of some, the duty which has mainly occupied us on the Defences of Washington, has been as honorable as any, and more laborious than the average. And though not permitted to see within our term the close of the war, we have been allowed to have a hand in the greatest battle, and the most disastrous to the enemy, of any fought in the East, and can go to our homes, feeling that with glorious successes in the West, and the opening of the Mississippi, the "back bone of the rebellion" is indeed broken.

And now with prayers for the speedy triumph of the Good Cause, in the service of which it is honor enough to have had a share, with heartiest good wishes for his comrades in arms, for many of whom he has formed friendships which will be life long, and with kindest regards for the "gentle readers" who have received with such kind interest his hasty and unstudied sketches, your correspondent brings this series to a close, and takes his leave of camps and army correspondence.

Yours, G.

Benedict wrote this letter on his last day of Federal service. Neither he nor the official records say when he arrived at Brattleboro, but it was probably on or about July 10, as he traveled and worked with General Stannard. The 12th Vermont had arrived at 6:00 A.M. the day before, and the men rested for the day. That was not the case for the regimental staff and company officers, as they had to fill out their muster rolls, property sheets, ration returns, and other paperwork. On July 10, the 12th Vermont had an inspection in which the company commanders checked the condition of each soldier's issued government property, which had to be returned to the quartermaster. This included rifles, bayonets, cartridge boxes, and knap sacks. The soldiers kept only the uniforms they wore, their personal effects, and any gear they wanted to buy. The cost for any government property a soldier lost during his service came out of his final pay. On July 11, Governor Holbrook reviewed the 12th Vermont in its last dress parade, which was also witnessed by many friends and relatives of the officers and men in the ranks of the regiment. It was at about this time that news of the New York City draft riots reached them. Two hundred men from the 12th Vermont volunteered to go back to New York City to help restore order. Before they could be sent, however, the 14th, 15th, and 16th Vermont Regiments arrived in the city, and the 12th Vermont was no longer needed. Major Austine inspected the muster rolls and kept an eye on the equipment turned in on July 12 and 13, and the 12th Vermont's outprocessing continued in a flurry of equipment cleaning and paperwork. On the night of July 13, the 13th Vermont Regiment arrived to prepare for their mustering out of the service, and they shared stories about Gettysburg that night.

In his July 14 letter, written during his last hectic days of service, Benedict gives more details about the battle of Gettysburg. He recounts the medical care on the battlefield, with the 2nd Vermont Brigade's surgeons working until they fell asleep on or between patients. Local barns were pressed into service as field hospitals and soon were overcrowded with wounded men. The surgeons and other medical staff worked in poor conditions with crude instruments and sometimes insufficient medical supplies to treat all the wounded needing care. Still, they managed to save many men who would have died on the battlefield without them.

For some reason, Benedict did not write in his letters about the wounding of Maj. Gen. Winfield Scott Hancock, which he had witnessed, although he described the incident in future writings about Gettysburg. As the Confederate infantry advanced past the 2nd Vermont Brigade's position on July 3, Hancock rode to General Stannard's command post to give him the order to start a flank attack. By the time Hancock got there, the 13th and 16th Vermont were deploying. Hancock, who was mounted, and Stannard who was not, were conversing in shouts over the sounds of rifle and cannon fire when a Confederate minié ball passed through Hancock's saddle and struck him, driving a nail and other parts of his saddle into his thigh. Hooker and Benedict caught him as he collapsed off his horse, lowered him to the ground and out of the line of fire. Hancock was bleeding profusely, and Stannard and his staff officers worked to stanch the flow. Fifteen minutes later, a surgeon reached the group. He extracted a nail and then closed the wound.[22] When the fighting ended, Hancock's staff got an ambulance and then found a private residence where he could recover until they arranged to get him to a general hospital. Hancock was one of a total of 51,112 casualties on both sides in this battle.[23]

Benedict's visit to the part of the battlefield where he had fought only a few days before probably took place after he checked on the brigade staff, which was marching off with the I Corps as it moved out to pursue Lee and the Army of Northern Virginia. Benedict left the battlefield to watch over General Stannard on the train to Baltimore and later to Washington. That was the beginning of their journey home to Vermont. Stannard recovered at the Army General Hospital in Brattleboro, along with other soldiers who needed long-term care.

Benedict compares what he saw on the battlefield to Matthew Brady's photographs of the Antietam battlefield, which had been made public by the time Benedict entered the army. These photographs created a stir, because it was the first time many saw what the aftermath of a battle looked like. Gettysburg had almost twice as many casualties as Antietam, and Benedict depicts it as a far greater bloodbath. This was not Benedict's last visit to the Gettysburg battlefield that year. He returned in November 1863 for the dedication of the National Cemetery at Gettysburg. Although Benedict left the Gettysburg battlefield, the battle did not leave Benedict; it had become a part of his life.

CHAPTER 8

Mustered Out

On the night of July 13, 1863, as the 12th Vermont escorted the 13th Vermont from the Brattleboro train station by torchlight, elements of the Army of Northern Virginia crossed the rain-swollen Potomac River back into Virginia. General Lee had waited two days for General Meade to attack the Confederate army's defense position near Williamsport and Falling Waters, Maryland. Lee hoped that such an attack would incur heavy losses to Meade and soften Lee's defeat at Gettysburg. Meade had been in command for less than three weeks and had lost his two most trusted corps commanders, and he was in no mood to attack the wounded Confederate army. Attacking Lee, who was dug in, was not a wise decision for any commander. Meade's caution led to another command decision that has been debated since the Civil War: whether Meade let Lee and his army slip away. On the morning of July 14, the majority of Lee's army was back in Virginia, and Union cavalry attacked Maj. Gen. Henry Heth's division, which formed the Confederate rear guard. Thus, the first Confederate units to fight at Gettysburg also wound up being the last to fire shots in the campaign.

Meanwhile, in Brattleboro, Vermont, the 12th Vermont was mustered out of Federal service. The men had turned in their government property, the company and regimental paperwork was squared away, and the troops received their pay and train tickets home. After mustering out, the 12th Vermont had a final regimental formation, with Colonel Blunt addressing the troops one last time, then dismissing the command to the individual company commanders. After a few words from their company commanders, the men received their discharge papers and were dismissed for the final time. The mood was more somber than when they had come to Brattleboro for their mustering in, as the 12th Vermont had lost sixty-six men to disease or injury and sixty-five more had been discharged for disability.[1]

In any case, the men were all a little older, wiser, and more experienced than before they had left Vermont. Some got on the trains with family members who had reached Brattleboro a few days earlier, such as Mary Farnham, who arrived the day after the 12th Vermont and waited for Roswell's discharge. The townsfolk of the soldiers' communities greeted the returning men with welcome-home parties. There was usually a banquet at which the town fathers thanked the men for their service with speeches and a good meal. Then these soldiers–turned–civilians went home, some for the first time in nine months, and finally were able to sleep in their own beds, without half a dozen of their comrades nearby. The next day, the men returned to work on their farms or at the jobs they had left behind less than a year before.

While the 12th Vermont returned home, the 14th, 15th, and 16th Vermont Regiments guarded the streets of New York City after the draft riots. But finally, it was time for them to go home, too, and they were mustered out of the service. Benedict and his fellow members of Company C escorted their sister company, Company A of the 13th Vermont Infantry, from the train depot to the town hall for their welcome home about a week after the 12th Vermont's. The men of Company A were greeted as returning heroes after having fought at Gettysburg, but this honor cost the company four dead, four wounded, and one missing.[2] The *Burlington Free Press* reported this event on July 22:

> The arrival this morning of company A, of the 13th Regiment so much of the company as went from this neighborhood—was attended with a greeting on the part of the citizens of the place like in extent and enthusiasm with the one given to Company C of the 12th on Wednesday last. The fire companies were out preceded by the Jericho Band. Company C under the command of Lt. Wing, formed a military escort, with the Westford Drum Corps, and a procession of the citizens brought up the rear. The streets were through with the citizens of the place, male and female on foot, in carriages, and on horse back all hearty in welcoming and honoring the men who had served their country so well, and done honor to themselves and the state on the battle-field of Gettysburg.
>
> Assembled in the park the returned soldiers were greeted with welcome and thanks on the part of their fellow citizens in a pertinent and eloquent speech from Sullivan Adams, Esq. He referred

in appropriate terms to the good service done by the company and especially to the gallantry they had displayed in the recent battle. Their enlistment at a time when not drafted men but volunteers were asked for by the government, their bravery and success upon the field, their readiness, when they had almost reached their homes to again turn back and aid in crushing treason in New York City, their entire career as soldiers proved that they were true patriots and loyal men—an honor to the State of Vermont, deserving of distinguished honor from their fellow citizens. Mr. Adams also spoke in terms of the highest praise of the [2nd] Vermont brigade and sketched its career. Captain Lonergan on behalf of himself and men responded to the welcome that met Company A of the 13th, on its return. He spoke with justifiable pride of the achievements of his own men, and of the 13th regiment. The honor which had been accorded the 13th by other Vermont regiments was alluded to as having been especially grateful to the soldiers and their officers. The battle of Gettysburg where he had fought for and helped secure a triumph from the flags whose inspiration cheered him on the field, had numbered among the days on which it was fought, the proudest day of his life. Captain Lonergan described the movement of the troops and the success which won so much honor for the Union causes and for Vermont. In concluding he called for three cheers for Gen. G. J. Stannard, commander of the [2nd] Vermont Brigade which were given with a will. Cheers were also given for Captain Lonergan and for Company A.

The morning was very fine, and the national flag streaming in the sunshine on all sides, with the stirring notes of Yankee Doodle and other popular airs from the band and the drum corps added to the earnest good feeling of all present, made the occasion pass in an unusually pleasant manner.

By the time all the Vermont nine-month regiments were mustered out of service, most of the Army of the Potomac had moved back to Virginia. The 1st Vermont Brigade from the VI Corps was detached for temporary duty to New York City to garrison and enforce the local draft laws for the rest of the summer. In the fall of 1863, the Federal government called for more troops, and Vermont started to raise another infantry regiment and also sent more soldiers into the Vermont infantry regiments still in the field. The raising of the 17th Vermont in the spring of 1864 was difficult, and less than a quarter of the men who had served in the nine-month regiments joined the 17th Vermont. George Benedict, George Hagar, and Richard Irwin did not reenlist, feeling that they had done their part in fighting the Rebellion. But Benedict had a continuing interest in the battle of Gettysburg, and in mid-November 1863, he traveled to Pennsylvania to report on the dedication of the National Cemetery at Gettysburg for the *Burlington Free Press.* A few days after this event, he wrote his last wartime letter for the newspaper.

Gettysburg, Pa., Nov. 20, 1863.

Dear Free Press:

I left Philadelphia for the classic ground of Gettysburg on Tuesday morning last, and about noon was dropped, together with a number of pilgrims for the National Mecca of the time being, at Columbia, on the banks of the Susquehanna. A bridge a mile and a quarter long spanned the waters there on the 29th of June last; but on the appearance of a brigade of rebel infantry on that day near Wrightsville on the opposite shore, the structure was fired to prevent their crossing, and completely destroyed to the stone abutments. Consequently travelers across that way must depend upon the ferry.

There is, or was on Tuesday last, a choice between a steamboat of two-horse power, and divers rowboats of two man power. I chose the former of course, and with eighteen others, ladies and gentlemen, stepped on board the staunch and elegant (by a figure of speech) Steamer *Union,* Capt. Duke. There were many who would fain have taken passage with us, but they were refused by Capt. Duke as sternly as old Charon drove back the unhappy shades who thronged the shores of Styx. Nineteen souls, or bodies rather, was the capacity of his steamer, and not another could gain admittance though they waved greenbacks in bunches before his eyes. The *Union* moved away from under their eager noses, with the grace of a high pressure water fowl, and we, her favored passengers, looked complacently on their disappointment, as we left them behind to the tender mercies of the wherrymen. We had a little fear lest our steam shallop might be overloaded, for two of the ladies were of well nigh the weight of four average mortals; we had apparently a momentary fear of rebel privateers, dispelled however, by Capt. Duke's prompt assurance that no hostile Alabamas vexed honest craft on those waters; but we had not the slightest fear of being outstripped on our passage over. Alas for the folly of short-sighted followers of the steam demon! Our captain forgot to turn the damper in his smoke-pipe; the steam, in spite of eager poking and much feeding with pine chips, ran rapidly down, the wheels of the *Union* turned with slower stroke, the plashing of oars was heard behind us, and soon with ill concealed smiles and tongues thrust banteringly into their cheeks, the friends we left behind us first lapped, then passed, then distanced the *Union* and her chop-fallen load. Never mind. We got over, and after a collision with a canal boat, occasioned by our rudder declining to work at the most criti-cal moment of the passage, we made a safe landing. 'Twill be all the same a thousand years hence, as if we had outstripped the world in oars. And I needn't and wouldn't have given so much space to our passage of the Susquehanna, were it not for the moral of the tale, which the astute readers of the FREE PRESS can not fail to per-ceive and apply.

We took at Wrightsville a "one-horse" railroad to York, and then a one-and-a-half horse railroad to Gettysburg, reaching there through much delay and tribulation at ten o'clock at night—to find the "hotels" overflowing, and our crowd swelled by two or three hundred other pullers at time's foretop, who confidently supposed that thirty-six hours start of the big rush would give them the pick of the public accommodations of Gettysburg, dependent on private hospitality for food and shelter. I fared well enough, however, and so I trust did the rest.

The next day I came to the battlefield. I went first to the scene of the first day's hard and costly fight. Guided by Major Rosengarten, then of Major General Reynolds's staff, I stood upon the spot where that brave and able general fell, while forming his line. I looked over the ground where, shortly after, General Doubleday, who succeeded to the command of the 1st corps, cut off and captured General Archer and a good share of his brigade, and maintained for an hour and a half of stubborn fighting his position until Howard's 11th

Corps came up, in time to save the 1st from utter destruction, but itself to be beaten back with the 1st to Cemetery Ridge, after a melancholy loss in killed and wounded and prisoners. We passed next to the south, along the ridge on which Lee formed his lines on the second day. The fields, then trampled by many thousands of ill-shod rebels, have regained in that portion of the battleground, in a great measure, their former condition; the fences have been put up, and the plough and harrow have obliterated the deep cannon ruts. We crossed over the fields in front of Rogers house, on which Sickles made his ill-advised advance on Thursday and which he left strewed with the bodies of his own men and that of the enemy. We climbed "Little Round Top," among the boulders at the base of which still lie the bones of some of the rebels, slain by Crawford's men of the Pennsylvania reserves, on Thursday afternoon and which in that portion of the battleground alone failed to find burial. I reached the top of Round Top just as a fine national flag was flung to the breeze from a tall flagstaff erected on its very summit. Then passing towards the center I stopped of course, on the ground held by Stannard's men of the Vermont 2nd Brigade, and on which they flanked and shattered the rebel column, three full divisions massed in probably the heaviest and most desperate charge of the war. The battleground here remains much as it was left at the battle's close—clothing, cartridge-boxes, bayonet-sheaths, and soldiers' accoutrements by the thousands still strew the ground. The low breastworks of rails still remain, and the skeletons of horses covered by the skin, are scattered unburied as they fell.

Thence to Cemetery Hill, on the left of which grounds of the National Cemetery have been laid out. I found easily the position allotted to Vermont on the north-eastern slope of Cemetery Hill. NINETEEN of the bodies of our brave boys have been removed from the spots where they found hasty burial, and re-interred here, and the trenches are open for the remainder. Their remains are placed in plain wooden coffins in trenches walled with stone at the head and feet and each body marked by a numbered stake, to be replaced in due time I suppose by a suitable headboard or stone. The work of re-interment is going on over the whole ground. About 1,200, hardly a third of the whole number of our dead, have thus far been collected; but it is intended that the work shall be completed before Winter.

I must hasten to the close of my letter, as I hastened to the close of my day's work; for the sun was sinking as I passed over Wolf Hill on our right, down into the hollow, where Geary and Wadsworth literally "piled the ground" with rebels slain, on Thursday night and Friday morning. Their bodies lay thick, thick among the granite boulders, with blackened faces and staring eyeballs, when I was last upon the spot. They have since been collected in trenches and such inscriptions as "45 dead Rebs buried in this pit," rudely written on the "blazed" trunks of the oaks.

I need not describe the proceedings of yesterday. Mr. Everett's polished discourse; President Lincoln's simple and touching dedicatory speech; the generals and governors and grandees present— all of this you have already had in the city papers. And you have heard of the sad sequel—the sudden death of a man and boy killed by the explosion of a shell from the field. The principal trade of Gettysburg, by the way, is in these unexploded shells, often with charges still intact, and the wonder is that more casualties have not already occurred from accidental explosions.

The toot of the locomotive which is to take me hence, warns me away.

Yours, G.

Traveling to Gettysburg for Benedict was an adventure in itself. After the battle, many people from the North went to Gettysburg to care for wounded relatives or to find their remains to bring home. The dedication of the National Cemetery brought another mass influx of people. About 15,000 people from the North traveled to Gettysburg for this event, crowding the town in which 2,500 people had lived before the battle.[3] The scarcity of lodging shows that the dedication was a major event for the area and that Gettysburg had indeed become a Civil War Mecca.

Benedict now visited those parts of the battlefield that he had missed the first time. His guide, Maj. Joseph G. Rosengarten, an aide on General Reynolds's staff, had witnessed the general's death and was a good person to explain what had happened to the I Corps on Seminary Ridge on July 1. Neither man had taken part in the second day's fighting, but it was easy to see what had happened, with all the discarded equipment and decomposing horses, still there. When the two men came to the area of Pickett's charge, it was Benedict's turn to tell the story.

Benedict's letter gives the sense that the land was slowly healing itself. Tourists, souvenir hunters, and local residents picked up anything left by the two armies, until a militia regiment was assigned to guard the area and quartermaster and ordnance troops recovered the remaining government property on the battlefield. By the time of Benedict's November visit, the Union army had recovered 24,864 muskets and 10,589 bayonets, as well as other articles, including knapsacks and field artillery pieces.[4] A dozen or so civilians, including the two mentioned by Benedict, were killed after the battle by the mishandling of weapons or ammunition taken from the battlefield.

Edward Everett was the keynote speaker at the dedication ceremony. Everett, considered one of the best public speakers of that day, was from Boston, and he had an illustrious career, having served as president of Harvard, secretary of state, senator, congressman, and governor of Massachusetts. Benedict wrote more about the events of that afternoon, including President Lincoln's speech, in the November 23 *Burlington Free Press:*

> The Dedication at Gettysburg on the 19th was successfully carried out according to the previous arrangements. The day was fine and an immense throng was present. There was a great military and civic procession to the cemetery where the military formed around a stand on which was the President of the United States, members of his cabinet, Governors of States and other eminent civil and military dignitaries. The dedication exercises consisted of a funeral dirge by the band, a prayer by Rev. Mr. Stockton, the Oration by Hon. Edward Everett, the dedicatory address by the President, another dirge and the benediction.
>
> The dedicatory Address by President Lincoln is reported as follows:

> Fourscore and seven years ago our Fathers brought forth upon this Continent a new nation, conceived in liberty and dedicated to the proposition that all men are created equal. [Applause.] Now we are engaged in a great civil war, testing whether that nation, or any nation so conceived and so dedicated, can long endure. We are met on a great battle-field of that war. We are met to dedicate a

portion of it as the final resting-place of those who here gave their lives that that nation might live. It is altogether fitting and proper that we should do this. But in a larger sense we cannot dedicate, we cannot consecrate, we cannot hallow this ground. The brave men, living and dead, who struggled here have consecrated it far above our power to add or detract. [Applause.] The world will little note nor remember, what we say here, but it can never forget what they did here. [Applause.] It is for us, the living, rather to be dedicated here to the unfinished work that they have thus far so nobly carried on. [Applause.] It is rather for us to be here dedicated to the great task remaining before us, that from these honored dead we take increased devotion to that cause for which they here gave the last full measure of devotion; that we here highly resolve that the dead shall not have died in vain; [applause] that the Nation shall under God have a new birth of freedom, and that Governments of the people, by the people, and for the people, shall not perish from the Earth. [Long continued applause.]

After the dedication, Benedict does not say whether he spent more time on the battlefield or returned home. It is likely that he went to Washington, D.C., because he later writes of meeting General Hancock at Willard's Hotel five months after his wounding, and that was the time of the National Cemetery's dedication. During this meeting, he and Hancock talked about the battle and Hancock's injury. Hancock told him that a few months after his first surgery, he was still in pain, so the surgeons operated again. This time they extracted a minié ball and a wooden plug.[5] Benedict left this interview with a thank-you note from Hancock, who was impressed by the soldier and writer. After the war, Hancock told George Hooker that "no braver or cooler man than Benedict served in the Army of the Potomac. Brains and bravery make the perfect soldier; Benedict combined the two."[6]

This meeting and his visit to Gettysburg marked the beginning of Benedict's interest in and work on the battle's history. During his visit, before the dedication of the National Cemetery, Benedict met with and showed John B. Bachelder what he knew about the battle.[7] A month later,

Benedict began corresponding with Bachelder and continued to do so for the next several years. Bachelder became the official historian of the battle of Gettysburg and was the first to gather information on the battle, starting a few days after the armies had left the field. Bachelder talked with wounded of both sides at the numerous Gettysburg hospitals that had sprung up after the battle. Later that year, he received permission to stay with the Army of the Potomac while it was in winter quarters and interviewed most of the commanders, of corps, divisions, and regiments, who had survived the battle and campaign. After the war, Bachelder corresponded with commanders and staff officers from both sides, compiling an impressive collection of eyewitness accounts on this battle before his death in 1894.

Benedict did the same in Vermont, getting the first accounts of the battle from Col. Francis Randall of the 13th Vermont, Col. William Nichols of the 14th Vermont, Col. Redfield Proctor of the 15th Vermont, and Col. Wheelock Veazey of the 16th during the winter and spring of 1863–64.

While Benedict was researching and collecting information on the battle of Gettysburg, the Civil War continued. His further wartime efforts included serving as a recruiting officer for northern Vermont and eastern parts of upstate New York. In the battle of the Wilderness in the spring of 1864, the 1st Vermont Brigade lost half of its effective strength, which shocked the state. Then it seemed like the war had come to a standstill at the siege of Petersburg, as each side waited for the other to leave. In the fall, Confederate general Jubal Early's advance up the Shenandoah Valley and subsequent attack on Washington's defenses caused Lt. Gen. Ulysses S. Grant to send the VI Corps to strengthen the Union capital's defenses. Under Maj. Gen. Philip Sheridan, this force engaged Early's troops and destroyed this Confederate force in the Valley at Cedar Creek. The 1st Vermont Brigade fought with distinction at the battle of Cedar Creek, where Early's troops launched a surprise attack that almost destroyed the Union force there on October 19, 1864. However, Union troops rallied, then counterattacked, crushing Early's corps. This battle prevented a military disaster that could have turned the 1864 election against Lincoln. He was the first president to be reelected since Andrew Jackson, and this signaled that the war would be fought to the end.

While the war raged in the South, Vermont got a taste of it on its own soil in the St. Albans Raid. On November 18, 1864, a group of ten Confederates raided the small city of St. Albans, some twenty miles from the U.S.–Canada border. St. Albans had direct railroad service to Montreal, where these raiders were based. The men robbed three banks, then tried to burn down the town. The fire failed to catch, and there was growing resistance among the townspeople after one was killed by the raiders. They left with $200,000 in greenbacks before a mob of enraged Vermonters could capture or kill them. The raiders crossed the border but were interned by the Canadian authorities. A patchwork of militia units was assembled to protect the border against further Confederate raids. Benedict was mobilized in this situation and became the aide-de-camp for Colonel Proctor, who commanded this motley collection of semiarmed, semitrained men. In a month or two, Benedict was released from this mobilization, although he served a few more years in the Vermont militia after the Civil War.

In late March and early April 1865, the end of the war was in sight. For nine months, the armies had waited each other out, but the Confederate position started to crack after their attack on Fort Stedman on March 29, 1865. Soon after, Lee and his army evacuated Petersburg, and Richmond fell to the Army of the Potomac on April 3, 1865. Benedict and others waited for word by telegraph that General Lee's army was defeated and the war was over. This news came over the telegraph at 1:00 A.M. on April 10, 1865. It spread quickly as church bells began to ring, proclaiming the end after four years of war. People filled the streets of Burlington on that crisp morning, as dozens of bonfires were started, including a very large one near town hall on Church Street in the center of town. This began a day of rejoicing in Burlington, along with all of the North. The joy was short-lived, however, as on April 15, word of President Lincoln's assassination reached Vermont. The news brought profound shock and sadness. It was the first murder of a president of the United States. Many Northerners felt as though it had been a death in the family. Benedict's accounts of Lincoln's assassination in the *Burlington Free Press* were bordered by heavy black, like a mourning band, a common practice at the time in letters telling of the passing of a close relative. On Wednesday, April 19, Burlington had an official day of mourning, and local churches conducted memorial services for the slain president.

As the emotions over the war's end and the president's assassination began to subside, a feeling of normality returned as men went back to their civilian lives. Many of them got married and started families. Benedict married his fiancée, Katherine Pease, in Rochester, New York, on December 22, 1864. Mary Frances, Benedict's daughter from his first marraige, then seven years old, now had a mother. In 1867, a daughter, Martha, was born to the couple, but the baby died within the year. On New Year's Day, 1872, Katherine gave birth to a son, George Wyllys, who was named after his grandfather.

Benedict became the owner and editor of the *Burlington Free Press* in 1866 and remained so for the next forty-one years. During that time, he made this paper the most circulated and influential in the state of Vermont. This paper also helped him in his politic endeavors. He served as a state senator from Chittenden County from 1869 to 1871. After his term of office, he became a kingmaker in Vermont politics. He was a high-ranking member of the state's Republican Party, and his newspaper shaped public opinion in Vermont's most populated region. As a Republican delegate from Vermont, Benedict traveled to Chicago to the national Republican Convention to nominate James Garfield and Chester A. Arthur, who were elected president and vice president in 1880. Benedict was appointed collector of customs for the district of Vermont from 1889 to 1893, during the Harrison administration. One appointment that was perhaps closest to his heart was in 1879, when Gov. Redfield Proctor appointed him state historian for the Civil War.

In the next decade, Benedict researched and wrote three books on Vermont in the Civil War, while continuing his other family, political, and business matters. He wrote and published *Vermont in the Civil War*, vol. 1, in 1886; *A Short History of the 14th Vermont*, in 1887; and *Vermont in the Civil War*, vol. 2, in 1888. In 1895, he edited the Civil War letters he had written thirty years before, and republished them as a book titled *Army Life in Virginia*. These books joined Benedict's first book *Vermont at Gettysburgh*, published in 1870. He also spoke on the subject of Vermont in the Civil War. His first of many speeches was on March 10, 1864, on the battle of Gettysburg. His most memorable speech was in 1892, on a new holiday that was an outgrowth of the Civil War: Memorial Day. That same year, he received his greatest honor from his wartime service when he was awarded the Medal of Honor for his actions at Gettysburg nearly thirty years before. He served on the executive committee of the Medal of Honor Legion of the United States. But one of the happiest events of his life, was the birth of his grandson and namesake, George Grenville Benedict II, in 1900.

At the turn of the nineteenth century, Benedict's health was slowly eroding. In the winter of 1906–1907, Benedict, now eighty-one years old, and Katherine, sixty-two, went South for their health, spending the winter in St. Augustine, Florida. In February while they were there, Benedict had a heart attack. He slowly recovered and, by April, felt it was time to return home to Vermont. On April 4, they stopped at Camden, South Carolina, on their way North, for a few days. On the night of April 7, Benedict had another heart attack around midnight. Katherine gave him nitroglycerin tablets and called for help, but while she waited, he collapsed and died in her arms. She wrote in her diary, "My poor husband was gone." She returned to Burlington, Vermont, a few days later with his body. His funeral was one of the biggest the town had seen. Katherine, Burlington, and indeed, the whole state of Vermont mourned his passing, but his spirit lives on in his Civil War writings.

NOTES

INTRODUCTION
1. George G. Benedict's Pension File, National Archives, Washington, D.C.
2. Company C Descriptive Rolls, 12th Vermont Regimental Books, Record Group 94, National Archives.

CHAPTER 1: A CALL TO ARMS
1. Francis Lord, *They Fought for the Union* (New York: Bonanza Books, 1960), 124.
2. Office of the Adjutant General, General Order No. 10 (printed in the *Vermont Chronicle*, August 19, 1862). The remainder of Burlington's quota was filled by a company raised by John Lonergan, which became Company A, 13th Vermont.
3. Descriptive Rolls, 12th Vermont Regimental Books.
4. Special Order No. 2, September 30, 1862, 12th Vermont Regimental Books.
5. Descriptive Rolls, 12th Vermont Regimental Books.
6. Report on Col. Asa P. Blunt's Sword Presentation Speech, *The Caledonian* (St. Johnsbury, Vermont, October 10, 1862).
7. Telegram from Secretary of War Edwin M. Stanton to Governor Holbrook, September 22, 1862, Record Group 94, National Archives.
8. Ralph O. Sturtevant, *A Pictorial History of the 13th Vermont Regiment* (Burlington, VT: 13th Vermont Regiment Association, 1910), 34.
9. John D. Billings, *Hard Tack and Coffee* (Boston: George M. Smith and Company, 1887), 44.

CHAPTER 2: CAMP AT EAST CAPITOL HILL

1. Thomas L. Livermore, *Numbers and Losses in the Civil War, 1861–1865* (1900; reprint, Carlisle, PA: John Kallman Publishers, 1996), 92.
2. Roswell Farnham, letter of October 9, Farnham Papers, Special Collections, University of Vermont.
3. General Order No. 3, August 19, 1862, Casey's Provision Division's Order Books, Record Group 94, National Archives.
4. Adjutant and Inspector General, *Revised Roster of Vermont Volunteers Who Served in the Army and Navy of the United States during the War of Rebellion* (Montpelier, VT: U.S. War Department, 1892), 223.
5. Company F Personnel Loss Section, 12th Vermont Regimental Books.
6. Letter of October 4, 1862, Farnham Papers.
7. George G. Benedict, *Vermont in the Civil War,* vol. 1, (Burlington, VT: Free Press Printing Company, 1883) 25.
8. Richard Irwin, letter of November 1, 1862, Irwin Letters, Special Collections, University of Vermont.

CHAPTER 3: CAMP VERMONT

1. Charles Cummings, letter of November 10, 1862, printed in the November 20, 1862, *Brattleboro Phoenix.*
2. George I. Hagar, letter of November 8, 1862, Hagar Letters, Special Collections, University of Vermont.
3. *Green Mountain Freeman,* December 10, 1862, Vermont State Archives, Montpelier, Vermont.
4. Regimental Order No. 11, November 23, 1862, 12th Vermont Regimental Books.
5. George I. Hagar, letter of November 9, 1862, Hagar Letters.
6. Discharge Sections, 12th Vermont Regimental Books.
7. Travel pass, Benedict Papers, Special Collections, University of Vermont.
8. George I. Hagar, letter of December 5, 1862, Hagar Letters.

CHAPTER 4: CAMP AT FAIRFAX COURTHOUSE

1. Livermore, *Numbers and Losses,* 96.
2. Robert B. Johnson and Clarence C. Buel, eds. Battles and Leaders of the Civil War, *The Opposing Armies at the First Bull Run* (Secaucus, NJ: Castle, 1887), vol. 1, 195.
3. Richard Irwin, letter of January 8, 1863, Irwin Letters.

4. B Company, 14th Vermont Company Orderly Book, Special Collections, University of Vermont.

5. Personnel Loss Sections, 12th Vermont Regimental Books.

6. General Order No. 4, December 25 1862, 14th Vermont Regimental Books, Record Group 94, National Archives.

7. Richard Irwin, letter of December 28, 1862, Irwin Letters.

8. "B," letter of December 25, 1862, published in the January 1, 1863, *Rutland Weekly Herald*.

9. Maj. Gen. Samuel Heintzelman, Report of January 3, 1863, *Records of the War of Rebellion,* Operations in N. Va, W. Va, MD, and PA, 706.

10. George Bigelow, letter of January 2, 1863, published in the January 11, 1863, *Burlington Times.*

11. Ibid.

12. Brig. Gen. Edwin H. Stoughton, Report of December 29, 1862, *Records of the War of Rebellion,* Operations in N. Va, W. Va, MD, and PA, 717.

13. George I. Hagar, letter of January 27, 1863, Hagar Letters.

14. Roswell Farnham's Pension File, National Archives.

15. Mary Farnham, letter of December 21, 1862, Farnham Papers, Special Collections, University of Vermont.

16. Roswell Farnham, diary entry of December 13, 1862, Farnham Papers, Special Collections, University of Vermont.

17. Mary Farnham, letter of December 21, 1862, Farnham Papers, Special Collections, University of Vermont.

18. Ibid.

CHAPTER 5: CAMP AT WOLF RUN SHOALS

1. George G. Benedict, furlough request form, Benedict Papers.

2. General Order No. 8, January 20, 1863, and General Order No. 9, January 23, 1863, Casey's Division Order Book, Record Group 94, National Archives.

3. George I. Hagar, letter of February 6, 1863, Hagar Letters.

4. Special Order No. 55, February 5, 1863, 13th Vermont Regimental Books, Record Group 94, National Archives.

5. Mary Farnham, letter of February 17, 1863, Farnham Papers, Vermont Historical Society.

6. Ibid.

7. Morning Report Section, 16th Vermont Regimental Books, Record Group 94, National Archives.

8. Personnel Loss Sections, 12th Vermont Regimental Books.

9. Col. George Hooker's Medal of Honor File, National Archives.

10. Casey's division telegram, March 30, 1863.

11. Casey's division telegram, April 13, 1863.

12. 12th and 13th Vermont Regimental Books.

13. Special Order No. 5858, Headquarters, Department of Washington, April 15, 1863, Record Group 94, National Archives.

14. XXII Corps, telegram of April 15, 1863, Record Group 94, National Archives.

CHAPTER 6: CAMP AT UNION MILLS

1. George I. Hagar, letter of April 22, 1863, Hagar Letters.

2. Livermore, *Numbers and Losses,* 98.

3. Francis T. Miller, ed. *The Photographic History of the Civil War,* vol. 4, *Prisons and Hospitals* (Secaucus, NJ: The Blue and the Grey Press, 1987), 195.

4. Mark Nesbitt, *35 Days to Gettysburg: The Campaign Diaries of Two American Enemies.* (Harrisburg, PA: Stackpole Books, 1992), 32.

5. Roswell Farnham, letter of May 10, 1863, Farnham Papers, Special Collections, University of Vermont.

6. 2nd Vermont Infantry Brigade, telegram to Corps Headquarters, May 10, 1863, Record Group 94, National Archives.

7. Richard Irwin, letter of May 19, 1863, Irwin Letters.

8. Ibid.

9. Sturtevant, *Pictorial History,* 167.

10. Benedict, *Vermont in the Civil War,* vol. 2, 436.

11. Ibid., vol. 1, 83.

12. Roswell Farnham, speech of June 29, 1892, Farnham Papers.

13. John William, diary entry of June 14, 1863, William Papers, Vermont Historical Society, Montpelier, Vermont.

14. Benedict, *Vermont in the Civil War,* vol. 2, 439.

CHAPTER 7: ON THE FIELD OF GETTYSBURG

1. George I. Hagar, letter of June 23–24, 1863, Hagar Letters.

2. Brig. Gen. George J. Stannard to George G. Benedict, June 27, 1863, Brigade Telegrams, Record Group 94, National Archives.

3. George G. Benedict, *Army Life in Virginia* (Burlington, VT: Free Press Printing Co., 1895), 160.

4. Benedict, *Vermont in the Civil War,* vol. 2, 440.

5. Edwin B. Coddington, *The Gettysburg Campaign: A Study in Command* (New York: Charles Scribner's Sons, 1968), 234.

6. George J. Stannard diary, July 2 1863. In David and Audrey Ladd, *The Bachelder Papers: Gettysburg in Their Own Words,* vol. 1. (Dayton: Morningside House, 1994), 54.

7. *Vermont Standard,* July 24, 1863

8. Stannard diary, July 5, 1863. In Ladd, *Bachelder Papers,* 57.

9. Capt. Asa Foster, pension file, National Archives.

10. Benedict, *Army Life in Virginia,* 172.

11. Benedict, *Vermont in the Civil War,* vol. 2, 459.

12. Map of July 3, 1863. In Ladd, *Bachelder Papers,* vol. 1.

13. George G. Benedict, Medal of Honor File, National Archives.

14. Stannard diary, July 3, 1863. In Ladd, *Bachelder Papers,* vol. 1, 57.

15. *Burlington Free Press,* July 11, 1863.

16. Benedict, *Vermont in the Civil War,* vol. 2, 489.

17. Roswell Farnham, letter of July 4, 1863, Farnham Papers, Special Collections, University of Vermont.

18. Richard J. Irwin, letter of July 6, 1863, Irwin Letters.

19. Roswell Farnham, letter of July 3, 1863, Farnham Papers, Special Collections, University of Vermont.

20. Roswell Farnham, letter of July 3, Farnham Papers, Vermont Historical Society, Montpelier, Vermont.

21. Roswell Farnham, diary entry of July 4, 1863, Farnham Papers, Special Collections, University of Vermont.

22. George G. Benedict, "Hon. George B. Benedict Relates His Memories of the Great Battle," *Boston Journal,* February 15, 1893.

23. Livermore, *Numbers and Losses,* 102.

CHAPTER 8: MUSTERED OUT

1. 12th Vermont Regimental Books.

2. Company A Personnel Loss Section, 13th Vermont Regimental Books.

3. Gregory A. Coco, *A Strange and Blighted Land: Gettysburg, the Aftermath of a Battle* (Gettysburg, PA: Thomas Publications, 1995), 121.

4. Ibid. 335.

5. Benedict, *Army Life in Virginia,* 184.

6. George Hooker, letter of September 19, 1891, George G. Benedict, Medal of Honor File.

7. Benedict, "Benedict Relates His Memories."

BIBLIOGRAPHY

MANUSCRIPT SOURCES

National Archives, Washington, D.C., Record Group 94

Medal of Honor Files
Lt. George G. Benedict
Col. George Hooker
Capt. John Lonergan
Col. Wheelock Veazey

Pension Records
Lt. George G. Benedict
Col. Asa Blunt
Q.M. Harry Brownson
Lt. Col. Roswell Farnham
Capt. Asa Foster
Col. George Hooker
Maj. Gen. George J. Stannard

Telegraphic Records (1862–63)
Brig. Gen. John J. Abercombie
Col. Asa Blunt
Maj. Gen. Silas Casey
Maj. Gen. Samuel P. Heintzelman
Col. Redfield Proctor
Col. Francis V. Randall
Brig. Gen. George J. Stannard
Brig. Gen. Edwin H. Stoughton

Unit Records
12th Vermont Infantry Regiment Descriptive Rosters and Order Books
13th Vermont Infantry Regiment Descriptive Rosters and Order Books
14th Vermont Infantry Regiment Descriptive Rosters and Order Books
15th Vermont Infantry Regiment Descriptive Rosters and Order Books
16th Vermont Infantry Regiment Descriptive Rosters and Order Books
2nd Vermont Infantry Brigade Correspondence and Order Books
Casey's Division Correspondence and Order Books (1862–63)
Abercrombie's Division Correspondence and Order Books (1863)

University of Vermont, Special Collections, Bailey Howe Library, Burlington, Vermont
George G. Benedict Papers
Roswell and Mary Farnham Papers
George I. Hagar Letters
Richard Irwin Letters

Vermont Historical Society, Montpelier, Vermont
Charles Cummings Papers
Roswell Farnham Papers
John William Papers

NEWSPAPERS
Boston Journal, January 1893–February 1893
Burlington Free Press, August 1862–November 1863
Burlington Sentinel, August 1862–August 1863
Burlington Times, August 1862–August 1863
Brattleboro Phoenix, August 1862–August 1863
The Caledonian, August 1862–August 1863
Green Mountain Freeman, August 1862–August 1863
Rutland Weekly Herald, August 1862–August 1863
Vermont Chronicle, August 1862–August 1863
Vermont Standard, August 1862–August 1863

OFFICIAL PUBLICATIONS

U.S. War Department. *Revised Regulations for the Army of the United States.* Washington, D.C., 1861.

———. *War of the Rebellion: Official Records of the Union and Confederate Armies.* 128 vols. Washington, D.C. 1880–1901.

———. Vermont Adjutant General's Ofice. *Report of the Adjutant and Inspector General (P. T. Washburn) of the State of Vermont, from November 1, 1862 to October 1, 1863.* Montpelier, Vermont, 1863.

———. Adjutant and Inspector General. *Revised Roster of Vermont Volunteers Who Served in the Army and Navy of the United States during the War of Rebellion.* Montpelier, Vermont, 1892.

BOOKS

Benedict. George Grenville. *Army Life in Virginia.* Burlington, VT: Free Press Printing Co., 1895.

———. *A Short History of the 14th Vermont Regiment.* Bennington, VT: Press of C. A. Pierce, 1887.

———. *Vermont at Gettysburg.* Burlington, VT: Free Press Printing Co., 1870.

———. *Vermont in the Civil War.* 2 vols. Burlington, VT: Free Press Printing Co., 1883 and 1886.

Billings, John D. *Hard Tack and Coffee.* Boston: George M. Smith and Company, 1887.

Boatner, Mark M. *The Civil War Dictionary.* New York: David McKay Co., 1987.

Casey, Brig. Gen. Silas. *Infantry Tactics.* Washington, D.C.: U.S. War Department, 1862.

Coco, Gregory A. *A Strange and Blighted Land: Gettysburg, the Aftermath of a Battle.* Gettysburg, PA: Thomas Publications, 1995.

Coddington, Edwin B. *The Gettysburg Campaign: A Study in Command.* New York: Charles Scribner's Sons, 1968.

Coffin, Howard. *Full Duty: Vermont in the Civil War.* Woodstock, VT: The Countryman Press, 1993.

———. *Nine Months to Gettysburg.* Woodstock, VT: The Countryman Press, 1997.

Cooling, Benjamin Franklin III, and Owen H. Walton II. *Mr. Lincoln's Forts: A Guide to the Civil War Defenses of Washington.* Shippensburg, PA: White Mane Publishing Company, 1988.

Fiebeger, Col. G. J. *The Campaign and Battle of Gettysburg.* West Point, NY: U.S. Military Academy Press, 1915.

Harrison, Kathy G., and John W. Busey. *Nothing but Glory: Pickett's Division at Gettysburg.* Gettysburg, PA: Thomas Publications, 1993.

Ladd, David, and Audrey Ladd. *The Bachelder Papers: Gettysburg in Their Own Words.* 3 vols. Dayton: Morningside House, 1994.

Livermore, Thomas L. *Numbers and Losses in the Civil War, 1861–1865.* 1900. Reprint, Carlisle, PA: John Kallman Publishers, 1996.

Lord, Francis. *They Fought for the Union.* New York: Bonanza Books, 1960.

Marshall, Jeffrey D. *A War of the People: Vermont Civil War Letters.* Hanover, NH: University Press of New England, 1999.

Nesbitt, Mark. *35 Days to Gettysburg: The Campaign Diaries of Two American Enemies.* Harrisburg, PA: Stackpole Books, 1992.

Palmer, Edwin. *The Second Brigade; or, Camp Life.* Montpelier, VT: E. P. Walton Co., 1864.

Pfanz, Harry W. *Gettysburg, The Second Day.* Chapel Hill, NC: The University of North Carolina Press, 1987.

Poirier, Robert G. *By the Blood of Our Alumni: Norwich University Citizen Soldiers in the Army of the Potomac.* Mason City, IA: Savas Publishing, 1999.

Stewart, George R. *Pickett's Charge.* Boston: Houghton Mifflin Co., 1959.

Sturtevant, Ralph O. *A Pictorial History of the 13th Vermont Regiment.* Burlington, VT: 13th Vermont Regiment Association, 1910.

Wert, Jeffry D. *Mosby's Rangers.* New York: Touchstone Books, 1990.

Wiley, Bell Irwin. *The Life of Billy Yank: The Common Soldiers of the Union.* Baton Rouge: Louisiana State University Press, 1978.

Williams, J. C. *Life in Camp.* Claremont, NH: Claremont Manufactures Co., 1864.

INDEX

Page numbers in italics indicate illustrations.